KITCHEN ECONOMICS

KITCHEN ECONOMICS

Women's Regionalist Fiction and Political Economy

THOMAS STRYCHACZ

The University of Alabama Press   Tuscaloosa

The University of Alabama Press
Tuscaloosa, Alabama 35487-0380
uapress.ua.edu

Typeface: Minion Pro

Cover image: Detail from "Prang's aids for object teaching–The kitchen" (Boston: L. Prang & Co., ca.1874), lithograph; Library of Congress, Prints and Photographs Division
Cover design: David Nees

Cataloging-in-Publication data is available from the Library of Congress.
ISBN: 978-0-8173-2058-4
E-ISBN: 978-0-8173-9293-2

To Kathryn, Nicholas, Daniel, Angie, Alexandra,
Isabel, and now Dolores and Raymond

CONTENTS

ACKNOWLEDGMENTS

The first ingredients for *Kitchen Economics* were slow-cooked together over many years of American Culture Association meetings, where the Food and Popular Culture panels, so ably curated by Beverly Taylor, allowed me to explore some of its overarching ideas. Two sabbaticals from Mills College, plus a strategically timed course release, arrived at ideal moments—and I'll always be grateful to Mills's students for years of classroom exchanges that inspired so many of these ideas.

Many individuals provided invaluable help at crucial junctures. The anonymous reviewers at *Legacy* gave excellent feedback for my article on Sarah Orne Jewett. Two anonymous reviewers for the University of Alabama Press were extremely helpful and perceptive. Gary Scharnhorst, series editor for UA Press, also provided useful advice. A particular thank you to Kim Magowan, who gave the manuscript a most scrupulous and brilliant reading.

Since years of work don't exist in a vacuum, a special thank you to Kathryn Reiss and the rest of my family, who were unremittingly supportive, encouraging, and confident about the value of the project.

KITCHEN ECONOMICS

INTRODUCTION

Female Regionalist Writing and Aeconomia

The first sentence of Rose Terry Cooke's "Miss Beulah's Bonnet" (1880) has Miss Beulah warning the village hatmaker who is going to refurbish her aging Leghorn bonnet: "I don't want to be too fine, ye know, Mary Jane,—somethin' tasty and kind of suitable."[1] Miss Beulah's idiom of aesthetic restraint—"tasty" (but not too fine)—proves a durable metonym in a story where a good deal of the drama accrues around the challenges to her kitchen economies. Drawing "more than half [her] subsistence from the garden and orchard" (197) and relying on stewing up the hens in the barn once their laying days are over, Miss Beulah barely copes with the unexpected arrival of her widowed niece and three children from the city, especially when dividends from a "small amount of money carefully invested" (197) fail to appear. Great-nephew Jack, in particular, pushes her careful household management to the limit. Like some fairy-tale Hansel, hungry and "longing for gingerbread" (207), or like Jack the Giant Killer, Jack and his "preternatural appetite" (207) reach almost mythic proportions. As Miss Beulah laments: "Tain't no use a-tryin' to fill him. He's holler down to his boots. . . . If he grows . . . accordin' to what he eats, he'll be as big as Goliath. . . . I don't begrudge the boy reasonable vittles, but I can't buy butcher's meat enough to satisfy him noway" (210). Harboring unreasonable desires that Miss Beulah cannot satisfy in the marketplace, this "holler" Goliath underscores by contrast what would appear to be the distinctively female virtues of Miss Beulah's household economy—frugality, self-sacrifice, controlled appetite, and restrained urges—as she seeks to feed five people with virtually no money. She even refuses to replace the Leghorn that Jack arranges to have squashed. It is only at the very end of the story that what Mary Jane calls the "tastiest bunnit . . . I ever see in my life" (213)—sent by Miss Beulah's great-niece Sarah, now working in Chicago and making "great wages" (213)— begins to imply the encroachment of new market economies on Miss Beulah's austere life.

Such frugal kitchen and household economies are familiar to readers of late nineteenth-century female regionalism in the United States. Works such as Sarah Orne Jewett's *The Country of the Pointed Firs*, Mary Wilkins Freeman's "A Mistaken Charity," and Alice Dunbar-Nelson's "Mr. Baptiste" accustom us to characters who tout the value of relying on their own produce and resources and who make a virtue of economizing. "'Out of debt, out of danger,' mother always said" (209) observes Miss Beulah when she refuses Mary Jane's offer to extend credit to her. Harriet and Charlotte in "A Mistaken Charity" subsist on pumpkins, berries, and dandelion greens. Mr. Baptiste makes his living by bartering discarded fruit in the kitchens of New Orleans. A mythos of parsimony invests these stories, often accompanied by a residual or elegiac republicanism whereby an ethos of self-sufficiency, autonomy, and virtue is put to the service of the greater good. Miss Beulah's obdurate independence goes hand in hand with her self-sacrificing attempts to stretch her household affairs to accommodate four more people. She "nigh about worked her head off for 'em, and never charged a cent o' board" (212). We might think of the story as a miniature American Georgic that invokes a "discourse of rural virtue," the marks of which were "sedentary farming . . . and embeddedness in [simple] market relations."[2]

Most scholars interested in the socioeconomic contexts of late nineteenth-century US literature find stories such as this one—with its barn full of hens, an ancient (and not too fine) bonnet, a small sum in the savings bank, and a psychic allegiance to "goin' without" (213)—largely out of step with its historical moment. The consensus narrative has the United States set on a frenetic path to modernity, undergoing critical transformations characterized by the increasing subordination, or at least exposure, of cultural and psychic economies to the exchange relations of the marketplace. Following Eric Sundquist's precept that the "age of realism in America is the age of the *romance of money*,"[3] the most persuasive scholarly narratives about late nineteenth-century historical change in the United States reveal the "incorporation" of the American economy and culture under the advance of corporate capitalism;[4] the rise of monopolies and an increasingly centralized economy; the competing demands of labor and capital; debates about the equitable distribution of national wealth and the currencies (gold, silver, paper) appropriate to efficient market exchange amid enormous increases in GNP; heightened social anxieties amid rapid shifts in social mobility and immense influxes of immigrants; the opening of new markets encouraging ever greater consumer choice and new "cultures of consumption" in an era when Western societies were beginning for the first time to "contemplate abundance";[5] "complex alterations of human value,"[6] as Americans turned from disciplined expenditure to "consuming desire" bolstered by an increasing reliance on credit and debt;[7] "frantic panoramas" of fractured cultural forms and mass public discourses;[8] emergent constructions of selfhood wherein unfulfilled human beings sought therapeutic outlets for their anxieties;[9] new psychic structures of fantasy as individuals turned from small, local markets to shopping in new, exotic, theatricalized department stores geared toward the "arousal of free-floating desire";[10] a desire for authenticity amid an epidemic of "counterfeit" cultural forms;[11] new economic forms beginning to allow, indeed encourage, women to express their desires by consuming commodities;[12] new constructions of "economics" as the science of subjective (and infinite) wants and desires; and an "aesthetics of consumption"[13]—new narrative and representational strategies suitable to the fractured social relations of an onrushing modernity. Amid such tumultuous economic times and swirling social and psychic changes, Miss Beulah's commitment to self-sacrifice and penurious living seem residual, incidental, disconnected. The story, like other female regionalist writings, contrives little more than a "counterworld to 1890s modernity."[14]

Richard Brodhead and others argue that the allure of counterworlds constitutes the very appeal of such writing to late nineteenth-century urban elites who wished to ignore, or displace, the historical reality of a United States riven by competing voices, values, and class and economic interests. From this perspective, stories such as "Miss Beulah's Bonnet" with its homogeneous small-town population proceed on the basis of unexamined assumptions favoring white racial privilege, middle- and upper-class status, and Anglo-American cultural supremacy at a moment when many elite Americans felt that the social order was under threat from "big business, class conflict, ignorant plutocrats, and dirty immigrants."[15] Cooke's generous villager, Miss Beulah, therefore represents the work of many female regionalists for whom "country refuges, quaint villages, and the lures of tradition, community, and authenticity" offered the "solace of continuity and cultural stability" to urban elites apprehensive about the loss of their cultural identity and authority.[16] Deceptively simple accounts of idiosyncratic yet cohesive village life conjure up a "vision of a unified social totality" in which (white) villagers promote nativist (Anglo-American) values;[17] they set out to construct a new, stable social order based on "deeply racialized and nationalistic" categories;[18] their assaults on economic extravagance reflecting (white) anxieties about racial and sexual "irregularities";[19] they may even symbolize "manifest domesticity," a disciplinary regime that "entails conquering and taming the wild, the natural, and the alien" and that is therefore "related to the imperial project of civilizing."[20] That "social totality" might signify an imaginary nation as, at a moment of massive cultural, socioeconomic, and psychological transformation, American culture "returned to and reified a monologic national historical narrative, a unifying, triumphalist vision of the past."[21] From this perspective, it is clear why Miss Beulah's Leghorn turns out to be her "mother's wedding bunnit" (196). Her desire to refurbish it rather than taking another on credit connects her economical lifestyle to a ceremonial embrace of traditional folkways and thus to an idyllic, mystified vision of American values.

Yet a "mythos of parsimony" fails to do justice to "Miss Beulah's Bonnet"— and to female regionalist fiction—as a complex site of economic representation. The story's plot is constructed around a question that political economists from Adam Smith to Thomas Malthus, David Ricardo to John Stuart Mill placed at the center of their theoretical agenda and that late nineteenth-century neoclassical economists tackled anew: how to maximize the utility of scarce resources. Miss Beulah's crisis is precipitated by her niece's desire to "save a good deal of money if she could spend the summer with Aunt Beulah" (198) in order to allow her daughter Sarah to save for her wedding. She rents her house and by moving in with Miss Beulah is "spared the expense of board and lodging for her family" (198). Miss Beulah, in turn, solves her crisis through economic triage: no twenty-five-cent circus for Janey, serving cheap "pudding and johnny-cake" (210), and putting off the acquisition of a new bonnet. She finds "other uses for money this year besides bunnits" (208). Both Miss Beulah and her niece turn out to be rational economic agents, the niece a woman of "unusual common sense" (198), Miss Beulah facing her economic dilemma by "arrang[ing] it logically" (209). They are more homo economicus than Jack, with his gargantuan appetite, ever seems likely to be. Making scarcity and an orderly response to it by rational agents central to the plot, the author shifts focus away from the *archaism* of a one-bonnet woman to the *arche* of economic analysis: to the rational decision-making processes that undergird such considerations, which are supposed to define homo economicus and are capable of being formalized in abstract terms as universally acknowledged laws of economic behavior.

One of my goals in this book is to restore the formal discourses underpinning female regionalist writing by resituating it within traditions of classical political economic thought: premodern and Enlightenment political economy (Plato, Aristotle, Thomas More, John Locke, Thomas Hobbes, Baron de Montesquieu, Jean-Jacques Rousseau) as well as later works by classical political economic thinkers who specifically addressed the conditions of market society, such as Smith, Malthus, and Mill. For a century after Adam Smith, political economists sought to construct and to constitute their authority through a body of formal knowledge focused on the workings of markets and the behavior of individuals within them. David Ricardo was a central figure here, he and his disciples looking to derive "irrevocable and universal" laws of economic behavior such as the "law of diminishing returns, the law of population growth, the law of wages, the law of capital accumulation, the law of rent, and the law of markets."[22] Some principles enjoyed widespread assent. First, humans act rationally to maximize the utility of their limited means. Second, as J. S. Mill argued, nature is miserly so that resources are always scarce.[23] Third, the fact of scarce resources entails competition between economic agents. Fourth, economic agents want to accumulate wealth while avoiding the pain or disutility of labor. Fifth, competitive markets reveal the aggregated operations of self-interested actions. Sixth, markets produce the best allocation of resources and the best method for accumulating wealth on the grounds of their superior efficiency.

But political economy meant more than the search for a set of laws or codified theories about how market economies function. In general, classical economists formed a body of thought aimed at answering broad questions about how a healthy polity might organize a productive distribution of resources and wealth for the common good; they were intellectually attuned to interpreting economic activity as the product of interdependent members of a social group. As J. S. Mill observed, the discipline of political economy was focused on the "nature of Wealth, and the laws of its production and distribution," including the "operation of all the causes by which the condition of mankind, or of any society of human beings, in respect of this universal object of human desire, is made prosperous or the reverse."[24] Even Adam Smith, whose incisive account of the self-interested economic agent led to hegemonic constructions of homo economicus in the nineteenth century, saw humans as social beings constructed within and contributing to a civil society.[25] Self-interest, for Smith, defined the behavior of humans participating in markets; it was not the *core* principle of human identity. Political economy recognized its roots in "*oikos*, the Greek from which we derive ecumenical (all in this together), economics (material providing), and ecology (interdependence of all the creation)."[26]

The rational economic choices Miss Beulah makes are aimed at the *oikos* in this sense. But that signifies more than a generous spirit. We can legitimately speak of a "kitchen commonwealth" because the story develops the thinking underpinning her hard choices in abstract terms. Having refused the village hatmaker's offer of credit, Miss Beulah apportions her remaining stock of money according to a rigorously worked-out list of priorities: Forgoing a trip to the circus saves twenty-five cents; giving up a new bonnet means she has the fifteen dollars promised to Sarah, five dollars due for charity, and twenty dollars in her will for Janey. This leaves "no margin for daily expenses" (209). The point here is not that she enters the market in order to subsist. The logic of the market determines her choices. In structural terms, Miss Beulah's economic assumptions accord with a post-Malthusian analysis of commonwealth in which the economic dilemma becomes, fundamentally, how to divide a means of subsistence under threat from ever greater population pressure. Miss Beulah's household operates as a domestic version of one influential outgrowth of Malthusian thought: David Ricardo's wages-fund theory. Ricardo considered wealth distribution a zero-sum game whereby the various classes of society competed for a determinate sum of capital: more investment in capital goods meant less money available for hiring labor. Miss Beulah makes the same assumption in terms of distributing her limited (in fact, diminishing) capital among her "increased family." Like wages-fund theory, the rational choices she has to make commence with a set of assumptions (a fixed sum of capital), confront the same problems (a scarcity of resources), and work toward the same solutions (distributing resources unequally among competing priorities). Parsimony is a logical response to scarcity.

What I call "kitchen economics" resists the counterworld characterization of female regionalism by situating the kitchen and the *oikos*—the broad ensemble of household arrangements to which kitchens metonymically refer—in relation to the broad questions political economists raised in formal idioms and in more public venues about the economic life of polities. How might polities be modeled? How do they change over time? How might resources and wealth be more productively distributed? These fictions construct female subjects and the domestic spaces and social roles they occupy in firm relation to political economic thought. That, in turn, entails new approaches to the issue of gender in assessing the ideological orders of female regionalism. In looking askance at Jack's prodigious appetite, for example, Rose Terry Cooke joins many other female regionalist authors in considering how economic systems cater to a supersized male appetite that is detrimental to the common good. These works frequently contest the identification of *men* with the paradigmatic figure of homo economicus and the supposition that theories of economy organized around that figure bear the imprimatur of natural and universal law. The terms of that challenge are complex and often contradictory. "Miss Beulah's Bonnet" reverses the gendered logic of economic man only to resurrect it in a different form. In setting Miss Beulah's rational economies against Jack's inordinate appetite, the story represents her as an unexpected heir to traditions of classical political economic thought that Jack seems to have abandoned. One question the story raises is therefore whether gender constructs desiring or rational beings in different ways. Could femina economica in the kitchen ground a universal set of economic laws that apply equally to men and women—for instance, that all human beings are naturally competitive, or rational, or acquisitive—despite the social codes that place men and women in different domains?

Approaching the kitchen commonwealth through the logic of political economic thought puts my approach at odds with most appraisers of domesticity in female regionalist writing. Long a key category in feminist hermeneutics, women's domestic labor has generated crucial debates about the economic and cultural value of the homework economy—about the value, for example, of caring labor or of unpaid domestic labor, or about the (de)valuing of domestic roles.[27] The role of the anomic housewife bound to kitchen drudgery often represented women's social repression. Charlotte Perkins Gilman (1898) argues that women's "labor in the household has a genuine economic value" for men (though not for women), since it "enables men to produce more wealth than they otherwise could."[28] Women create an "enormous class of non-productive consumers." Betty Friedan reprised many of Gilman's arguments in *The Feminine Mystique* (1963). But second-wave feminist analysis also came to position domesticity as a lynchpin for understanding and reclaiming the richness of women's cultures. Work in the home "has at its base an epistemology of domesticity whose tenets embrace moral, practical, and compassionate labor."[29] Women-centered languages, ceremonies, and traditions emerging out of the female-dominated spaces of kitchen, garden, and drawing room signified to many feminists a socially discounted but culturally powerful form of resistance. Its separateness from the realm of patriarchal relations meant that domesticity could even function as a privileged space of critique.

Feminist appraisers of female regionalist writing often accepted this logic. They interpreted its focus on domestic cultures as a gnosis;[30] as a sign of the vitality and complexity of women-centered epistemologies; as a figuring forth of the subversive shapes of "female relational reality;"[31] and as a female world of love, ritual, and community in which "mutual support and productive work grant mothers and daughters self-respect and love."[32] It becomes possible to read household activities as a critique of alienated labor under conditions of market capitalism—a "precapitalist, preindustrial matriarchal community," running "counter to the urban, upper-class, capitalist, industrial, male-dominated civilization" of the late nineteenth century.[33] This approach has been updated in theoretically sophisticated ways. Catriona Sandilands's queer, ecofeminist reading of Jewett emphasizes the notion that it is *only* when "apart"—apart, that is, from a "dominant (male) society"—that "women together can develop a critical and reflective distance on processes of social and natural change."[34] For Judith Fetterley and Marjorie Pryse "place" is understood to be a socioeconomic realm dominated by white men and subject to their ideologies of nation, property, and power. The trope of decenteredness—writing "out of place"—allows them to realize the counterhegemonic possibilities of regionalism. Domestic spaces, for them, manifest a "propertyless condition" in a "location, space, and place that is disconnected from ownership."[35]

Even the most nuanced studies of nineteenth-century domesticity emphasize the dissociation of bonnets, hens, and kitchen life from the exchange relations of the marketplace. Nancy Glazener observes that women who worked at home had the "rare privilege of producing and laboring for the immediate use of their household, which meant that their labor could function symbolically (though not actually) as labor outside of capitalist relations."[36] Andrew Lawson concurs, arguing that realist writers suffering the vicissitudes of the United States' turbulent transition to free market capitalism looked to posit the "salient facts of the household economy and of local exchange against the alienating abstractions of the capitalist market."[37] The useful materialities of everyday household affairs could link "republican virtue to the political economy of the freehold."[38] Adapting one's household economy to old hens and homegrown produce promises to resist the perilous lure of new debt-inducing credit systems. Here too home labor has limited oppositional value. Confined to rural enclaves relatively insulated from the dislocating forces of hegemonic capitalism, exchange relations are merely "bypassed or stalled."[39] Even Beth Sutton-Ramspeck's ambitious study of "literary housekeeping"—female writers employing the domestic realm to lay claim to the "marketplace and halls of government"—is mediated through issues considered pertinent to middle-class women, such as "making the food supply safe, 'cleaning up' society, [and] improving the human race through 'public motherhood.'"[40] In this she follows the logic of Lora Romero's "idiom of social housekeeping,"[41] which accorded nineteenth-century middle-class women a contestatory discourse by making domestic orderliness a source of articulate resistance to a semibarbarous and brutal masculinity, while supporting the broader disciplinary procedures whereby middle-class women (and men) sought to consolidate their cultural authority.

When it comes to assessments of female regionalism, most scholars take "kitchen" (and "*oikos*")—the realm of bonnets, orderly domestic activities, women's work, women's communities, and economizing—and "economics" as incongruous, even contradictory, terms. In *Kitchen Economics* I recognize the economies of the household and the role of the female household manager as the problematic of a complex and varied relationship to political economic thought. To theorize that relationship, I introduce the concepts of aeconomia and femina economica. Deriving from the Greek roots of "economy" (*oikos* + *nomos*, one who manages a household), the terms are tropes of productive tension. The contrast between the hat Miss Beulah refuses to take on credit and the tasty Chicago bonnet suggests that her household aeconomia cannot be merely conflated with a market economy. And as figures of difference, these terms retain a capacity for critique. Miss Beulah's struggle to accommodate Jack's supersized appetite condemns a city boy's voraciousness and arguably implicates, and genders, a city market culture along with him. The story bears an affinity here to Charlotte Perkins Gilman's critique of an "unnatural appetite," an "excessive hunger" in American society, which metaphorizes unnaturally accentuated sex-distinctions caused by an "abnormal economic relation" between men and women.[42]

Unlike Gilman's argument about the decidedly noneconomic functions of women's domestic spaces, the terms "aeconomia" and "femina economica" characterize women as economic beings and position their domestic affairs in oblique relation to an array of cultural practices and knowledge systems signifying "the economic." What complicates the critique of supersized male appetites in "Miss Beulah's Bonnet" is Miss Beulah's identification with economic man, the self-interested, competitive, rational economic agent central to classical economic thought. And what complicates *that* identification is Miss Beulah's response to her niece's daughter, Janey, for whom this "poor spinster's repressed affection" and her secret "love of beauty . . . all blossomed" (199). Janey's admiration at the end of the story for the new Chicago hat ("Pitty, pitty bonnet!" [213]) signifies the potentially frightening impact of a market economy burgeoning with appetites impossible to satisfy—but also the moment at which appetite and desire begin profitably to invade Miss Beulah's subsistence economies and open up her psyche to values incommensurate with restraint and careful management. In pointing to such moments of economic relation as a presence and problematic, these terms resist the counterworld logic that female regionalist writings simply stand outside the hegemony of (white male) market relations, whether one reads that stance as a prelude to critique; as an important, but residual, counter to the disturbing advent of market capitalism; or as a fictional realm too far removed from exchange relations to allow a productive critique of them. Their characteristic idioms affiliated with the formal discourses and abstract laws of political economy, kitchen activities, to paraphrase Glazener, take on symbolic functions inside, rather than outside, capitalist relations and market ideologies. Kitchen commonwealths are counterparts of, not counterworlds to, modernity.

One of my primary concerns in this book is the complicated modalities of that affiliation. While political economists in the nineteenth century could always represent their knowledge as a constellation of abstract principles capable of formal expression, I approach that body of thought as a set of widely disseminated narratives that structured countless inquiries into, assumptions about, and illustrative fictions of economic life. Here, representations of "the economic" compel a culture's attention through "large narrative structures" that join "economic issues to political, social, and psychological concerns."[43] The rhetorical strategies of formal nineteenth-century political economic thought often exhibited what to today's economists would be a nonchalant reliance on story, anecdote, hearsay, even fable. Political economic thought had the ability to "range freely across the economic and the non-economic, to incorporate the social and the psychological into their analyses, to move from historical narrative to theoretical discourse without apology."[44] It provided a "wide canvas on which political economists once created pictures of social existence and discussed the relations that defined the way their world worked."[45] Persuasive fictions about the natural characteristics of homo economicus— "arguments about what the nature of man is or should be"[46]—or the natural progression of human civilizations underwrote political economic law and constituted its claims to truth.[47]

Narrative exposition proved a potent way to bring the formal knowledge systems of political economy into semiformal and popular discourses. Harriet Martineau's nine-volume work, *Illustrations of Political Economy* (1832–34), which cast economic principles in fictional form, proved to be an enduringly influential popularization of political economy across the nineteenth century. Writers in journals such as *Atlantic Monthly, Harper's, Scribner's,* and *Century* often drew upon political economic principles, articulating them formally but also reimagining them as anecdote, fiction, parable, fable, and travelogue. Many popular works that sought to address pressing socioeconomic questions of the late nineteenth century followed suit. Henry George's *Progress and Poverty* (1879), William Graham Sumner's *What Social Classes Owe to Each Other* (1883), and Andrew Carnegie's "Wealth" (1889) all depended on paradigmatic fictions to advance their arguments. So did Charlotte Perkins Gilman's *Women and Economics*, published to "universal acclaim,"[48] a complement to the scores of didactically conceived Martineau-like fictions that illustrated her economic theories over the course of her career.[49]

Laura Brown's concept of a "cultural fable" is particularly valuable in explaining how political economic thought penetrated a variety of cultural registers. A "set of related figures that have a distinctive structure," cultural fables are "generated collectively in many texts over a period of time." They are also responsive to the debates, events, and discourses pertinent to particular historical circumstances. A cultural fable "can be said to tell a story whose protagonist is an emanation of contemporary experience and whose action reflects an imaginative negotiation with that experience." The eighteenth-century figure of Lady Credit, for example, associated the female body with a "powerfully realized and influential cultural expression of fluctuation and excess, distinctive aspects of the experience of modernity."[50] Lady Credit accommodated cultural anxieties imaginatively and represented them across many different cultural realms. Some political economic fables are relatively formal and consciously articulated features of political economic thought. But the concept helps to explain how propositions about economic life articulated abstractly in formal knowledge systems were disseminated across a vast range of cultural activity through a repertoire of recurring situations, tropes, and characters, and through the typical plots that disposed them in a logical relationship to each other. Miss Beulah is a rational economic agent not in direct relation to Adam Smith or J. S. Mill but in relation to an immense cultural "storying" about fundamental economic principles.

This book is structured around three such cultural fables. In chapters 1 and 2 I examine stages theory, or stadialism—a description of *how* societies evolve, and how they *should* evolve, in stages over time, generally understood in terms of a linear and progressive movement from savagery (characterized by hunting and gathering), barbarism (settled agriculture), and civilization (commercialism, industrialism, and market economies). Political economic principles underpinned the logic of these stages. Assuming that humans were fundamentally motivated to exchange goods with each other, stadialists argued that the historical process was shaped by the efficiencies accruing to a division of labor and to a competitive market system presided over by the civilizing effect of capital. That logic finds persuasive expression in the formidable cultural mechanism of what I call a "plot of polity": at once a formulaic story of how historical progress gives rise to a civilized polity, a coordinating logic capable of disclosing how events are causally and temporally linked, and a narrative structure that can be disclosed, and governed, only from the standpoint of an observer at the end of the narrative/historical process.

In chapter 2 I trace the complex workings of stages theory as it structures two of Mary Wilkins Freeman's stories, "The Revolt of 'Mother'" and "A Mistaken Charity." The account of political liberalism in "The Revolt of 'Mother'" charts Mother's shift in status against geopolitic transformations on the one hand (colonists moving from the Old World to the New) and Hobbesian and Lockean narratives of the emergence of civil society on the other—only to find that the two narratives do not match. "A Mistaken Charity" crosscuts its attempt to bring republican principles of self-sufficiency and civic virtue to bear on contemporary discourses about charity with its two elderly heroines' perplexing embrace of a "savage" gathering lifestyle. Stadial thinking also contributes to analyses of Jewett's accounts of Green Island (chapter 4) and the Bowden reunion (chapter 7), the latter of which has become a touchstone for scholars' criticisms of what seem to be nostalgic, nationalistic, and even racist constructions of history in female regionalist writing. The Bowden reunion, together with the Green Island chapters, shapes a much more speculative treatment of historical plots of evolving civilizations than scholars have yet recognized. They also work to rebut the common accusation that female regionalists are broadly nostalgic for a simpler, more rural past.

The second cultural fable is the topos of the fabulous island commonwealth. This staple of economic modeling from Thomas More's *Utopia* (1516) to Daniel Defoe's *Robinson Crusoe* (1719) has been employed to explicate abstract economic laws as well the development of human societies. In chapter 3, "'Supposing an Island': Political Economic Topographies in Stowe and Jewett," I look briefly at Jewett's "The King of Folly Island" (1888) and in detail at Harriet Beecher Stowe's *The Pearl of Orr's Island* (1862), a novel that introduces what amounts to a subgenre of island fictions within New England female regionalism.[51] I argue that female regionalists persistently tapped traditions of political economic thought embedded in island realms. Regionalists also built on a long history of broader island-discourses in the United States. *Pearl*, for example, ties fables about how civilizations develop to contemporary discourses about the economies of Caribbean islands, which in the postbellum era were frequently invoked to expound on American economic power, colonial aspirations, and nationalist and racial ideologies. It is Stowe's "Caribbeanism" that upsets *Pearl*'s attempt, or perhaps yearning, to establish a utopian commonwealth on Orr's Island. It also underwrites the migration of political economic thought into the kitchen.

In chapter 4, "The Kitchen Economics of Green Island in Jewett's *The Country of the Pointed Firs*," I continue to explore the trope of the island commonwealth by looking closely at the excursion to Green Island, where Mrs. Todd and the narrator collude with Mrs. Blackett to produce a chowder feast. The episode's modality is fabulist—an oneiric account of harmonious communities, of digging potatoes, and making chowder in an "old kitchen" somewhere over the sea. But the contexts it engages are very much of the late nineteenth century. Invoking More's *Utopia*, and building on Stowe's sense that the kitchen can be a privileged site of political economic knowledge, the Green Island chapters fashion a kitchen economics out of abstract political economic principles amid contemporary debates about how the United States might organize a more productive distribution of resources and wealth. Favoring balanced distributions, moderate sums, and stable measures of value, Jewett nonetheless includes as part of her distinctively-speculative political economy an acknowledgment of the growing hegemony of market capitalism and the (neo)classical ideologies of insatiable human wants and mandatory capital accumulation that supported them.

In chapters 5 and 6 I focus on the complex cultural fable of the body politic by studying narratives about eating and drinking in the political economic mode that Catherine Gallagher terms "bioeconomics"—the tendency among classical political economists to focus on "interconnections [between] populations, the food supply, modes of production and exchange, and their impact on life forms."[52] Metaphors of food production, distribution, and consumption constantly invoke the body politic, and have done so for millennia. Aristotle, contemplating the ideal of the city, observed that the many people who constitute it "can when joined together be better . . . just as dinners contributed [by many] can be better than those equipped from a single expenditure."[53] Green Island chowder-making (as well as Bowden reunion gingerbread) claims that heritage. They are feast fables in which raw materials brought together from several sources combine with kitchen work to delineate a speculative commonwealth. I pursue that inquiry in chapter 5 within the context of *the* feast that, in the United States, defines iconic national values: Thanksgiving. In "Talking Turkey: The Political Economy of Thanksgiving in Cooke and Stowe," I argue that turkey-day stories signify more than merely generic values of family, amity, and prosperity. They construct imagined histories; they write economics in a bioeconomic idiom, composing narratives about production, consumption, and distribution, about appropriate divisions of labor, gendered labor roles, and an imaginary body politic. Above all, they reconstruct the body politic under the sign of aeconomia. Perhaps the plurals, bodies politic and aeconomiae, are more appropriate. Cooke's *Huckleberries* (1892) contains no fewer than four Thanksgiving stories, ending with one ("How Celia Changed Her Mind") that seems to reverse the modality of the first three. Kitchen commonwealths in female regionalist turkey-day stories overdetermine the bioeconomic idiom that aligns Thanksgiving with broad national and economic significations.

In chapter 6, "Reconstructing the 'Fruit Sublime' in Dunbar-Nelson's 'Mr. Baptiste,'" I turn from New England feast days to New Orleans and the discourse of what I call the "fruit sublime." Through trade, travelogue, and political discourse, the metaphor of "ripe fruit" connects the extravagant tropical fruit production of Caribbean lands to the United States' long-standing attempts to dominate the broader Caribbean region. The fruit sublime implies, ultimately, abjection.[54] Mr. Baptiste, the title character of Dunbar-Nelson's short story, subsists in the interstices of the tropical fruit trade by bartering fruit that has been thrown away because it is overripe. His own abjection— he is unceremoniously thrown into potter's field at the end—invites us to recall a Caribbeanist discourse so richly imagined in the writings of US visitors to tropical lands that their peoples seem displaced into, or subsumed by, the fantastic fruits that are never quite theirs. Mr. Baptiste's kitchen bartering inscribes, and disrupts, the topos that in part underwrites the US discourse on Caribbean fruit, fruit lands, and, indeed, fruit people: a stadialist barter-to-capitalism plot of history that offers ideological support for the US presence in tropical fruit–producing lands. Inviting acts of historical reconstruction, "Mr. Baptiste" is a remarkable rewriting of the "Caribbeanist" discourse Stowe had tapped a quarter century previously.

I position aeconomia in an oblique and shifting relation to the cultural fables that inform female regionalist narrative. I do not read the "distinctive structure" of the cultural fable as a necessary constraint on the production of meaning—as the figure to which textual meanings refer. Instead, I read the process of signification as that which complicates the figure by actively participating in the construction of its meaning. What motivates this claim is the persistent engagement of female regionalists with *fable* and strategies of *fabling*. One could hardly construe the (bio)economic implications of Jack's gigantic appetite in "Miss Beulah's Bonnet," for example, without considering the effect of Cooke's playful fabling. The story incorporates numerous folk and fairy tales about poverty, widowed mothers, rascally boys, and undreamed of riches: Hansel, the resourceful Jack of Jack the Giant Killer, and the mischievous, cow-selling Jack of Jack and the Beanstalk. Such odd conjunctions of aeconomia and fable construct a whimsical and playfully disorienting narrative mode in "Miss Beulah's Bonnet." Somehow, Jack's "preternatural appetite" has to be reconciled with his fairy-tale avatars' misdemeanors and successes. That same narrative mode appears regularly in female regionalist fiction. Hansel and Gretel, notably, informs Sarah Orne Jewett's meditation on social and narrative economies in the gingerbread house scene at the Bowden reunion.

I explore the complex relationship between aeconomia and cultural fables about economics as a form of economic fabulism. Though fables seem a quintessentially counterfactual form—self-consciously moralizing, incorporating supernatural or magical elements, at odds with reality as we think we know it—they can possess substantial political content and work to deconstruct hegemonic representations of the polity.[55] In chapter 5 I employ Annabel Patterson's striking analysis of Aesop's "The Belly and the Members" in order to reconceive the trope of the body politic in female regionalist Thanksgiving fictions. Kitchen fabling can also be understood as *fabulism* in its more contemporary sense: a form that superimposes the fabulous and the everyday and exercises a broad critique of realism as a narrative form whose authority rests on its putative ability to represent social relations truthfully and absolutely, to present its "ordered significances . . . as immanent to society," and thus to contain social contradictions.[56] Fabulism problematizes what Roland Barthes called "writing degree zero": the urge of realism to make its acts of representation invisible, thus to make that which is represented seem universal and incontestable. This is not to conflate late nineteenth-century female regionalism with post–World War II magical realism but to argue that interpretations of aeconomia in female regionalist fiction must, like magical realism, take into account fairy tale and fable as a persistent presence in its construction of economic meanings.

Economic fabling as I analyze it here can be theorized profitably in terms of Michel Foucault's concept of *heterotopia*. In an early lecture "Des Espaces Autres" (1967), Foucault argues that, unlike the concept of utopia, there are actual places that can be conceived of "counter sites, a kind of effectively enacted utopia in which real sites, all the other real sites that can be found within the culture, are simultaneously represented, contested, and inverted. . . . The heterotopia is capable of juxtaposing in a single real space several spaces, several sites that are in themselves incompatible."[57] Though Foucault left this provocative idea largely unelaborated, the concept is generally taken to refer to real spaces that function outside of, or on the borders of, or in between community norms. These are sites where different kinds or conceptions of space can be superimposed, and where material realities can be imaginatively transformed. Heterotopia signifies "spaces of alternate ordering," which "marks them out as Other and allows them to be seen as an example of an alternative way of doing things."[58]

Female regionalist representations of the kitchen commonwealth open up an "other space" within what could otherwise appear to be the most mundane social sites of the kitchen and household. Aeconomia superimposes a curious mixture of abstract economic thought and fable/fabulism on the real quotidian sites of women's domestic activities, reconfiguring in the process their characteristic functions. Freeman's stories constantly evoke heterotopia. In "The Revolt of 'Mother'" Mother claims the barn as home, and indeed as a "kitchen of her dreams," in an odd superimposition of market and domestic activity. In "A Mistaken Charity," Charlotte and Harriet escape from the Old Ladies Home to their home—which turns out not to be "their" home any more. The most striking instance, however, is the gingerbread house at Jewett's Bowden reunion, a miniature version of the Bowden house and of the House of Bowden, which models various economic relations and which, in falling to ruin at the feast's end, captures the provisional and contested qualities of heterotopia as Foucault envisages them in his lecture.

Scholars often think of heterotopia in terms of its capacity to critique—to invert, contest, resist—social structures of order. I follow Robert J. Topinka's somewhat different emphasis. Topinka argues that heterotopian spaces are less sites of resistance than of "reordering," which provide "glimpses of the governing principles of order." Heterotopias "reconstitute knowledge, presenting a view of its structural formation that might not otherwise be visible," making "legible the ground on which knowledge is built by complicating that ground."[59] What I call economic fabulism does not necessarily function in contradiction to, or as a subversion of, cultural fable—indeed, it would follow from the logic of heterotopia that interpretations of such complicatedly imbricated spaces could not conform to a single orientation. In adapting the topoi of cultural fables, however, fabulism may well reveal the historical and cultural structures that make them pertinent and timely. The terms "aeconomia" and "femina economica" are also intended to work in this way: they open up for examination and put into question their relationship to "economics" and "homo economicus" so that the obviousness of the terms and the clarity of the oppositions begin to erode. Miss Beulah's recouping of the economic functions of homo economicus from Jack's appetite suggests one way in which the kitchen, by making space for what would seem distinctively Other, causes us to scrutinize the logic that separates the terms.

Topinka's analysis, however, implies a still broader inquiry into the very ground of our assumptions about economics—that is to say, what we *mean* by "economic functions" in the first place. The title of chapter 7, "Economics Gingerbread Style: Toward a Model Political Economy of the Kitchen," points to why this inquiry is necessary. It seems counterintuitive, oxymoronic even, to adapt a set of economic principles from the baking of a gingerbread house. One reason is that the discipline of political economy was itself subject to a late-century paradigm shift as neoclassical economics began to supersede it. To speak of the political economy of the kitchen requires a careful elucidation of how the "governing principles of order" of late nineteenth-century economic knowledge underwent a reordering that has defined the study of economics ever since. From the perspective of mainstream economics, some of the political economic contexts that might make stories about gingerbread houses and fabulous islands significant *also* read like fable, or at least as a mode of knowledge in serious need of scientific and mathematical upgrading.

The first manifestos of neoclassical economics published in Britain and the United States—William Stanley Jevons's *Theory of Political Economy* (1871) and Alfred Marshall's *Principles of Economics* (1890) prominent among them—did not disavow classical principles of economic thought so much as focus and narrow them into a "science" of markets. Three aspects of this transformation are of great consequence to the way we might articulate the "economic" meanings of a gingerbread house (or a bonnet, or fabulous island, or Thanksgiving feast). First, the new science of economics was able to quantify its insights by focusing solely on market behaviors. Though one can neither measure nor quantify desire nor account for why individuals have certain preferences, the choices they make in the market can be quantified. There, commodities are priced, affording consumers a way to evaluate their options. On that basis, economists could begin to consider their work a mathematically based science—indeed, the "only truly rigorous and scientific discipline across the social sciences."[60] Second, neoclassical economics shifted away from zero-sum wages-fund thinking by beginning to consider humans as creatures of infinite wants. What exercised constraint on human choice was neither a cap on the total capital available, nor some sense that humans naturally favored restraint, but granting "new prominence to the causes that govern the relative exchange values of different things." Economists, Marshall insists, should study how individuals allocate value differentially rather than absolutely.[61] Such thinking gave rise to what is often called the marginal revolution. Measuring the relative and shifting value of commodities or costs of production, marginalism focuses on the last amount an economic agent is willing to pay for a good before the marginal utility of another good supersedes it.

Third, a single-minded focus on the "mechanics of utility and self-interest" obviated broad discussions about what constituted the common good.[62] Neoclassical logic favored what has come to be called methodological individualism: "isolated, individual decision making in an austere, putatively universally applicable context," where the "universal" context was the assumption that markets have penetrated human life to the extent that all wants have to be represented by and in them.[63] Neoclassical economic practice therefore does not ask what the body politic should be or look like. Indeed, since questions of value are held to be relative and subjective, it is immaterial whether an individual allocates money to a cup of tea or to charity. This new focus on methodological individualism and mathematical formalism helped to empty out "much of the earlier social, institutional, cultural, and historical content that [political economy] was initially thought to embody."[64] As Marshall wrote in 1879, the "nation used to be called 'the Body Politic.' So long as this phrase was in common use, men thought of the interests of the whole nation when they used the word 'Political'; and then 'Political Economy' served well enough as a name for the science"—the point being that the discipline of political economy, along with the holistic principles it embraced, has begun to seem premodern.[65]

The hegemony of neoclassical economics means that historicizing female regionalist narrative within the context of political economic thought is to encounter a situation in which many of its "economic" insights have been superseded, disavowed, or traduced by what now counts as "economics." This is not to suggest that contemporary scholars of literature and culture celebrate the logic of neoclassical economic thought. Far from it. Nonetheless, the urge to read female regionalism in terms of a counterworld to modernity is generated by accepting a privileged discourse of economic knowledge that (1) understands frugality, moderation, self-restraint, and the common good as vestigial signs of a premodern world; (2) frames the most pertinent responses to the late nineteenth century in terms of the logic of a modernizing, corporatizing economy; (3) assumes a correlation between a neoclassical economic focus on subjective wants and the fractured subjectivities found in writers such as Henry James, Frank Norris, Stephen Crane, Theodore Dreiser, and Edith Wharton; and (4) promotes their work by virtue of their exemplary response to startlingly new economic conditions. That narrative of history is implicitly stadialist. In chapter 7 I explore this issue by considering the case of a handful of scholars who over the years have switched allegiance from one counterworld to another, their early embrace of the counterhegemonic implications of female regionalism giving way to a suspicion that this body of work is not so much oppositional to as out of step with the conditions of modernity. That construction of modernity is consistent with the same premodernizing narratives about historical change upon which the first neoclassical economists drew to substantiate their revolutionary ideas.

Moving toward a political economy of the kitchen therefore entails considering the pertinence of alternative economic discourses. At a moment in the twenty-first century when the discipline of mainstream economics has syndicated with neoliberal political practices to leave the United States with a market machine efficient at producing profits but with little or no aspiration to raise questions about what constitutes the common good, some economists have urged a return to the analytic and representational strategies of political economy as a way to restore the importance of history, society, narrative, interdisciplinarity, and a persuasive sense of what constitutes a commonwealth. So does ecohistory, which is to say "economics" reimagined from our historical moment of imminent ecocatastrophe, when a neoclassical economics advancing a philosophy of infinite wants and lacking any conception of commonwealth may be on the verge of providing ideological support for its own demise. Ecohistory written from what is conceivably the end of (written) history compels the emergence of different narratives about modernity. Intensifying calls for newly sufficient ways of living *now* allows a revaluation of (say) parsimony in the nineteenth-century kitchen commonwealth and of the historicizing practices that have assigned it premodern status. Jewett's gingerbread house focuses that revaluation. A heterotopian reflection on economic models and mode*ling*, model commonwealths and the laws that are thought to invest them, the gingerbread house enjoins a new consideration of the competing claims of today's economic models.

I proceed by way of case studies. Though I lean toward Sarah Orne Jewett and Mary Wilkins Freeman as the writers who most consistently and interestingly articulate a kitchen economics, my inclusion of Stowe, Cooke, and Dunbar-Nelson suggests that the boundaries of the discourse on kitchen economics cannot be fixed by writer, influence, or tradition. Kitchen economics exists as an important function of many female regionalist works. Moreover, various kitchen commonwealths incorporate political economic thought in different ways. The very concept of heterotopia precludes taking a single orientation. Nonetheless, acknowledging the potential overlap of political economic thought and the domestic spaces of female regionalism has at least two salutary effects. It resists the common counterworld hypotheses that look elsewhere to locate the most pertinent responses to an age of money. It also challenges the logic followed by so many literary and cultural histories of the period that the inevitable hegemony of market society is the only narrative about modernity worth telling.

1

PLOTS OF POLITY IN LATE NINETEENTH-CENTURY US POPULAR ECONOMIC DISCOURSES

Over the course of "Miss Beulah's Bonnet," Miss Beulah's economic travails plot onto a narrative of emerging modernity: subsistence and a parsimonious husbanding of resources yield by story's end to the pretty Chicago bonnet, seeming to mark a new era of irrepressible wants and freely circulating commodities. As such, the story stands as a provocation to stages theory, or stadialism, a metahistorical account of the evolution of human societies, which political economic thought employed to explain the emergence of civilized market societies, and which was supposed to *end* with the achievement of market society. In later chapters I elaborate the complex ways in which female regionalist writers adopt stadialism as a structural principle of their fiction and, in their kitchen commonwealths, frequently contest it. Fabulist narrative modes present a particularly potent challenge to stages theory insofar as that concept purports to establish the true plot of history along with the economic verities that are supposed to define it. I begin with some classic political economic accounts of stadialism, then analyze some of the complex purposes it served as a cultural fable. I also consider its limits, as new narratives of modernity arose in the late nineteenth century to challenge its explanatory power.

At a turning point in the history of economics, Adam Smith developed what he called the human propensity to "truck, barter, and exchange" into a description of the rational, competitive, self-interested economic agent, from whom he extrapolated a theory of how resources get distributed in a market economy: "It is not from the benevolence of the butcher, the brewer, or the baker that we expect our dinner but from their regard to their self-interest."[1] Smith's logic underpins a still broader account of social structure and, ultimately, a theory of how societies change through history. Self-interest urges humans wishing to exploit their talents and skills toward a division of labor, which makes itself felt by a widening discrepancy between a "rude state of society," in which "every man must have procured to himself every necessary and conveniency of life which he wanted," and those countries in which the efficiencies of the division of labor promote the "highest degree of industry and improvement."[2] The efficiencies accruing to a competitive market system were not, for Smith, universally to be admired. Profound costs attend a division of labor, since the "man whose whole life is spent in performing a few simple operations. . . generally becomes as stupid and ignorant as it is possible for a human creature to become"—a fate destined for most people in any "improved and civilized society."[3] It is in "barbarous societies" where each individual has to perform a variety of tasks that "invention is kept alive."[4] Nonetheless, a division of labor presides over the economic efficiencies of capital accumulation. More efficient production marks a crucial step beyond subsistence. Amassing a "general stock" beyond the requirements of "immediate consumption" frees humans from a hand-to-mouth existence.[5] From this stock a nation derives revenues and, reinvesting them, gradually grows its capital. This creates the possibility of commonwealth and allows civilization to emerge.

"Political economy," observes Regenia Gagnier, "held that the disposition to truck, barter, and trade transformed world history."[6] It did so in part by writing history, like Smith, in terms of stadialist narratives about the order and progress of civilization based on changes in the mode of subsistence. Classical political economy developed these schemas into what was usually understood to be a three- or four-stage process, plotting the evolution of societies from hunting and gathering (savagery) to pastoralism and settled agriculture (barbarism) and thence to commercial and market economies (civilization). Each stage was held to be characterized by growing specialization and increasing capital accumulation, and each corresponded with typical social and economic forms, which nineteenth-century social scientists elaborated in complex ways. Language sophistication; technology; systems of religion; architectural styles; gender roles; and familial, social, and political organization—all were invoked on a regular basis. Women were generally thought to be treated harshly in the earliest stages of human history. As the nineteenth-century anthropologist Lewis H. Morgan put it, men far back in time began to "exact fidelity from the wife, under savage penalties"; in the modern civilized family, where women have property rights, "woman has gained immensely in social position."[7]

Acquiring a concept of private property was thought to be axiomatic for societies making the step to civilization. As political economist Henry Wood wrote in 1894, the "*condition of civilization or barbarism among nations is in proportion to the security and inviolability of individual property rights.*"[8] Wood, like so many others, invoked John Locke's description of the emergence of property, property rights, money, exchange, and civil society during the normal progression of societies from a state of nature to a liberal polity. Locke's problem was how to resolve the gap between the "first ages of the world," characterized by a "commons" in which "every man should have as much as he could make use of" because "there is land enough," and the appearance of money and market economies, characterized by accumulation and unequal ownership of property. Locke's fable—"supposing an island, separate from all possible commerce with the rest of the world," he begins—invokes a human fascination with some "sparkling pebble or diamond" which, it appears, individuals would naturally desire to possess and to accumulate. This process Locke presents, rhetorically, as a fait accompli. "And thus came in the use of money, some lasting thing that men might keep without spoiling, and that by mutual consent men would take in exchange for the truly useful, but perishable supports of life."[9] The desire to accumulate something in excess of a hand-to-mouth subsistence on the richly abundant commons allows humans to articulate a concept of enduring value ("some lasting thing" that exists "without spoiling"). New conceptions of value bring in the use of money, a general equivalent, which allows exchange; exchange, in turn, fosters competition for resources, acquisitive tendencies (for something "men might keep"), and newly efficient productive modes such as a division of labor. The advent of a general equivalent underpins the very concept of a civil society. It requires mutual consent to function and laws to adjudicate the accumulation of property it makes possible.

Given that systems of exchange seem foreordained, the final stage of civilization was considered the first to embrace fully the natural proclivities of humans toward exchange, self-interest, competition, acquisition, and contract. Homo economicus enshrined the concept of civilization, which in turn guaranteed the importance of political economic analyses of society and history. Stadialism was less an idea than a persuasive, massively particularized cultural fable composed of a web of interlocking ideas. Stages theory was crucial to the development of the human sciences from the second half of the eighteenth to the end of the nineteenth century.[10] It was also of consequence to semiformal and popular economic literatures of the late nineteenth century. Among its many effects, it underwrote a variety of narratives about imperialism, race, and national character. Stages theory was advanced to show how human civilizations should evolve, to describe how actual societies have evolved, and to show how and why some have failed to do so. It afforded a putatively scientific way to categorize, and place at the apex of a hierarchy of civilization, such forms of social privilege as white masculinity, the imperial sway of European nations, Anglo-Saxon and Anglo-American cultures, and the supremacy of the United States as a polity, nation, and economy.[11] It was also employed—though in increasingly complex ways—to address the economic problems of a rapidly industrializing economy.

The concept of a plot of polity helps identify key principles of stadialism as an abstract and idealized metanarrative of history. "Plot" implies a temporal sequence: One stage necessarily follows another, contributing to an entire narrative arc that an inevitable-seeming denouement—a civilized polity—completes. As important, it implies a coordinating logic. Each stage contributes to, and is secured by, the sense of a whole. Since each stage carries with it a stable sense of how it stands in relation to every other stage, a plot of polity can be entered at any point, and indeed reconstructed from a single stage, for it exists as a foreordained structure whether it is articulated as such or not. Any part of the structure may "speak for" another. Pastoralism (herding), for example, is more than a description of a human activity. It is a clarification of the schema that makes the description possible. It makes history preposi- tional: pastoralism is a stage *of*, the stage that led *to*. A plot of polity, however, easily mystifies its formulaic qualities—the sense in which readers come to it with its form and significance already known—since it adopts the ruse that it conforms to the shape of narratives that disclose how events are causally linked only after the plot has been apprehended as a whole. Civilized indi- viduals and imperial nations could claim the knowledge of what it took to move from one stage to the next because, and only because, they had reached the standpoint of the final stage. Stadialism justified imperializing activities not only on the basis of civilization but also on a nation's expertise in the long and arduous process of becoming a civilization that preceded it.

In this chapter I focus on four influential works that embraced stadialist thinking to underwrite their responses to US economic crises. In "Wealth" (1889), Andrew Carnegie argues that wealth should accrue to meritorious individuals in an advanced civilization. In *Progress and Poverty* (1879), a best seller in the 1890s, Henry George expounded a plan to increase social wealth by means of a single tax on land values. William Graham Sumner's *What Social Classes Owe Each Other* (1883) made him one of the most promi- nent apologists for laissez-faire capitalism in the 1880s and 1890s. At cen- tury's end, Charlotte Perkins Gilman's *Women and Economics* (1898) was touted as the "first real, substantial contribution made by a woman to the science of economics" by exposing what that "science" had always missed: the economic systems it purports to analyze are profoundly gendered.[12] For these writers, political economic principles could be plotted onto a schema of evolving civilizations. But they had to work hard to restore faith in that schema when the concept of modernity was announcing itself as a disconti- nuity, as a shocking rupture with the past.

"Wealth" was the era's archetypal capitalist's signature work. It inspired hundreds of Carnegie's lectures on both sides of the Atlantic.[13] Proposing that wealthy capitalists should become philanthropists, he also argues that such largesse comes at the cost of inveterate inequalities of condition between rich and poor. These are the consequences of capital accumulation. Helping to make his account an extraordinarily adaptable response to specific capital/labor crises of the 1890s is stages theory, the structuring logic of which is announced in the first paragraph via Carnegie's description of his visit to a Sioux village. The visit places the imprimatur of real facts, places, and names on the explanatory power of stadialism. The Sioux inhabit a liminal site (the prairie) wild enough to represent the very first stage of human society—as Locke theorized, they live in a state of propertyless equality—but also colonized enough to welcome a visitor from the last stage. Observing the "wigwam of the chief"—its poverty barely distinguishable from others in the village—allows him to juxtapose the "change which has come with civilization" with the "old conditions" experienced by the Sioux. "Indians are to-day where civilized man then was," he asserts.[14]

Carnegie's casuistry about the progress of civilization—civilized man *then* was not actually civilized—begins to reveal some of the complex ways in which stages theory works in "Wealth." Carnegie implies that the historical process can only be understood, and represented, by those who have traversed its stages. The fact that "civilized man then" went on to achieve civilization is what makes him capable of looking *back*, thus representing and formalizing the entire process. The Sioux are debarred from speaking of stages they have yet to experience. In fact they are displaced from the entire schema of historical progress they are supposedly there to represent, for the Sioux's old conditions are not the old conditions once experienced by (now) civilized man. Civilized men did not have other civilized men present at the inception of their civilizing process. If the Sioux are to progress though the stages of history, it will be under the tutelage of those who have already mastered the process. The first stage of history no longer authentically exists. It is therefore the prerogative of civilized man to speak to the endpoint of the process (i.e., modernity) and its *arche*—which helps explain how "civilized man then" comes to replace a group Carnegie should by the logic of his own schema construe as his savage progenitors.

Ancillary to modern social systems, the Sioux play a vital and multifaceted role in Carnegie's first paragraph. They ratify the first stage of the rhetorical schema—or the fact that there *was* a beginning to the process the schema describes, for a plot of polity requires a beginning in order to guarantee its logic of sequence. The Sioux also confirm that theory can be conjoined to historical fact. Invoking a centuries-long history of expropriating and colonizing Native American lands, Carnegie observes that the "old conditions" of (poverty-stricken) egalitarianism are passing under the civilizing influence of capital accumulation. And the passing of the Sioux's egalitarian lifestyle demonstrates that stages theory grasped the historical process correctly. Because stadialism produces a formulaic plot where one part can always imply another in a sort of narrative bait-and-switch, the inevitable demise of equality under the old conditions of poverty on the prairie underwrites the legitimacy of the new: profound class inequalities under the rich but unevenly distributed capital accumulations of industrial society. Carnegie's presence on the prairie limns a beautifully circular logic: The inexorable process of history is guaranteed by the fact that it already has happened. One function of a plot of polity told from the standpoint of its completion, its telos revealed, is that the historical process can no longer be perceived as a site of contest and question. If modernity feels like a rupture to those suffering under it, it is an inevitable rupture.

In an unsettling challenge to his own stadial model, Carnegie also recognizes the "changed conditions of this age."[15] One of these is *perpetual* progress and change: "Always we are hoping that we need expand no farther, yet ever we are finding that to stop expanding would be to fall behind; and even to-day the successive improvements and inventions follow each other so rapidly that we see just as much yet to be done as ever." The benevolent capitalist's concern is for the "future progress of the race."[16] Rather than implying a mandatory progress from one stage to the next, modernity here begins to be conceived as a rupture with the past. By writing into accounts of history a new stage of ongoing expansion, Carnegie essentially creates a prior stage of *early* capitalism. One crucial effect here is to demote industrial workers who might once have been thought to stand at the acme of human civilization to the status of the Sioux; "savage" Sioux and "civilized" workers are equally out of touch with modernity and its new stories of capital accumulation, to which Carnegie emerges as the sole civilized guide. But Carnegie generates doubts about his own rhetorical schema. Since there is "as much yet to be done as ever," the commanding retrospective glance from the end of history that he employs to position the Sioux and the industrial workers itself falls under suspicion. The end seems to have become a step along the way, oriented toward a more or less unknowable future.

A broad late-century debate aimed at resignifying the civilizing function of capital plays an important role in Carnegie's revised stadialism. Adam Smith had argued that accumulating capital impelled humans to move beyond a "rude state of society." Classical economists struggled with the long-term implications of capital growth. Thomas Malthus's bleak socioeconomic vision of a burgeoning population overwhelming resources emphasized the competing claims made on a limited common stock and the unequal portions falling to the lot of various social groups as populations increased in size. The Ricardian doctrine that wages fall as rents rise, for instance, indicated that the distribution of accumulated capital among the nation's major economic stakeholders—landlords, capitalists, laborers—was guaranteed to be a zero-sum game in which increased benefits accruing to one class ensured a loss for another. Malthusian and Ricardian analyses predicted a dismal future governed by an increasingly static economy and a logic of diminishing returns. To allow for "future progress," late nineteenth-century writers began to reconceive this problem in terms of *limitless* accumulation, an idea that had the potential to solve the problem of diminishing returns by promising to float all socioeconomic boats simultaneously. Carnegie argues in "Wealth" that the Law of Accumulation of Wealth observes no natural limit. One must earn profits on capital or go bankrupt. "To stand still," like the Sioux on the prairie, "is impossible."[17] It is a striking instantiation of his future-oriented stadialism. The prospect of unlimited capital makes it possible to argue that all might prosper even under conditions of increasing inequality. More quietly, Carnegie suggests that classical economists who privileged slowing or even static economies misunderstood the very logic of a plot of polity, which appears most intelligible not in terms of a fixed stage but in *moving* from stage to stage.

Social scientist William Graham Sumner provided ideological support for the positions Carnegie espouses in "Wealth" by also arguing that class differentiation and inequality are inevitable. Stages theory supplies verification. Early humans were equal to each other under conditions of savagery, living off the "spontaneous fruits of the earth"; but they also subsisted thereby "at the sport of Nature." It is the "power of aggregated capital" that "made . . . civilization possible" because capital represents "labor accumulated, multiplied into itself—raised to a higher power."[18] This multiplying effect is crucial. An exponential increase in capital accumulation remains the only logical solution to the bleak Malthusian calculus that population growth increases geometrically but subsistence arithmetically. Capital, that "human energy stored or accumulated" in the form of skill, knowledge, technology, social organization, and money, can fend off economic collapse.[19]

At this important step in his argument, Sumner dispenses with the wages-fund notion of classical political economy. Capitalists do not appropriate their capital from a finite common stock. Their efforts generate "millions more of wealth, many-fold greater than their own."[20] Sumner's analysis leads to his support for continually increasing amounts of capital concentrated in the hands of skilled capitalists and capital-rich corporations. It also leads him at times, tentatively, toward the notion that human individuals are creatures of insatiable wants.[21] Capital accumulation cannot take place without self-denial. But self-denial in an era of accumulations so massive that no individual could possibly use it all would logically end the process. The exigencies of capital growth lead Sumner to conclude that the first accumulation of capital "is slow, but as it proceeds the accumulation becomes rapid in a high ratio, and the element of self-denial declines."[22] Self-denial must recede if the economy is to go on generating ever-larger amounts of capital in order to keep pace with an increasing population.

In the best-selling and influential *Progress and Poverty* (1879)—in 1933 John Dewey observed that its millions of copies gave the book "a wider distribution than almost all other books on political economy put together"—Henry George builds his argument, like Sumner, around processes of extraordinary capital accumulation. He arrives at wholly different conclusions.[23] One of its best-known passages (in book 4) employs the prairie as a privileged site of inquiry as George sets out to demonstrate the principles underlying David Ricardo's law of rent, which concerned, in part, the way in which land values grow as population pressure increases. George begins by describing the arrival of a single inhabitant on uninhabited land, an example couched (like Locke's "supposing an island") as fable: "Here, let us imagine, is an unbounded savannah." His goal is to explain the inexorable process of acquiring and concentrating capital that leads to civilization. He relies on the same narrative that informs Smith and Sumner. The single inhabitant must perforce accomplish every task by himself. And because the first inhabitant must be "his own blacksmith, wagonmaker, carpenter, and cobbler," George argues that "though nature is prolific, the man is poor." But as soon as more occupants arrive on the land, the "wonderfully multiplying efficiency" of the division of labor means that its "productive powers" are "equivalent to the multiplication of its original fertility by the hundred fold and the thousand fold."[24] Efficiencies accrue to people who settle near each other, leading eventually to an urban center where the highly developed infrastructure and benefits of intellectual and cultural stimulation bestow ever-increasing added value on subsequent exchanges. Though the fundamental nature of the land owned by the single original inhabitant may not change—in fact its productivity may decrease—its locational advantage must increase. In this sense George "reconceive[s] land itself as a potentially limitless social resource."[25]

In an important recuperation of economic equilibrium, George also contends that dramatic advances in social development lead to economic actors who are able to shuck off their natural human proclivities for wanting ever more. Bioeconomic principles underpin George's reasoning. His narrative of developing civilizations begins with the isolated and limited human body forced inefficiently to perform every task for itself. The end of his narrative imagines an ideal economy in terms of the healthy appetites and satisfactions of a metaphorical body politic. The "social organism secretes . . . the necessary amount of capital just as the human organism in a healthy condition secretes the requisite fat." And "accumulated wealth seems to play just about such a part in relation to the social organism as accumulated nutriment does to the physical organism." George's position derives from, and would seem to be made imperative by, his interpretation that nature contains sufficient resources (given steady improvements in human ingenuity) to support a burgeoning population. Taking issue with the common assumption that a parsimonious nature places absolute limits on production, thereby guaranteeing misery as the population grows, George asserts that the "injustice of society" is in fact the "cause of the want and misery." What prevents the reader's inevitable rejoinder—that George conjures infinite ("thousand fold") social capital and therefore potentially unlimited population growth from finite natural resources—is the postulate of a human agent who is ultimately capable of restraining unlimited desire. For George, potentially limitless capital accumulation depends on the assumption that humans situated within a rational distribution of wealth will naturally come to control that accumulation when it exceeds "necessaries."[26]

At its most radical, Charlotte Perkins Gilman's *Women and Economics* reorganizes similarly conventional stadial features within a disorderly plot of polity designed to unmask the hegemony of male interests in economic life—the way in which the "female of genus homo is economically dependent on the male. He is her food supply." Gilman's fable of how humans managed the first step of sociality in a "rude state of society" is instructive. To begin with "primitive man and his female were animals, like other animals," Gilman says. "She ran about in the forest, and helped herself to what there was to eat as freely as he did" until man "instituted the custom of enslaving the female; and she, losing freedom, could no longer get her own food nor that of her young." In many respects Gilman's fable accords with a well-understood stadial schema in which, as Lewis Morgan put it, "savage penalties" were exacted on women in a state of savagery.[27] Following this same plot, Gilman shows that a "differentiation [division] of labor" and "exchange of product" lead to the "great engines of modern industry" and bring about a "civilized State" in which "citizens live in organic industrial relation." Or *should*. Since managing the "elaborate machinery of trade, commerce, government" could not be done by women in their "present degree of economic development," the outcome of the stadial plot turns out to be a simulacrum only. Performing it properly is an ideal to which humans should aspire, and a problematic that needs to be resolved.[28]

Most obviously, by confirming the identity of economic man as *man*, Gilman denies the stadial logic that the benefits of a civilized state accrue to all its citizens—as Morgan supposes when he argues that women have gained "immensely" as civilization has advanced.[29] Instead, Gilman argues, "human progress has been accomplished by men. Women have been left behind."[30] The consequences are immense. Male domination of the economic system assaults the notion that each stage conforms to a particular set of defining characteristics and breaks the coordination of one stage with another. So the "male human being is thousands of years in advance of the female in economic status," while "such economic processes as women have been allowed to exercise are of the earliest and most primitive kind."[31] In the late nineteenth century, economic progress and primitive conditions appear coeval once the gender of the economic actors are taken into account. But Gilman also works to differentiate economic progress from civilization. Men are "in advance" but also hypostatized at what stadialist thinkers agreed to be an early stage of history by virtue of men's brutal treatment of women. The concept of advance here becomes unmoored from the familiar linear plot that is supposed to anchor it: economic progress cannot be correlated with progressive gender relations since the final stage of history bestows property rights on men but not women. The very concept of sequence disappears. At least, it does so until the modern age adopts the plot of polity that should have guided it all along. For Gilman, aligning advanced and primitive stages occupied respectively by men and women promises a practical solution to inequality—it would allow women to manage the great modern engines of industry—but would also restore the interpretive power of the metahistorical schema. The narrative of history is one of male domination, but the metahistorical narrative supposed to explicate human progress is not. At the heart of Gilman's argument is an important move to recuperate stadialism as a way to expose the deficits of male domination.

Carnegie, Sumner, George, and Gilman rely on familiar stadial principles—the emergence of a general equivalent, capital accumulation, a division of labor—to underwrite their economic thinking. But each of these writers constructs modernity in such a way as to put pressure on that model of the progress of civilizations. George takes Ricardian logic counterintuitively in the direction of infinitely increasing (social) capital and capitalism itself in the direction of severely constrained property rights. Sumner and Gilman intimate a remade homo economicus—Sumner observing a new psychic terrain of infinite wants ("self-denial recedes"), Gilman challenging an "advanced" society that still privileges economic man. And Carnegie reaches something of an aporia. The account of historical change that establishes him as a privileged observer butts up against a competing sense of a historical continuum proceeding into an unknowable future. This may be to grant Carnegie the authority due to a proleptic thinker; but the very logic of a plot of polity that resolves in civilization falls apart.

A cultural fable still potent enough to underwrite an array of popular economic texts at the end of the nineteenth century, orthodox stadialism was nonetheless beginning to show the strains of new constructions of civilization and history. The rise of neoclassical economic thought offered one such increasingly powerful challenge. Curtailing the power of stadial thinking is in fact at the forefront of Jevons's and Marshall's early efforts to challenge the historicizing practices of political economy and end, as Marshall says, a focus on the body politic when "men thought of the interests of the whole nation." Like other popular economic thinkers, their focus is on the irruption of modernity and the wholly new modes of analysis it seems to demand. Jevons asserts, "I am for thorough reform and reconstruction," betokening an end to the "prestige of the false old doctrines." Marshall follows suit. "Modern economic theory" must address rapidly changing industrial conditions which promise a "collective freedom" from an "old order of life." These formulations show a residual stadialism shaping their early work. In the 1890 edition, Marshall sets out a familiar history of world civilizations to capture what is "characteristic of the modern age": the glacial pace of "custom in a primitive society" gives way to the "quickly changing circumstances of modern industry."[32]

This narrative of human history progressing from primitive conditions to modern market life proves to be no more than a gesture. Later editions of *Principles* banish it to an appendix. The challenge modernity poses to a stadial metanarrative of history is key. Recognizing that the "economic problems of the present generation" derive from "social changes that are of recent date," Marshall speaks to the "folly of attempts to revive the old rules."[33] Marshall does more here than deny that present-day economic problems can be understood or resolved by situating them within a linear plot of polity: he destroys its entire logic. Were modernity to be conceived of as a new stage, it could no longer be done in terms of stages theory, since there is at least one stage—modernity—that evades its coordinating logic. Marshall consigns a metahistorical narrative to history as a prelude to the much broader erasure of history that neoclassical economic thought would ultimately accomplish. Defining its purview solely as the science of exchange, economic thought in the twentieth century would simply assume the universality of the principles it now took for granted: methodological individualism, subjective and relative values, utility functions, rational economic behaviors, (perfect) markets. Consigned to a vague premodernity were older classical economic ideas:

historicist and holistic thinking; moral and ethical considerations about the good of the body politic; informal, nonmathematical narratives; and grand metanarratives such as the orderly progress of civilization.

An immense cultural fable concerning the historical stages supposed to govern the emergence of civilization, nineteenth-century stadialism was always more than mere historiography—more than an abstract description of how history was supposed to unfold. It ramified through a vast interlocking network of formal and imaginative works. Political economic principles— the importance of a division of labor, of capital accumulation, of the emergence of money—were organized and granted legitimacy within a narrative that eventuated in the inevitable appearance of market economies and homo economicus. The concept of an orderly plot and readers experienced in its familiar outlines were seminal to the cultural life of this fable. This conception of history did not sit well with new conceptions of modernity. Modernity, it seemed, had to be represented by a rupture with its past: a new focus on infinite wants and unlimited capital accumulation argued either for a new stage of human history or for a new kind of economics focused entirely on marketplace behavior. Subsequent chapters of this book take up two important questions. They examine how the cultural fable of stadialism meshes with the fabulist plots of female regionalism, beginning in chapter 2 with the signs of an unsettling turn-of-the-century shift in stadialist thought on full view in Freeman's "An Autobiography" (1917), which scripts several mismatched economic stories in its enigmatic assessment of her career. I conclude that chapter with an analysis of two of Freeman's late-century stories in which the superimposition of aeconomia on political economic thought eventuates in decidedly eccentric plots of polity. In the final chapter I deal with the broader theoretical question such an analysis begs—but which the brief account here of neoclassical antipathy toward stadialism anticipates—which is how the hegemony of neoclassical economics strips a concept such as aeconomia of its economic meaning and value.

2

FABULIST PLOTS OF POLITY IN
FREEMAN'S "THE REVOLT OF 'MOTHER'"
AND "A MISTAKEN CHARITY"

In a 1917 *Saturday Evening Post* article, Mary E. Wilkins Freeman referred to "The Revolt of 'Mother'" (1890) as a sort of fable—a "big fib," a story that "is not in the least true."[1] "There never was in New England a woman like Mother" (75) writes Freeman, referencing her "impossible" title character. It would seem logical to interpret this disavowal as a sign of a feminism incompletely realized. Though it looms large, Mother's revolt against her stultifyingly patriarchal husband is contained once by the neat rapprochement between the pair at the end of the narrative and then twice, nearly thirty years later, by Freeman's public refusal to countenance the story's more radical implications. "Revolt" expresses a will to liberty that gets realized, but frustratingly. Mother desires more. What she wants and gets is an improved domestic enclosure—in fact a "kitchen of her dreams"—in which to cook Adoniram's dinner.[2] This topos of rebellion fading into what appears to be a renewed commitment to ideological conformity surfaces frequently in Freeman's stories. Candace in "A Village Singer" battles her township—but only to regain her position in the church choir. Hetty in "A Church Mouse" and Louisa in "A New England Nun" want rooms of their own. They get a church sanctified by its late-blooming spirit of charity in Hetty's case, a metaphorical nunnery in Louisa's.

Regionalist fictions that seem to move toward reclaiming essentialized and stable identities are "vulnerable to some of the charges voiced by current postmodernist critiques of rootedness."[3] Over time scholars have become less confident about the progressive and liberatory aspects of Freeman's work, preferring to couch their analyses in terms of the "ambivalence" of "unresolved and paradoxical polarities,"[4] of "undecidable or purposefully 'unreadable' images that both affirm and negate,"[5] of "conflicting voices,"[6] and of stories that subvert "feminist as well as patriarchal assumptions."[7]

Put like this, Freeman's 1917 article proves the worth of Mary Kelley's argument in *Private Woman, Public Stage* (1984) that nineteenth-century "literary domestics" imbued with ideologies of private domesticity maintained a vexed and anxious relationship with their own public voices. Freeman appears unable to decide how to pose a critique of women's position in or out of the kitchen as she veers from a nineteenth-century fiction committed to a "kitchen of her dreams" to a twentieth-century disavowal of it—a troubled posture that manifests in the details of the article, which criticizes Mother, salutes the good sense of a real farm-mother of the day who "would never have dreamed of putting herself ahead of Jersey cows," and who "usually buys Father's clothes for him" (75), while also conveying an unmistakable sense that the "real" Mother's obsession with cows and Father's clothes is charmingly outdated.

Not surprisingly, Freeman's rather uncompromising rejection of the past has posed a conundrum to scholarly approaches committed to historical exegesis. It inspired Charles Johanningsmeier to challenge Richard Brodhead's new historicist argument in *Cultures of Letters* that Freeman's work, like that of other female realists, achieved its cultural status by appealing to the elites who read journals such as *Harper's* and the *Atlantic*. As Johanningsmeier ably argues, Freeman was always astute about finding diverse markets for her writing.[8] By 1917, she had a vast new mass market readership through the *Saturday Evening Post*, a magazine then experiencing the most dynamic growth in its history.[9] Conversely, some feminist scholars have managed the disturbing sense that "An Autobiography" deconstructs an important female writer's life and career by assuming that the author must be ironic or "duplicitous."[10] That supposition brings into harmony the earlier and later parts of Freeman's career and preserves the recuperation of history as a celebratory narrative of women's lives within a politics of continuity and tradition.

Such emphases overlook two issues that are key to my interpretation of "A Mistaken Charity" and "The Revolt of 'Mother.'" First, the fact that Freeman looks back nearly three decades to her 1890 story places a premium on processes of, and narratives about, historical change. By denigrating her earlier fiction and implicitly poking fun at the farm women who favored Jersey cows, Freeman speaks to the late nineteenth century and her early career in terms of rupture. Both seem little more than historical footnotes to her current claim on modernity, which the article links to a refreshing new ability to tell the truth, expose old fables, and rewrite literary history. Second, generally ignored, or displaced into an account of Freeman's engagement with markets for fiction, is the fact that the *Post* article plots its account of changing times against a history of economic transformations. Freeman insists that the story is "impossible" and "sacrifice[s] truth" precisely because it does not embed Mother within the material conditions real "New England women of that period" would have confronted. They would have "lacked the nerve" to move into the "palatial barn" not because they dare not challenge their husbands but because they "coincided with their husbands in thinking that sources of wealth should be better housed than consumers. That Mother would never have dreamed of putting herself ahead of Jersey cows which meant good money" (75). Women would "have held the household reins," which, far from signifying a regime of cooking and cleaning, implies their prominent status as rational, calculating agents playing an active role in managing the family's sources of wealth. "Women capable of moving into that barn would have had the cottage roof raised to insure good bedrooms," Freeman avers; "there would have been wide piazzas added to the house. . . . Mother usually buys Father's clothes for him. He knows he would be cheated were he to attempt it" (75). Perplexingly for interpretations that have read "Revolt" as a challenge to women's limited opportunities, Freeman seems to be arguing that the story was nowhere less truthful than in implying that New England women had limited opportunities.

One plausible explanation, following Johanningsmeier's assessment of the author as a shrewd businesswoman who always wrote with an eye to what would sell, is that Freeman, in order to appeal to the *Post's* more consumer-savvy twentieth-century readership, positioned late nineteenth-century New England women on the cusp of a consumerist revolution. Committed like their husbands to a preconsumerist ethos, these women set out to conserve material signifiers of value—the cows, for instance, which "meant good money." Yet they also responded to the pull of market forces that generate status from luxuries such as "wide piazzas," remodeled houses, and dream kitchens, and that, by 1917, make it possible for Freeman and her readers to recognize a significance the farm wives might not fully register: the difference between "sources of wealth" and "consumers." The emergence of an explosive consumer capitalism might have urged Freeman to see Mother's revolt as being less revolutionary than the actual changes experienced by women under conditions of modernity, which had ruptured the logic that sources of wealth had to be "housed" in the farm, the cows, the house, the barn.

Freeman's best example of a consumerist awakening in New England is her own fabling. "I sacrificed truth when I wrote the story, and at this day I do not know exactly what my price was. I am inclined to think gold of the realm" (75). Freeman hints that she was bought off, either by the imperatives of commercialism or, more ominously, by a market ideologically opposed to the idea of women writers telling the truth. Some have read this passage as the anxious confession of an author compelled toward artistic achievement and therefore "plagued" by the "issue of debasing her art for mercenary considerations."[11] The fanciful trope of "gold of the realm" suggests a contrary emphasis: a fabulous payoff. In solidarity with the nineteenth-century farm women she approves, Freeman shows herself to be a canny operator in the marketplace. Unlike those women, her younger self seems already invested in an ethos where extravagant profits can be made from fictions that have no basis in reality. Such value is provisional and contingent on the consumer; it cannot be housed and conserved like Jersey cows, the farm women's source of wealth. And Freeman is still attuned in "An Autobiography" to the fluid ways in which truths can be marketed. She adopts an attitude of full disclosure by asserting that she was once willing to fudge the truth for gold of the realm. But she neglects to mention that her revelations come courtesy of yet another financial transaction with a journal more interested in entertainment and selling copies than in detailed analysis. These are revelations on the model of celebrity culture: a scandalous truth about an already well-known story guarantees its future as an even better-known story.

From a celebrity-market perspective, the question of whether Freeman is being ironic matters only in the sense that it is unanswerable and thus continues to provoke discussion. Freeman the fabulator (or big fibber) generates capital both financial and cultural from seeming to lay her old fable to rest, which takes shape instead as an ineluctable commodity. It possessed market value as an 1890 fiction and does now again, at least potentially, as a 1917 succès de scandale. Freeman refuses to assign either transaction a stable value. She receives an unspecified amount for "Revolt" and does not even mention that she is being paid for the 1917 article. And for good reason. If the market logic governing "An Autobiography" does not house value in a dollar price, as if her writings were so many Jersey cows, neither does it presume that value is lost by the author appearing to rip up her own literary roots. Instead, Freeman floats or "un-houses" the value of her writings as symbolic capital, freeing readers to grapple with the question of whether "Revolt" or her recantation of it is the bigger fib, and in the process making her meanings endlessly provisional, provocative, debatable. The fact that scholarly disagreements about "An Autobiography" have consolidated it as one touchstone of the meaning of her work shows how successfully she read the marketplace.

"Revolt," recanted, turns out to be imbricated with and thoroughly contextualized by market forces; neither fib nor fable is exempt. Freeman's mercurial consideration of modernity in "An Autobiography" shows that interpretations of those economic forces are contingent on, and reciprocals of, particular understandings of history and historical change. At least two histories of her relationship to her own work emerge. One is an explicit claim on a plot of modernity marked by a rupture between the unrealistic older work and the truthful commentary on which she says she is now able to embark. It lays out an incipient stadial narrative. Like Carnegie at the beginning of "Wealth," Freeman seems to position herself at the end of history, from which stance the inadequacies of all previous stages can be known and disclosed. The new capacity for truth-telling that modernity makes possible allows her to recognize the unrealistic aspects of "Revolt." But the same piece ensures that "Revolt" is both brought to mind in, and situated as, an economic fact of the early twentieth and the late nineteenth century; the story was once saleable and the scandal of it is now profitable again. The story's economic value as it was invested and then reinvested in the marketplace across a span of nearly three decades seems to be a marker of continuity, not of abrupt change. From that point of view, as Carnegie trenchantly observed, there is no longer any privileged end. Negotiating this metanarrative of history—that is, how Freeman envisages the very process of historical change—would therefore seem crucial to understanding the piece. The question is whether her 1917 economic self registers an abrupt break with the nineteenth-century farm wives or discovers a relationship between her work and their longing for wide piazzas—or whether she is still trying vainly to recover the stable value that was once thought to inhere in a cow or a published story.

My analyses build on this complicated insertion of text into (economic) history. They adopt as the keystone of their interpretive orientation the sort of sophisticated, exploratory play with the unfolding of economic forces in history that Freeman demonstrates in her *Post* article. The domestic space proves to be the crucible of this inquiry. But it reads that space differently from most approaches to how Freeman represents domestic labor in the home, which generally emphasize her refusal to fully embrace modernity. Lorne Fienberg contends that Freeman's female characters can "emerge from their homes to test the value of their entrepreneurship and their goods publicly in the marketplace" but that, in line with the classic appraisal of the female realist representation of women's work, they "return to the domestic sphere to enact alternative personal economies." Consequently it becomes possible to "defy the patriarchal system of valuing commodities over a woman's capacity for love and creativity." One important exception is Monika M. Elbert, who describes an author enmeshed in the logic of consumer capitalism. Fetishizing household goods and other commodities in a failed effort to "compensate for their thwarted creativity or stunted sexuality," the "prototypical Freeman protagonist" is the "collecting, spending, and greedily acquisitive woman."[12]

Elbert, however, hypostatizes Freeman's insouciant play with historical schemas. "An Autobiography" stages the kitchen economy of the household (and barn) as a mobile space capable of staging heterogeneous economic discourses and practices, and capable of problematizing stadial narratives and other conventional conceptions of history. In my analyses of "The Revolt of 'Mother'" and "A Mistaken Charity" I reenact that logic by tracing complex links between economic discourses and diverse plots of polity. "Revolt" positions Mother's transformation of her domestic economy within the neatly linear accounts of history favored by liberal political theory, only to confuse them with an escalating number of "parallel cases" that serve to question the very logic of linear developments. The there-and-back-again plot of "A Mistaken Charity"—to the Old Ladies' Home and then back home—similarly perturbs the relationship between its resolutely premodern characters and what appears to be the inevitable advent of modernity. Both stories help pose the key issue I explore in chapter 7: why and how we as scholars deploy plots of modernity in order to structure our interpretations.

The stories also point us toward the productively unsettling possibilities of economic fabling. James Bucky Carter has pointed out the prevalence of a "fairy-tale discourse" in what is usually considered Freeman's "exemplary realist or local color texts," adding that Freeman is "often not working with a stoic realism but within the boundaries of magical realism."[13] Carter is correct, though I draw different conclusions from his insight. As Freeman's *Post* analysis of "Revolt" shows, an impossible fable—a big fib—can open up economic issues and possess both monetary and symbolic value. The rhetorical play of "An Autobiography" demonstrates that a process of fabling does not have to resolve into fantasy; it can place the reader under interpretive pressure to negotiate new positions. Freeman's fables are exploratory political acts. Rather than resolving economic questions within formulaic safe endings, they mystify straightforward accounts of political economy. This frequently places Freeman in a position of critiquing a male-dominated tradition of political economy. Her fictions also engage core assumptions of political economy—including its own fabulist urges toward supposing an island or imagining an unbounded savannah—which dramatize possibilities of reading historical processes in diverse ways. Freeman's fabling/fibbing determines the shape of a political economy problematically suited to, or perhaps suited to the problematics of, the late nineteenth century.

THE ECCENTRIC SCRIPT OF "HOME": DISORDERLY AECONOMIA IN "A MISTAKEN CHARITY"

Charming, often hilarious, "A Mistaken Charity" (1887) tells the tale of two elderly sisters taken by do-gooder Mrs. Simonds from the poverty of their tumbledown house to the smart establishment of the Old Ladies' Home—before they run away! The story slips easily into the realm of the fantastic.

The comic-epic overtones of Harriet and Charlotte's return home are particularly striking. In the story, modeled on *The Odyssey*, the pair escape from captivity, overcome obstacles, and receive providential aid from a man who chances by and drives them home. Warming to her Odyssean role on the trip back, Harriet proves to be a magnificent liar.[14] "A Mistaken Charity" also draws upon a fairy-tale narrative mode that consistently places Freeman's work within the "boundaries of magical realism."[15] Most obviously, the story revisits "Hansel and Gretel." Mrs. Simonds first plays the wicked stepmother, relocating the sisters to the miserable Home, and then the witch. Mrs. Simonds appears in the story with a basket of doughnuts and soon has the "two forlorn prisoners" being fed on "finely flavored nourishing soups."[16] In order to return home, Harriet slips the key into her pocket, like Hansel secreting a handful of pebbles, and later lies, like Gretel, to effect their escape. Like Hansel and Gretel, the pair "ran away" (244) from the prison of the Home. They "took their bundles, stole slyly out, and were soon on the highroad, hobbling along, holding each other's hands, as jubilant as two children, and chuckling to themselves over their escape" (246). After the fortuitous intervention of the helpful driver—a white duck plays a similar role in "Hansel and Gretel"—the story concludes with their joy at being home.

Events in the story's fantastic register can evoke economic issues. Many plot details of "Hansel and Gretel" resonate with the sisters' economic distress. Harriet and Charlotte are poor and in want, and Mrs. Simonds steps conveniently into the role of the uncharitable stepmother by seeking to address the poverty of the "two children" through a drastic relocation. The Home's finely flavored fare, like the fairy tale's house made of bread and cake, proves perilous. It forces the sisters to exhibit hitherto undiscovered resources in escaping and returning to the "common, coarser food" they prefer at home. It is possible to read the fairy tale as a special case of the sisters' blunt republican defiance of money, market forces, and unnecessary luxury. "I guess they'll see as folks ain't goin' to be made to wear caps agin their will in a free kentry" (246), Harriet says, chuckling about the discarded lacy caps they had been forced to wear. That resistance issues in an iconic economic self-sufficiency. The delight the sisters derive from the pumpkins, apples, and currants in their garden patch "was not merely that they contributed largely towards their living. . . . They were their own, their private share of the great wealth of nature, the little taste set apart for them alone out of her bounty, and worth more to them on that account . . . than all the richer fruits which they received from their neighbors' gardens" (238). The value they place on their garden patch receives a peculiar emphasis, having less to do with subsistence than the fact of the "private share" it offers for "them alone." The tiny garden patch pitches a grand claim: it yokes together political freedom and economic self-sufficiency, claiming the Jeffersonian dream for two elderly women in their battle against mistaken coercive powers.

One effect of these allusions to fairy tale and myth is potentially to tap into a compelling but nostalgic political imaginary, evoking and marketing republican virtues long lost to the late nineteenth-century United States. The story's fabulist excesses—reading Mrs. Simonds as a fairy-tale witch and the Home as a perilous confection of cake and candy—seems to close down its purchase on the material circumstances of the elderly poor in a brutal get-ahead capitalist society. Timeless plot imperatives, moreover, might be thought to enact a containment strategy in tandem with the plot's drive toward an emotionally satisfying resolution. Once we align Harriet's lies with Odysseus's or Gretel's, those stories guarantee the sisters' return home and exert pressure on us to read their falling-down house as home. Locking its characters deep in an oneiric realm of ancient fables, the story seems another big fib.

In my analysis I challenge the supposition that the story neatly resolves its ideological material by arguing that Harriet and Charlotte are eccentric domestic economists. Their patchwork aeconomia is pieced together from their little "patch" of ground and from their neighbors' generosity; they survive under a "patched" (237) roof. Home becomes heterotopia, a site of confusing and jostling signs. They begin at home, and struggle mightily to return home. But they are homed in a house that belongs to another. The narrative works similarly. Its inventive, peripatetic magical realism intertwines fabulism and political economic discourses in a fluid hybridity. This is particularly evident in the story's competing plots of polity. The story counters an onrushing modernity, epitomized by the orderly, hygienic, market-based regime of the Old Ladies' Home, with not one but two backward-looking metahistorical schemas. A residual Jeffersonianism organized around a late nineteenth-century discourse of the virtuous, because Anglo-American, poor seems fashioned to lament a vanishing republican innocence. Yet a playful reverse-stadialism returning the two sisters to the very origins of human sociality threatens to upset the entire coordinating logic fundamental to stadialist plots. The story's embrace of a political fantastic butts up against its wayward and fantastic plot of polity.

Surviving amid bleak conditions, then mustering the strategic sense to make their way back home, Harriet and Charlotte derive much ideological capital from their affinity with the resourceful Hansel and Gretel. Though "A Mistaken Charity" appears to esteem the lives of "poor . . . and common people" (236) working hard in the "primitive country fashion" (237), it happens to pick the one event of the sisters' lives when their commonality with an optimistic American ethos of can-do shows most strongly. If their modus vivendi is (barely) that of the yeoman farmer, their potential is unambiguously entrepreneurial. Here too, the structure of fairy tale can lead us to embrace a faintly ridiculous—though emotionally satisfying—cultural and economic fantastic. One consequence would be the diminishing of what some scholars have seen as the rebelliously feminist energies of the sisters' actions.[17] Like the Grimms's tale, which ends with the now-rich children living happily ever after in their (step)motherless home, "A Mistaken Charity" could be said to parlay rebellion into an entrepreneurial outburst that is admirable but, the story assures us, not going to happen again.

A much commoner appraisal of the limitations of Freeman's work already exists in the new historicist critique of female realism, which generally reads it in terms of a nostalgic or even panicked flight from modernity. It is worth thinking through the logic of such a critique in terms of the story's insistent Jeffersonianism. The entire rhetorical apparatus concerning the sisters' living independently on, and receiving a private share of, their own land is at odds with a historical moment when Americans' interactions with the workplace were undergoing profound transformations. It is pretty to think that two "poor old souls" (238) might fend for themselves. That fancy is at variance with the facts about US poverty in late nineteenth-century. It is at odds with the reality of a workforce growing increasingly dependent on industrial wages and corporate salaries, and simply obfuscating when set against the macroeconomic forces that were sweeping the United States into the interdependencies of a global economy. If the story half acknowledges its own myth-making by leaving intact the modern regimen of the Home, which the two heroes can fantastically escape but never transform, Harriet and Charlotte's atypical household in the "old place" (236) evokes a nostalgic rural self-sufficiency that was by late century increasingly unviable.

The mythic grandeur the story bestows on its poor old souls may then derive in part from a specific contemporary discourse celebrating the "frugal spirit" of the "self-respecting poor."[18] This thematic was persistently evoked in the elite journals for which Freeman often wrote. It was especially prominent during the 1880s as anxieties about massive influxes of immigrants, rising labor agitation, and spectacular increases in capital flow and investment after the financial crisis of 1873 began to occupy the attention of cultural commentators.[19] Writing concepts of economic value into a national imaginary about the virtuous poor proved to be one powerful response. Writer after writer claimed frugality, self-sufficiency, and industriousness as native American values, unlike the "unassimilated alien element" of European-born immigrants.[20] Workers were self-motivated in the "early days of the republic . . . so great was the mobility of the laboring population, so high their intelligence, so frugal were their habits, so enterprising, alert, and industrially ambitious."[21] Such ideals were readily accommodated to New England—a common move in the strategic construction of this region as the epitome and embodiment of American values. In one New England mill town, a writer observed, "old customs prevailed, and the community was homogeneous" while "democratic equality prevailed, and society as yet was not divided into classes between which the lines were sharply drawn. . . . Under such circumstances, labor disturbances could not occur."[22] The very concept of a separate working class tended to come under fire in such accounts. The "real American workingman usually refuses to act as a workingman at all" but instead "simply as an American citizen."[23] And in those days "everybody worked."[24] Both positions implied a contrast with immigrants. Lazy, divisive, and un-American, "foreigners, with paralyzing caste-ideas crushed into them" now make the toil of "New England women" in cotton mills "every year more difficult and disagreeable."[25] They "come into the land to trouble it . . . [and] create turmoil for no good reason."[26]

The disruptive presence of immigrants is one reason why commentators writing from and to American cultural elites often pushed the paradise of communal American values into the past. They were prevalent in the "early days of the republic," during the "last century,"[27] and "half a century ago."[28] The important effect of these elegies to (supposedly) disappearing American principles is to "invent a tradition." They served to "establish continuity with a suitable historical past" in an attempt to allay anxieties over the rapid pace of social change.[29] Imagining social relations as having been complete seemed to guarantee their permanence. Since they were of the past, they were no longer subject to dispute. They could, therefore, provide a template for addressing and resolving intransigent social conflicts and ideological contests. At a time of chaotic social transformations, the trope of the self-respecting poor pointed up all that was now wrong with the laboring classes. It defined a group too homogenous, too dedicated to the ideals of republicanism, too content with a frugal lifestyle, and too industrious to be troubled by class, racial, and ethnic strife.

Looked at from this perspective, Harriet and Charlotte's mundane life of independence and even their one striking rebellion exemplify the fabled virtues of the American working poor. The sisters are exemplary American workers: industrious, frugal, self-sufficient, shunning a luxurious lifestyle. They live apart from the marketplace. Indeed, the crux of their rebellion is that they insist on choosing a life devoid of material luxuries. It is here that their identification with their parents' house, crumbling into the ground though it might be, signifies most effectively. Their dedication to the "natural ruin" (236) of the house, outside which Harriet grubs in the dirt for dandelions, is a powerful evocation of what it means to be grounded in the American soil, which safeguards their livelihood and undergirds their tough-minded independence. The advanced age of the sisters and of the "little house in which they had been born and lived all their lives" (235) plays an important role in this topos. Harriet and Charlotte are native-born, so old that they are symbolically speaking coeval with the origins of a "free kentry," predating both the age of mass immigration and the debate about immigration that forces other writers in other venues to articulate precisely what an American value is. Their Anglo-American republicanism is self-evidently home-grown.

Though the story pays tribute to what appears to be idiosyncratic lifestyles on the verge of extinction, the values the sisters represent might be thought to undergo something of an apotheosis as the story moves toward its emotionally compelling climax. The sisters' obdurate independence rises to near mythic grandeur at the moment they are supposed to be exiting the terrain of history. The plot's conclusion participates in this ideological salute by taking leave of the sisters at their moment of glorious return. They have inhabited this land from time immemorial; the story leaves them still, and now forever, in possession, unchallenged by the threat of further transformations of their lives. The story closes with their Jeffersonian independence staunchly preserved, the "free kentry" reclaimed, and they its exemplary citizens, honored by the people who work for that republic, such as the "good friendly folk" (237) who help them out with gifts of food. The plot of "Charity" might be thought to fashion the sisters' return into a "means of imaginative national unification" as it interpellates its readers into a symbolic citizenry along with the friendly folk.[30] That interpellation is no doubt complex. If urban middle-class readers of female regionalism constitute the "implicit norm against which the actions of the characters are judged,"[31] then attitudes toward what the narrator calls "people of their stamp" (245) might well celebrate their virtuous poverty by way of their alterity, by virtue of the fact that their mode of resistance to modernity is too much of an oneiric fable to have material consequences. Nonetheless, the author seems to insist that the concept of the (Anglo-American) virtuous poor does not belong solely to the distant past.

Compelling as this fairly characteristic sort of new historicist reading might be, it does scant justice to the complex details of "A Mistaken Charity." This becomes apparent as soon as we begin to gender its economic and political registers. The story's acerbic critique of the disciplinary practices underpinning nineteenth-century principles of middle-class womanhood sits uneasily with the sense that it forms an unambiguous salute to Anglo-American republicanism, precisely because middle-class women's commitments to the domestic sphere played such an important discursive role in fables of republican order. Imposing a regime of psychic and bodily order on its "forlorn prisoners," the Home is an embodiment and reductio ad absurdum of ideologies of the bourgeois home as it tries to turn them into "nice old ladies" (244). Harriet and Charlotte's health and appetite come under scrutiny—"nourishing soups" replace the "common, coarser food" (244) they prefer—and so does that indicator of class status, their taste, which the institution attempts to educate by means of "finely flavored" soups, "more delicately served" (244) fare, and sumptuary codes in which they have to be "more particular about their dress" (244. They are forced into "delicate neckerchiefs" and "new black cashmere dresses," while "white lace caps" (244) cover their hair. Coordinating a female psychic and bodily economy with a clean, tranquil, orderly domesticity, the Home operates a sort of textbook version of Catherine Beecher's *Treatise on Domestic Economy* (1841), in which a woman's regulation of self, house, and household codifies and enacts middle-class routines of social existence. Such power resides partly in the promise of a "comfortable" and "even luxurious" (244) lifestyle. Harriet and Charlotte are initially the victims of "disciplinary intimacy."[32] They are bound to their newly routinized lives by the "kindness and attention" (245) of the "good folks" (244) who run the Home. As they "shy out" (246) the door Harriet finds the perfect riposte to this exercise of soft power: hanging their caps, the material sign of their nice lady-hood, on the bedposts, she testifies to and ridicules the reifying practices of "home."

The story does not support a thoroughgoing subversion of ideologies of home. It poses alternatives in the shape of the sisters' living arrangements at the "poor little house" (236) in which they grew up and to which they return. Those alternatives—in the spirit of "grim humor" (246) with which Harriet adorns the bedposts—are a carnivalesque version of the Home. Back home, the organic rhythms of nature make for a wholly irregular domesticity. Under a patched roof where "rain and snow had filtered through" (236), the sisters live in a house where "nature had almost completely overrun and obliterated the work of man" (236). A "tiny garden patch" contains a "straggling" (237) row of currants, and Harriet's pumpkins at the end of the story "hev run all over everything" (249). Dinner at the start of the story means grubbing for dandelion greens. Such irregularities repeat in the sisters' characters and histories. Their unmarried state in this story seems socially suspect. Freeman carefully distinguishes between their "poor, ordinary, and homely" lives, which match "plenty of men in the place" (236), and the "fault" of Harriet's "blunt, defiant manner" and Charlotte's "reputation of not being any too strong in her mind" (236), which appear atypical. One consequence of not being married is that their rights to a home are precarious. A "rich man" (235) owns the mortgage they can no longer afford, and they are subject to the whim of the married (Mrs. Simonds) and the once-married (the rich widow).

As Fetterley and Pryse argue, the decentering potential of regionalist writing can effect a potentially explosive critique of the ideological sites of marriage, heterosexuality, and property rights.[33] This odd conjunction in "A Mistaken Charity" of home/Home/"home"—this house that is more home than the Home, but still not theirs—does precisely this. It establishes the possibility of a practicable but irregularly constituted household outside middle-class norms while revealing the disciplinary powers that work by way of the Home to make "home" conform with its powerful ideological underpinnings. It also immediately exposes as crucially flawed the hypothesis in so many assessments of female regionalism that domesticity necessarily implies a structure of social order and psychic control. The sisters' housekeeping and gardening implies an eccentric script of domesticity: a house that cannot be kept clean and dry, a garden that straggles everywhere, a home they do not own, a household in which any heterosexual interest died off long ago, and, perhaps most important, a domestic lifestyle that is always under threat, always provisional. One further consequence of the sisters coming home to a "home" that is not Home is therefore that the eccentric script denies the orderly resolution of the plot. The story's ecstatic finale—"O Lord," sobs Charlotte as they come home, "thar is so many chinks [of light] that they air all runnin' together!" (249)—provides closure only to the extent that we are able to forget the precariousness of the "home" to which the two elderly sisters return, and which remains "home" only through the acquiescence of those who, like Mrs. Simonds and the rich man, wield true social power. In this sense the plot itself acts as a hesitant disciplinary agent, inviting us to ignore, but never quite erasing, the difference that makes the eccentric household arrangements so potent and so fragile a counterhegemonic force.

The economic details of Harriet and Charlotte's lives support a decentered interpretation of ideologies of home. Far from being exemplars of the Anglo-American self-respecting poor, the claims they exercise on their home and on their political rights are deeply problematic. Rhetorically consistent with Jeffersonian republicanism and with contract-based political liberalism, the notion of a "private share of the great wealth of nature" which is "set aside for them alone" runs headlong into the quotidian facts of their lives. A "rich man who held a mortgage on the little house" gives them "the use of it, rent and interest free" (235). So while they live "free," they do not live free of the marketplace that grants their mortgage to the rich man in the first place. And if a small taste of nature is set aside for them, it is because the rich man, not nature, allows them their own pumpkins. The story does not merely hint at their lack of property—it describes the loss of their house in detail. The sisters were property owners. Harriet had been "swift and capable about her work" (237) (sewing and mending) and amassed a "little hoard of earnings," all of which "went to the doctors" (237) for Charlotte's eyes and Harriet's rheumatic fever, whereupon the rich man secured their mortgage. The market has already exacted a toll. In doing so it sets in motion an array of rhetorical incongruities. They live free in their house though it is no longer their house, and they are emancipated from the free market to the extent that the market has already appropriated the property that gave them, in lieu of marriage, a modicum of status. A rift therefore opens between the sisters' emotionally compelling loyalty to a rhetoric of private possessions and the material losses that support a different interpretation of the facts.

Indeed, the entire plot of possessive individualism may be a ruse. The sisters' undoubted passion for freedom is not matched by the access to the free market required of the liberal subject. They are not smallholders; the control they exercise over their home is always and already a fantasy. And they are not self-sufficient. The pattern of their lives runs counter to the myth of upward mobility whereby hard work is supposed to deliver success. But neither does it fit the discourse of virtuous poverty. In economic terms the sisters have been on a long downward trajectory. The author charts their devolution from self-sufficiency to dependence on charity, mistaken or otherwise. Harriet and Charlotte make a poor case for being representative American citizens—types, even, of American revolutionaires creating a "free kentry"— whose work habits, attachment to the American soil, and ability to "show some sperrit" (241) but not foment labor disturbances all lay out values that hegemonic discourses taught immigrants they would do well to emulate. The sisters' desire to return to a life of labor on land no longer theirs—however little they realize it—seems neither an anxious reconstruction of, nor nostalgia for, a time when American workers truly worked hard and, in working hard, showed that they were truly American. In fact, the sisters not only embrace an alienated existence and land that is now the rich man's but also fight for it. In so doing they lead us to an interpretation—more somber than most feminist readings of Freeman—of women (and readers) co-opted into a fable of economic and political independence in which the difference between (prison) Home and (free) "home" is no more than a difference between kinds of disciplinary regimes. "Charity" becomes a twisted version of "Hansel and Gretel": a grim fairy tale in which the two children escape Home only to find their way back to a gentler version of it.

Charity, the story's key trope, reprises this complex play with the material economic contexts of Harriet and Charlotte's lives. At first glance, the sisters seem to reside in a realm of charitable actions separable from market relations. Allowing them to live in the house for free, the rich man's "small and trifling charity" (235) matches the largesse of other neighbors. The narrator tells us that "one would donate a barrel of apples from his abundant harvest to the two poor old women, one a barrel of potatoes, another a load of wood for the winter fuel, and many a farmer's wife had bustled up the narrow foot-path with a pound of butter, or a dozen fresh eggs, or a nice bit of pork" (237). Even Mrs. Simonds's local acts of charity—distributing homemade doughnuts—seem wholly benevolent. She specifically states that she requires nothing back from the sisters. Such gifts of food and fuel can carry potent cultural meanings. They are material, useful, and by seeming to stand outside relations of exchange, immune to the troubling challenges that an unruly capitalism was making to rural homes and urban lifestyles alike.

The community's gifts are not, however, truly off-market. Mrs. Simonds's charity, in particular, strongly implies the existence of a mistaken market for good works. Mrs. Simonds is "hand in glove with officers of missionary boards and trustees of charitable institutions" (243) and holds a "partnership in good works [with a rich widow], with about an equal capital on both sides, the widow furnishing the money, and Mrs. Simonds . . . the active schemes of benevolence" (242). The story positions Mrs. Simonds and the widow as entrepreneurial agents of the market as they look for a "new project" (242) to fund. They foment a heady mix of capital and imagination as they set up a general partnership in benevolence (along with a limited partner in the rich man). Harriet and Charlotte are useful to the extent that they are penniless. Their insertion into a comfortable middle-class lifestyle at the Home requires not merely an ideological investment in nice-ladyhood but "entrance fees" (242) the sisters could not possibly afford. The charitable pair exemplify a process of creating cultural capital within ideologies of middle-class womanhood. Investing money in the sisters, and then refraining from making money off them, confers on the charity-givers prestige and status. From this point of view, the story foreshadows the views of many historians who have seen the participation of middle-class women in charity work as an way for them to gain a voice in public, political, and sometimes economic matters, but in such a way as to bring into existence a web of ideological differences from the poor.[34]

It therefore seems unlikely that Harriet and Charlotte returning "home" from the Home frees charity from the coercive powers of the market, recalling female middle-class readers to an aspirational charity work unsullied by mercenary impulses. The relationships that bind Mrs. Simonds to the market in fact extend through the entire community of friendly folk and include actions more scrupulously generous than hers. Though the farmers' economic well-being is quietly marked, they have a surplus to give the sisters because they live above the subsistence level. The best indication of this is the recipients of their charity, the sisters themselves. Having lost their "little hoard of earnings" (237), they are unable—and as far as the story allows us to know, the only characters unable—to give charitably to others. This minor-seeming point about the farmers' surplus is of great consequence to the story because it introduces stadialism to the unfolding of its plot. In stadial thinking, the progression of humans from hunting and gathering to settled agriculture was "one of the greatest events in human experience" since, "for the first time," humans could count on "unlimited subsistence." Farming led to settled communities, thence to surplus, thence to some method for exchanging goods and protecting one's ownership of them, and thence to civil society. The abundant harvest that allows many a farmer's wife to donate produce to the sisters invokes a cultural fable that purported to explain the logic of such abundance.[35]

What makes the stadial plot relevant to "A Mistaken Charity" is Harriet and Charlotte's symbolic reversion to the most primitive forms of social organization. The sisters' one hope is to keep a "roof over their heads, covering on their backs, and victuals in their mouths" (236). And they pursue that goal in ancient ways. We first see Harriet as a gatherer, "searching for dandelion greens among the short young grass" (234) and waiting for trees and bushes to bear fruit. The family have always "grubbed for their living" (236). Their one salute to later stages of human subsistence comes from growing a few pumpkins, which Harriet "contrived every year to raise" (237). Their return "home" can be read as a return to a different sort of "ancient . . . habitation" (235), the primeval shelter: "nature had almost completely overrun and obliterated the work of man, and taken her own to herself again, till the house seemed as much a natural ruin as an old tree-stump" (236). One motivator of the sisters' refusal of exchange relations is therefore their "savage" condition. They have no money or property: they occupy a stage of history prior to the introduction of money or property relations.

A well-worn plot of polity emerges in the interstices of the story. As gatherers, Harriet and Charlotte live a hand-to-mouth, barely viable existence. As agriculturalists, the farmers obtain a surplus, part of which they are able to give others gratis. With the advent of commercial and capitalist society, the "old home" (242) is replaced by the "luxurious" Home with its entrance fees, cleanliness, middle-class appurtenances, and cultural capital. The question that the sisters' return "home" raises is *how* we read this plot. It invites us to read it as a somewhat ironic but still straightforward acknowledgment of the power of stages theory. The sisters' lives seem admirable because, locked into the past, they refuse the logic of exchange (of "home" for Home). But they cannot hope to be relevant to their own historical era. Their obdurate but fading resistance is aligned with the "ancient . . . habitation" of myth and fairy tale for a reason. Tales suited to elemental origins jibe with the logic of the historical process to project the sisters' premodern lifestyles out of the historical moment and into a realm both attractively fabulous and indisputably remote. Like the backward glance Freeman bestows on the nineteenth-century farm women in "An Autobiography"—and like Carnegie's professed sympathy for the vanishing Sioux—the story construes itself as an elegy for "people of their stamp" (245) whose stories are almost completed.

That Harriet and Charlotte once had both money and property unsettles this conveniently progressive account of human history. Common feminist approaches might interpret Harriet's life as a grubber and gatherer as a critique of masculinist socioeconomics. Digging for dandelions is the direct consequence of the sisters' material loss of property. They do not occupy the first stage of human history naturally. They have been thrust there and persuaded that this is where they belong. Here, Freeman's narrative itself performs a sort of tricky symbolic dispossession. It seems to foreground a familiar stadial plot, stripping away the sisters' purchase on a modernizing society, while making it possible to see, in its brief glance at past material dispossessions, that stadialism might be the perfect ideological mechanism for proving that Harriet and Charlotte have no real place in this society—and for covering it up. It is the logic that naturalizes dispossession. It is the logic that Gilman seeks to expose in *Women and Economics* by showing how women have been excluded from a salutary metahistorical order.

The problem with reading either of these possibilities as the only interpretation of the story is that both accept a liberal story of civilization. They depend on seeing modernity as that which Harriet and Charlotte fail to acquire, or that which they have been excluded from. A third option is that the story places the very logic of stages theory under scrutiny. To admit the fabulist implications of the story—to associate Harriet with Hansel or Odysseus or a gatherer from the dawn of human civilization—is not necessarily to fall for a masculinist logic. It is to re-create stages theory as heterotopia. Like its play with home/"home"/Home, the story cross-cuts diverse narratives about the origins and development of human societies, placing them in uncertain relationships to each other. Harriet and Charlotte are elderly women from the youth of human civilization; "children" at the end of history; gatherers after their mortgage has been repossessed. Their characteristics are familiar enough to invoke powerful cultural fables—they plot onto recognizable sequences. But they do so in the wrong order. This places enormous pressure on nineteenth-century stadialist logic, whereby each stage of subsistence is supposed to correspond with characteristic social and economic forms: gender roles, familial organization, achievement of private property and a civil society, utility maximization, and much more.

The story opens a gap between the subsistence stage and the cultural forms that were supposed to be produced by it and representative of it. The sisters' eccentric aeconomia and the story's disorderly aesthetic—its strange amalgam of fact, fable, and fairy tale—conspire here to upend the coordinating logics and orderly progressions that are characteristic of stadial thinking. Harriet and Charlotte's economic freedom from want is caught between two models: one, their "private share of the great wealth of nature," reminding us of Jeffersonian republicanism; the other, grubbing for dandelions, of "savagery." Yet neither actually defines the sisters' subsistence, which is patched together from a natural wealth that is not abundant enough to survive on, from charitable gifts they pretend not to notice, from a private share that is not theirs. Gathering dandelions and touting the virtues of political liberty in a "free kentry," Harriet is a sort of republican savage, a civilized person without property, a femina economica who resists the notion that humans desire an ever-increasing surplus of capital and creature comforts but who nonetheless tackles her reduced circumstances as a rational agent. Denying the very possibility of fitting neatly into an organized category of judgment or knowledge, she grubs in the dirt at the start of the story amid jostling and discordant signs of home and primitive modes of subsistence, and ends by circling back to, and embracing, the very same disorderly aeconomia which the Home had promised to supersede.

BUILDING A "KITCHEN . . . OF DREAMS": PLOTS OF POLITY IN "THE REVOLT OF 'MOTHER'"

At the heart of "The Revolt of 'Mother'"—and the event that, unsurprisingly, has drawn most critical notice—is the symbolic exchange whereby Mother switches one home for another. In the process she encroaches on her husband's new barn, transforming it into a superior version of the weary domestic space she has been forced to inhabit for forty years, but also an odd simulacrum of the conventional middle-class household decades of instruction in a domestic imaginary had taught women to respect. Like "Charity," "Revolt" represents home as heterotopia. The barn is "home-like" (75) in at least four ways: (1) like the original home insofar as it boasts a stove, a kettle boiling, and a "table set for tea" (75); (2) "like" a home insofar as these signs of domesticity remain incomplete enough to cause Sarah Penn to ask her husband for windows, partitions, and furniture (77); (3) like the original home insofar as that space was only ever "like" a home; and (4) "like" a home insofar as there may never be a domestic space for women under patriarchy that constitutes a true home.

In looking "almost as home-like as the abandoned house across the yard had ever done" (75), the barn, among its other attributes, brings a peculiar confusion to the set of relations between home (as original) and "home" (as likeness, simulacrum). The barn does not seem quite like home without proper furniture, even though the house with furniture seems less like home than the barn will soon be. The home that the barn *could be* puts us in mind of the home that the house *could have been*. But where home is falls perplexingly into the in-between: perhaps in the empty yard Mrs. Penn traverses between the two structures, or projected outside the story altogether into whatever representation of utopian domesticity governs her desire for partitions, furniture, and a "kitchen of . . . dreams" (75). Adoniram, returning to the space he had thought his own, certainly stumbles into heterotopia. Nanny, nearly in hysterics, imagines her father confronted by a cow in the "house," while an aroma of cooking from the food he loves hangs over the "barn." Adoniram's frightened cry, "What on airth does this mean, mother?" (77), addresses the disorienting sense that ideological signs—mother, cooking, home—have been unmoored in such a way as to shuck off their relatively secure provenances and to put their meanings back into play. They have become mundane signs in search of a home.

This potent "unhoming" of the ideological meanings the nineteenth century attached to home and to woman's place in it led earlier feminist readers to confident appraisals of the subversiveness of Sarah Penn's posture—to see "Revolt" as an exemplary "feminist tale"[36] in which Mother struggles toward "self-expression and independence"[37] and claims the right to speak in patriarchal discourse.[38] Observing the logic of a plot that has Mrs. Penn ever more determined to secure her dream kitchen, later writers have reached for more ambiguous relationships between the redesign of space and female self-definition. The story, for example, might be said to demonstrate a "countercurrent of nostalgia for a lost patriarchy" beneath the "surface of feminist protest," or even to abandon feminism entirely.[39] Monika Elbert views Freeman's female characters as irrevocable "consumers" who try to fulfill themselves "through a burning desire to purchase, possess, or collect products with which the marketplace tantalizes them."[40] From that perspective, the story is proleptically aware of the stance Freeman would adopt in her *Post* article a couple of decades later. Mother's desire for a dream kitchen seems less protest than product placement.

The problem with all of these approaches to "Revolt" is that each flattens out the significance of its complex representation of *exchange*, either by assuming that the story describes a one-way journey from silence to self-empowerment, as earlier interpreters maintained, or by assuming that changes of place are always and already suspect, so that Freeman inscribed into her tale her ambivalences about consumerism or patriarchy or her audience, or had to represent the discursive structures that her cultural circumstances allowed. Yet in "Revolt" the principle of exchange does more than generate the primary plot mechanism. It constitutes the story's teleology. It underwrites Sarah Penn's actions, as she herself is hazily aware. Her own explanation for moving to the barn cites an exemplary moment of territorial exchange. She tells the minister that moving recalls the "right" of "our forefathers to come over from the old country 'cause they didn't have what belonged to 'em" (75–76). It is a remarkable claim on a remarkable historical antecedent. Announcing a precedent for her actions, she moves forward by looking back. And, as too few commentators remember, by gendering the forefathers' actions female, she makes property rights, "what belonged" to them and to her, the centerpiece of her resistance.

"Revolt" elaborates Mrs. Penn's brief revisionary history into a metanarrative in which the principle of exchange, woven into liberal plots of polity, serves both as a desired goal and the key to explaining historical change. The story recapitulates the emergence of social contract from a state of nature, marked by a shift from appropriation to propriety individualism, and issuing with the rise of civilization into a polity organized around the exchange relations of market society. By exchanging one place for another, Mrs. Penn enters into exchange relations and into the civil society that, according to schemas of political liberalism, market society enacts. One implication of this argument is that feminist claims for Mrs. Penn's self-empowerment and independence were on the mark, but that they are most visible and potent within Freeman's aggressive recuperation of politically liberal narratives for women. Property relations therefore come into play for women—as they do, for example, in Elizabeth Cady Stanton, Susan B. Anthony, and Matilda Joslyn Gage's monumental *History of Woman Suffrage* (1881), the first volumes of which overlapped Freeman's early career, and help to contextualize her strategies in "Revolt." It is even possible to argue along with Elbert that the story's embrace of symbolic exchange concludes within a consumerist paradigm. The distinction between the private home and the market (the barn, as a space of commerce) seems to be collapsing under conditions of modernity, and in the process all signs—home, the private space, women—are freed. But they are freed to become consumable and marketable. Freeman's *Post* article with its emphasis on selling her material for gold of the realm wryly adumbrates that possibility; so does Mrs. Penn's desire to turn "home" into a dream kitchen.

Yet "Revolt" complicates the central thrust of its own narrative. If one plot of polity leads characters relatively coherently from a state of nature to propriety individualism and consumerism, other schemas exist in the story to afford alternative interpretations of history and historical change. The story's narrative architecture rises out of a vast array of debatable copies and odd analogies: a barn that is "home-like," a new barn that unnecessarily doubles the old barn, an exchange of place that is like the American forefathers' move to the New World, and a proclamation of rights like the forefathers' claim on "what belonged to 'em." This is only a fraction of the narrative's play with analogies, many of which are specified in the text: historical figures (Webster, the Pilgrim Fathers), historical events (the siege of Quebec and the American Revolution), and biblical events (the siege of Jericho).[41] These multiplying instances, as they ramify through history and into fable, remind us more and more of Adoniram's bewildered "what on airth does this mean?" At its most startling, Sarah Penn's logic of analogy constructs a historical bricolage that challenges the sort of sequential, monologic, and male-dominated account of history with which the minister who comes to set her right is familiar. He could deal with "primal cases, but parallel ones worsted him" (76). What appears to be the story's attempt to historicize Mrs. Penn's actions contains within itself a critique of the very concept of a plot of polity. As "home" becomes heterotopia, the story progressively "unhomes" intellectual foundations rooted in hegemonic values and culturally persuasive ideologies of history, civilization, class, and gender. This approach certainly respects the tricky, shifting ground of Mrs. Penn's appropriation of the new barn, a move that her children consider wholly original, that she thinks of as a mere copy of her forefathers' enterprise, that the narrator places in the enigmatic category of "home-like," that Adoniram comes grudgingly to accept, and that the minister cannot conceive of at all. Given that Sarah Penn's new barn-politic possesses all the signs of a miniature commonwealth organized around the extension of exchange relations to women, one main task we face as readers of "Revolt" is to try to reconcile—or try to account for the irreconcilability of—"Revolt's" multiple constructions of history and political economy.

One interpretation of the conflict between Mother and Father in "Revolt" reclaims exactly what the bewildered minister seems most to miss: an orderly, linear history. Sarah Penn's actions map fairly straightforwardly onto classic liberal accounts of the emergence of contract and a civil society out of the uncivil natural conditions of mankind, which were characterized by Hobbes as the unregulated imposition of power by the strong over the weak, and by Locke as the insecurity of a state of affairs in which one's natural property in one's acquisitions can be alienated in the absence of a third-party constituency charged with the responsibility for adjudicating property claims, and in whose judgment all parties agree to abide. The capstone of Mrs. Penn's oration to her husband about the limitations of their cramped house is an accusation of broken contract. She invites him to ponder "if you think you're doin' right an' accordin' to what you profess. Here, when we was married, forty year ago, you promised me faithful that we should have a new house built in that lot . . . before the year was out" (69–70). Sarah Penn has at least three interwoven promises in mind: the marriage contract, the pledge to build a new house, and a biblically coded emphasis on Adoniram's religious duty to stand behind his word as a "professor" of faith.[42] Her rhetoric of faithful promises and "right" also adumbrates political economic narratives identifying the necessary emergence of contract, property rights, and systems of exchange from what Hobbes calls the "Naturall Condition of Mankind" and Locke the "State of Nature."[43] For Hobbes, humans must enter into a "pact, or covenant" in order to supersede the brutish "condition of meer Nature," which is a "condition of Warre of every man against every man."[44] The proper performance of contract—the core of Sarah's "you promised me faithful"—is called "*Keeping of Promise*, or Faith."[45] Its ultimate guarantor is a sovereign or "coercive Power" with "right and force sufficient to compel performance" lest individuals return to exercising their "Right of Nature," or that "Liberty each man hath, to use his own power, for the preservation of his own Nature."[46]

"Revolt's" backstory—the forty years preceding the events depicted in the narrative—presents an inverted account of this classic narrative. Adoniram gets it precisely backward. The Penns begin with contract—marriage (an exchange of vows) and a faithful promise (about an exchange of edifices)—but then devolve into a brutish state in which Adoniram acts like a lout (his speech is "as inarticulate as a growl" [64]), associates with animals (his wife accuses him of "lodgin' your dumb beasts better than you are your own flesh an' blood" [70]), and is determined to exercise his "right to all things."[47] If Adoniram seeks to play the role of a "coercive power"—the Sovereign's power, Hobbes insisted—in the Penns' household economy, then he sacrifices Hobbes's logic. He disavows, rather than defends, the contractual obligations he entered into upon marriage. He has the force to "compel performance" but not the right sufficient for the "Keeping of Promise." One consequence is that his wife emulates his willingness to live Hobbes's natural condition of mankind—that state of "warre" in which all persons have a "right" to whatever they can appropriate and defend, because all property is unsecured—by seizing the barn, overriding in the meantime her husband's legal claim, the minister's attempt to mediate the dispute, the townspeople's horror, and all sorts of other norms of a (supposedly) civil society.

"Revolt" begins with the Penns locked into a Hobbesian state of nature. Its denouement is distinctly Lockean. By assuming that the natural condition of humanity does not imply a state of war, Locke removes from his narrative of the emergence of contract the necessity for a coercive power embodied in the sovereign.[48] The instantiation of property rights and exchange relations provides the teleology for this shift of emphasis. In the "first ages of the world" what constrains individuals from appropriating and thus alienating another's property in a state of nature is not a common respect for property rights but an original "great common of the world."[49] Since no one could consume more than a small part of the vast territories open to human habitation, "it was impossible for any man . . . to intrench upon the right of another, or acquire to himself a property, to the prejudice of his neighbour, who would still have room for as good and as large a possession . . . as before it was appropriated."[50] Nonetheless, in a state of nature the "law man was under was . . . for appropriating."[51] Possessing "a property in his own person," man makes into his property whatever "he removes out of the state that nature hath provided" and mixes his labor with.[52] Subsequent stages of human society governed by money and property then arise. Relations of exchange provide the capstone to Locke's theory of historical progress. The "invention of money," supported by a framework of legal and political apparatuses, gave men the "opportunity to continue and enlarge" their possessions, allowed them to accumulate more than the basic necessities of life, and thrust them toward the benefits and privileges of civil society, among which is "freedom from absolute, arbitrary power."[53] Once Sarah Penn has been roused to annex the barn, the story's narrative arc seems to deliver the characters here: a set of shared agreements between Sarah and a suitably chastened Adoniram, who no longer wishes to exercise arbitrary power, installs, or perhaps resurrects the promise of, civil society. The couple receive their symbolic freedom under the tenets of liberal political theory.

How can freedom from arbitrary power eventuate from laying claim to and arbitrarily seizing another's property, as Sarah Penn does to the barn? The story's solution to this conundrum emerges from its fabulist play with Lockean first principles—from, in fact, the very position that Freeman ridicules in her 1917 article: that, economically speaking, the old barn was sufficient. "There's room enough in the old one" (73), Sarah Penn argues, a position corroborated by Nanny and the hired man: "Didn't need the new barn, nohow, far as room's concerned" (73).[54] What appeared to be a "big fib" in 1917—the notion that rational economic actors would choose to limit their capital investment—"Revolt" justifies by fusing together a civil society with a state of nature. The fact that there was "room enough" in the old barn implies conditions of plenitude—what Locke described as a shared "great common of the world" where, because all inhabitants may draw freely from unlimited room and resources, acts of accumulation are unnecessary, and no act of appropriation could alienate another's property. It would be impossible for anyone on the "great common" to "intrench upon the right of another, or acquire to himself a property, to the prejudice of his neighbour," since that neighbor would "still have room for as good and as large a possession . . . as before it was appropriated."[55]

Mrs. Penn seems to place her argument on this footing. There is already "room enough" in the old barn; therefore, her occupation of the new barn could not be construed as infringing on Adoniram's property. Indeed, the story's invocation of Locke's state of nature suggests that the new barn should not be construed as Adoniram's "property" at all. "Revolt's" final evocation of a landscape that "might have been an ideal one of peace" (78) because there is now room for everyone, wittily re-creates Locke's famous embrace of the North American continent as *the* latter-day example of what the "great common" must have been like for all humans living in a state of nature. "Thus in the beginning all the world was America," he proclaims, secure in his seventeenth-century faith in the infinite spaces the New World reputedly possessed.[56] The story's ending holds out the vague promise of writing "America" anew—but, as it were, in reverse, as if the story's readers are supposed to work backward from the capitalist and patriarchal relations of late nineteenth-century United States, under which Mrs. Penn in her old domicile made do with scarce resources, and toward Locke's vision of America in the first age of the world, where there is "room enough" for all and "before the desire of having more than man needed had altered the intrinsic value of things."[57]

The story's lack of confidence in the rapprochement between Mother and Father—the landscape "might have been" one of ideal peace—suggests that a different Lockean narrative about the progress of the liberal self under conditions of exchange more plausibly explains the story's economic logic. Mother undertakes an act of exchange (house for barn) to discover the importance of exchange in the abstract—and the new status that proprietary individualism brings with it. Her symbolic claim on exchange allows her to make a new claim on "herself" as an individual capable of entering into market relations with others, for the first time fully alive to the dictates of her natural, rational desire for a property in what she produces. Lockean theory helps to explain why the narrative, as well as Sarah's own oration, invokes so frequently and with such great particularity her domestic chores. She is shown cleaning the house, making shirts, cooking, and washing dishes, while her speech emphasizes her constant investments of labor into the household economy: "We ain't had no new paper on it [the walls] for ten year, an' then I put it on myself. . . . You see this room, father; it's all the one I've had to work in. . . . Father, I've been takin' care of the milk of six cows in this place" (69). In Lockean terms, Sarah Penn has spent forty years acquiring a property in the wallpaper, the milk, the food, and the house by virtue of mixing her labor with them. Her challenge to her husband is abstract—"I want to know if you think you're doin' right" (69)—but the story shows her acquiring a right by "doin.'" It defines the nature of her symbolic claim on "what belonged" to the Pilgrim Fathers. By this logic, her title to the barn/house lies not so much in the realm of an equitable return against her husband's broken promises as in the fact that her Herculean "feat" of shifting her entire household to the barn in a few hours supersedes any "property" Adoniram might have in an edifice that he neither designed nor built (74). She has worked harder for the barn than he. Her concluding call for Adoniram to provide furniture and partitions is less a demand on his money than an invitation for him to participate in the "owning" of the house/barn.

Shifting house also shifts the ideological meaning of Adoniram's role. It is he who has prevented his wife from entering into exchange relations and who thus runs afoul of the mechanisms that would eventually bring down any individual who, by attempting to exercise "power beyond right, which nobody can have a right to," violates the law of contract.[58] The outcome, Locke argues, is rebellion: "if a long train of abuses, prevarications, and artifices, all tending the same way, make the design visible to the people, and they cannot but feel what they lie under, and see whither they are going, it is not to be wondered, that they should then rouse themselves, and endeavour to put the rule into such hands which may secure to them the ends for which government was at first erected."[59] One effect of the new barn-politic glimpsed at the end of "Revolt" is to map the story's territorial preoccupations onto the polity of the United States, for her rebellion against Adoniram also implies a very specific subtext. Locke's "long train of abuses" leading a people toward resistance made its way into Thomas Jefferson's Declaration of Independence, which recapitulates Locke's argument about the right of a people, though slow to rouse, to secure a government and a civil society over against arbitrary power.

Sarah Penn's "rebellious spirit" (75), her determination to talk "real plain" to her husband, reminiscent of Tom Paine's rhetoric of "plain facts" in *Common Sense* (1776), her aggressive "don't tread on me" declaration of cultural and political independence ("I'm goin' to think my own thoughts an' go my own ways" [76]), her list of unanswered grievances, her peas shelled "as if they were bullets" (75), and her move to annex and transform the barn after her husband's forty-year refusal to listen to her just demands, suggests that her rebellion restages in miniature the War of Independence won by a different set of American forefathers. If Sarah Penn's repossession of Locke genders liberal political theory by claiming the privilege of civil society for women on the basis that women should gain property in what they produce through their investments of labor, then she also lays claim to, and genders, the historical conflict that was arguably most inspired by Locke's theories. Fomenting a new rebellion, the story reimagines her right to occupy and transform a space of her own in terms of America's right to self-government, and rewrites the American Revolution in terms of the radical revolution that should have been.

Two other documents surely stand behind "Revolt's" reterritorialization of American space, American history, and American thinking: the Declaration of Sentiments from the 1848 Seneca Falls Convention, and *History of Woman Suffrage*. *History's* "original undertaking"—the first effort to write a history of women's suffrage—is relevant to "Revolt" in several ways. The authors embed the history of women's liberation within a broadly liberal plot of polity, beginning with a Hobbesian regime governed by "brute force" and by "barbarous periods, when . . . 'might makes right,' was the law" and moving to "liberal principles of republicanism," which are characterized by the "theory of individual rights and self-government" and emphasize, just prior to *History's* account of Seneca Falls, American women's steps toward gaining property rights. It also writes the struggle to extend liberal principles to women as a peculiarly American story. The "Revolutionary Mothers" who protested against "being ruled without their consent" in the eighteenth century found "all arbitrary power dangerous and tending to revolution." They were spurred on by the success of the American Revolution: "Woman's political equality with man," the introduction contends, is the "legitimate outgrowth of the fundamental principles of our Government, clearly set forth in the Declaration of Independence," which formed the template for the 1848 Declaration.[60]

"Revolt" and *History* concur in terms of their metanarratives of history. In both, a Hobbesian state of "warre" yields to the promise of a Lockean civil society. A new contract arises between men and women, between mother and father. In "Revolt," however, that new contract is compromised by its un-Lockean conclusion. A fabulous idyll in which there is room enough for all cannot, for Locke, withstand the advent of exchange relations. In that respect "Revolt's" liberal plot of polity is incomplete, and Freeman's "An Autobiography" its true capstone, for the later work rewrites "Revolt" with an eye on the exchange relations that must come about when there is no longer room enough for everyone to have all they desire, so that a New England farm wife is forced to trade off Jersey cows and wide piazzas against "herself." To accept that land and other resources are scarce makes Mother's actions seem wholly uneconomic, even utopian, for they must constrain the future accumulations of goods that are sure to arrive if, as Locke argues and classical economists emphasize, humans are creatures who want more than scarce resources allow and have, in order to satisfy such urges, invented systems (barter, money, markets, exchange) to acquire more than they need to subsist.

If, in the near term, the old barn is still capacious enough for four Jersey cows, the economic process that the new barn represents (which Freeman cites in the *Post* article) is that four cows will lead to more cows, more milk, more hired men, and more property. Sarah Penn takes what Adoniram could make use of; she curtails his propensity to accumulate. This is one way to phrase the "big fib" Freeman describes in "An Autobiography." Her narrative of modernity is nowhere more clearly delineated than in the structural shift in economic logic that takes us from the fabulous and even utopian dream of a state of nature in which there is room enough for all—so that Mother can join the productive enterprises of the farm without cost to anyone—to the logic of scarcity, so important to Locke's metanarrative about the emergence of exchange relations, and the lynchpin of (neo)classical economics.

What cautions us against accepting too readily the linear thrust of this liberal plot of polity is Sarah Penn's long tussle with the minister who comes to set her "lawless and rebellious spirit" (75) to rights. When Mrs. Penn offers her uncompromising interpretation of her move from house to the new barn—"I think it's right jest as much as I think it was right for our forefathers to come over from the old country 'cause they didn't have what belonged to 'em" (75–76)—the minister's superior learning collapses. "He could expound the intricacies of every character study in the Scriptures, he was competent to grasp the Pilgrim Fathers and all historical innovators, but Sarah Penn was beyond him. He could deal with primal cases, but parallel ones worsted him" (76). That there are other ways of telling history beyond the minister's grasp of the country's fathers suggests that some histories belong to a *male* architecture of power incapable of housing Sarah Penn's new way of thinking and that, therefore, the logic of parallel cases needs to be gendered. Her attempt to place her shift of location in a historical context offers a riposte to her own earlier, bitter statement that when her daughter gets older she will "know that we know only what men-folks think we do, so far as any use of it goes" (66). The sudden possibility of Pilgrim mothers as well as fathers—the possibility of cases parallel to those that had seemed primal and unique—define new epistemological principles ready to occupy and fill out the position that the minister has proved incapable of entering. Readers are surely implicated in this appraisal of the baffled minister. The scene leads us beyond him—beyond the circumscribed interpretive strategies he exemplifies—to a different readerly stance where we become more alert and open to new ways of reading, knowing, and judging. Simple histories that refuse to contemplate the problem of parallel cases now seem distressingly antediluvian. Adironam himself takes one shambling step into that new territory at the end when he has to ask "what on airth does this mean, mother?" (77).

Sarah Penn's change of dwelling implies many other analogous relocations: fields of knowledge, interpretive stances we might adopt as readers, and given her own emphasis on eliciting historical contexts for her actions, new questions about how histories are narrated and constructed. Why, for example, do parallel cases confuse the minister's epistemologies and constructions of history, and why do primal cases enable his position in the social order as a bulwark of male power? The issue runs deeper than the fact that all historical innovators the minister knows about are male. A claim on primal sources of knowledge clearly offers support to concepts of hierarchy. Being by definition "like" nothing else, moreover, primal knowledge requires special exegesis and special exegetes; therefore it can be withheld. But Sarah Penn does more than challenge a principle of exclusion. She offers a multi-faceted threat to the minister's historical schema, not just because she claims the right to interpret history, but also because a history constructed out of recurring parallels could have no truck with unique origins. Mrs. Penn herself seems to have no inkling of this. In thinking about her actions as resembling the Pilgrim fathers, Sarah Penn seems to have in mind nothing more than a commonsense historiography. She assumes, like the minister, that primal cases and historical innovations naturally precede and inform—because they have in some way caused—subsequent events. Her actions are the consequence of a process begun by the forefathers. But the logic of an analogous situation—a situation in which two cases are truly parallel—shows that we might just as easily interpret the Pilgrim fathers by grasping the significance of her revolt, in which case her new world is a way of understanding theirs. Perhaps Nanny and Sammy are more acute than they know when overawed by what they think of as their mother's "purely original undertakings" (74): perhaps they might understand the Pilgrim fathers by studying their Pilgrim mother's originality.

Stanton, Anthony, and Gage's *History* once more usefully frames the story's explosive sense that it might be possible to start reading history in a non-linear fashion. By featuring in its opening chapters the first women's rights convention at Seneca Falls and its Declaration, *History* draws attention not only to an important historical event—another original undertaking, the opening salvo in the political battle for women's rights—but also to an important way of conceiving history in terms of parallel cases. Rewriting Jefferson's Declaration of Independence to proclaim that "all men and women are created equal," and replacing the crimes inflicted on the British colonies with the plight of women, the Declaration doubles, extends, and in a sense recolonizes Jefferson's revolutionary words. It is an act of mimicry that emphasizes both an original—the original, authentic meaning of the words that subsequent failures of the American republic to liberate women could not betray—and the power of a reconstructed copy, upon which the meaning of the original seems, paradoxically, to depend. *History* writes the relationship between women's suffrage and abolition similarly. It recounts the progressive entwining of the two movements. But if the "prolonged slavery of women is the darkest page in human history," then the struggle for suffrage is unique. Like abolition, it is a battle against prolonged slavery, but it also stands alone as the exemplary instance ("darkest page") to which all other similar strug-gles would have to be referred if the entire history of enslaving humans is to be grasped.[61]

The framers of the Seneca Falls Declaration quite consciously wrote wom-en's rights into being Jefferson-like or abolition-like. The Convention of 1848 was like the first abolitionist meetings, and like the revolutionary moment of 1776, hence the relevance of Jefferson's groundbreaking words. But not un-til these likenesses occurred could the fundamental principles of a liberal, American, republican narrative of history be truly contemplated. Historical processes become heterotopian. In the sense that Seneca Falls merely repeats a revolutionary moment that puts an end to a long train of abuses, the Decla-ration of Sentiment's repetition of Jefferson's Declaration highlights the con-vention's fidelity to a liberal account of history. It positions itself at the end of a long line of political advances by quoting Jefferson's own quotation of Locke and his recapitulation of Locke's argument about a people's right to end tyranny. But the Declaration's reconstructed version of Jefferson actually affords an alternative history: here, the "history of mankind is a history of re-peated injuries . . . toward women, having in direct object the establishment of an absolute tyranny over her." It is only when this long train of abuses is revealed, when this history of "repeated injuries" is told, that the concept of an "equal station" under the law begins to be manifest.[62]

This puzzling situation—an original undertaking (the first convention for women's rights) mimics previous revolutions, while a copy (the Declaration) authors for the first time a truly liberal narrative of history—begins to open up the complexity of Mother's shift to the new barn-politic. The fact that Sarah and Adoniram end up together in the new barn, (fore)father and (fore)mother together, suggest the possibility that one symbolic goal of "Revolt" is to build a new American commonwealth upon a Seneca Falls–like emphasis on an equal station between men and women. Mrs. Penn must therefore be mistaken when she argues that the occupation of the new barn looks back to the colonization of the New World where America's forefathers finally found what belonged to them. The true story of propriety individualism cannot be-gin to be told until Mrs. Penn occupies the barn. Mrs. Penn could not be re-peating the forefathers' actions, since their actions explicitly exclude women's property rights. Nor could she be copying the actions of the revolutionary founding fathers, whose principles might embrace her in the abstract but ex-cluded her (or her foremothers) when those principles were applied to the new republic. Like the Seneca Falls Declaration, the narrative of the Ameri-can Republic cannot be told until copies, or at least the right kind of copies, are understood as originals and until an extension of the liberal plot of polity registers with its audience.

Mrs. Penn's reterritorializing of the farm can be read as a progressive interpretation of history insofar as it disrupts the primacy of primal male-centered acts and makes it possible to explain the liberatory impulses behind world-changing events without sole reference to the ground-breaking activities of great men. They may in fact be understood with reference to hers. Yet that same logic would impose its own problematic reconstruction of history. If parallel cases are like Sarah Penn's act of subversive self-empowerment, it would seem necessary to salute the colonization of the North American continent as unreservedly as we might Mrs. Penn's expropriation of the barn. We might give instant assent to the very legitimate claim that Mother is typical of Freeman's "women protagonists [who] make their own choices and thereby engage in acts of self-definition that redesign their spaces" while still remaining wary of the implications of how those acts of self-definition might ramify. The story's redesign of history might well justify acts of colonization along with the assertion of property rights on the North American continent.[63]

Yet the logic of parallel cases in "Revolt" takes us beyond not only the baffled minister's fetish of singular instances but the neat historical reversals that both story and History imply. "Revolt" generates a surfeit of parallel cases. Sarah Penn signifies her expropriation of the barn in terms of her forefathers. The narrator adds many more. Mrs. Penn's oratorical expertise is associated with Webster (70)—Daniel Webster, obviously, who made strenuous efforts to maintain the Union in the decades leading to Civil War, and probably too that wordsmith Noah Webster, whose attempts to redefine the language of power (British English) in order to create a federal language stands behind Mrs. Penn's attempts to exercise her linguistic prerogatives. The Pilgrim fathers coming from the old country to the New World remind us of other reterritorializations. Some were relatively peaceful, notably the founding of the Commonwealth of Pennsylvania through its namesake, William Penn. Some were achieved through war, such as the 1759 capture of Quebec by Maj. Gen. James Wolfe (74). Sarah Penn's occupation of the new barn and the displacing of its supposedly rightful master also invokes the War of Independence. If we map the construction of the new barn onto Reconstruction—noting that Union follows an initial disruption (barn vs. house, father vs. mother, North vs. South)—another historical sequence becomes possible: the forefathers' taking "what belonged to 'em" in the New World; the Revolutionary founding fathers taking back what no longer belonged to Britain; a post–Civil War nation, putatively unified once more, giving back to a once-dispossessed people (African Americans) what belonged to them (their freedom and human rights); and capped by another group of dispossessed people (women) agitating still for a true commonwealth fit for men and women.

The story also invites numerous fabulist parallels. Sarah Penn's crowded house reminds us of the nursery rhyme of the old woman who lived in a shoe. The final lines of the story allude to Jericho, which "went down," like Adoniram, the "instant the right besieging tools were used" (78). Other tales from the Bible crowd "Revolt." Among Sarah Penn's forefathers are surely the leaders of Exodus, her forty years of domicile in the old house longing for her "kitchen of . . . dreams" consolidating our sense that she has been suffering domestic slavery, or perhaps just wandering in a domestic wilderness, while awaiting what her children think of as "uncanny and superhuman" (74) intervention. "It looks like a providence" (73), she admits at one point as events take Adoniram unexpectedly away just before the new barn is due to come into service. Wry parallels to Noah's Ark, another biblical story of peripatetic humanity, also resonate in the story. The architect designs the new barn "for the comfort of four-footed animals" yet "planned better than he knew for the comfort of humans" (74), while a rumor circulates in the town that "all four cows were domiciled in the house" (76). Unsurprisingly, the narrative concludes with a ritual cleansing—Mrs. Penn directs Adoniram after his return to "get washed" (77) and then, more particularly, "poured some water into the tin basin, and put in a piece of soap" (77)—all of which results in a post-diluvian landscape that "might have been an ideal one of peace" (78).

In its massing of so many historical, biblical, and fairytale-like contexts, the story places a great deal of interpretive pressure on any monologic reading of Mother's change of state, whether it is a liberal political economic narrative leading her to claim her property rights, or a conventional feminist argument that Mother struggles toward self-expression and independence, or the biblical references that lead Brian White to contend that Freeman is exploring the "liberatory possibilities of her religious tradition": the allusions to the Promised Land, Jericho, and Christ's parable of building one's house upon rock "point unerringly to a promised land waiting to be conquered and lead the reader to the very gates of fortresses whose walls may and must be besieged by women."[64] The problem is not that the story fails to provide evidence for such readings, but that the story's logic of parallel cases is heterotopian: it provides too many "like," but conflicting, cases. What, for instance, connects Christ's parable about building one's house on rock, Jericho, and Plymouth Rock (76)? What is the connection between the siege of Jericho, the siege of Quebec during the British expropriation of Canada from the French (during the Seven Years' War), and the Americans' expropriation of the colonies from the British a few years later? In what ways should we be making analogies between Mrs. Penn's revolutionary seizure of the barn and the acts of colonization practiced by her forefathers, whose legacy includes Father's domineering attitude toward the farm and his wife, not to mention the minister's ignorance? Even if we assume that Freeman took a relatively uncritical attitude toward colonization, there are surely good grounds for distinguishing between the British possession of the New World (through the forefathers), the British possession of Canada (through Wolfe), and the dispossession of the British from America (through revolutionaries determined to think their own thoughts and go their own ways). The same sorts of problems occur when we turn to a fabulist register. Mrs. Penn might play the part of a new Moses (or Noah) leading other women from domestic servitude to the promised land, but are we being invited to think of her avatars, Wolfe or Daniel Webster, as Moses figures too? Once we have recontextualized Daniel Webster as a historical and mythic figure, following the narrative's urging to place Mrs. Penn's actions within a matrix of parallel cases, would it not seem more useful to think of his determination to preserve the Union as an *impediment* to the sort of radical change that might lead "a people" to a promised land?

The very scene that inserts Mrs. Penn into history, granting her, and us, the capacity to read her move into the barn as a political act, also flattens history into a series of parallel cases which, the more we inspect them, seem less like hers, and less like each other, and possessed of varying degrees of revolutionary import. "Revolt's" narrative architecture features heterogeneous plots of polity. In this respect Sarah Penn must be seen as a piecemeal historian. Her domestic economy certainly suggests as much. Because she has a "scanty pattern" (71), when she makes new shirts for Adoniram, she has to "plan and piece the sleeves" (71). Moreover, her new home remains unfinished at the end of the story. It requires windows, partitions, and furniture (77), and the stove resides in the harness-room (75). The "great middle space" would make a parlor "fit for a palace," but only, "by-and-by" (75). We might read Mrs. Penn as an archetypal bricoleur, piecing together an incomplete structure out of shards of the past and one-upping the architect, who plans "better than he knew" for the future. From this perspective, the story comports with Fetterley and Pryse's argument that female regionalists developed the sketch narrative as a challenge to oppressive ideologies of centered form and market capitalism.[65] But that challenge, the logic of this story implies, must itself remain incomplete. The new barn-politic's representation of historical processes would have to include exchange relations among its perquisites. Once more, it fulfills its peculiar function of making a claim on originality—*this* model of commonwealth has never been seen before—and simultaneously looking back to rewrite, correct, confuse, but also borrow from, common narratives of how commonwealths evolve.

3

"SUPPOSING AN ISLAND"

Political Economic Topographies in Stowe and Jewett

Island fictions occupy something of a privileged position in New England female regionalist discourse. Sarah Orne Jewett acknowledged the formative influence of Harriet Beecher Stowe's *The Pearl of Orr's Island* (1862) and admired *Among the Isles of Shoals* (1873), by her close friend Celia Thaxter. These works inspired a long-standing fascination with islands, evinced in *A Marsh Island* (1885), "The King of Folly Island" (1888), and the compelling island sequences in *Country*: the four-chapter sojourn at Green Island when the narrator accompanies Mrs. Todd to see her mother, quickly followed by the tale of poor Joanna's self-imposed incarceration on Shell-heap Island. *Country*'s island topoi invoke a range of women's lived realities—the communion the narrator enjoys with Mrs. Blackett on Green Island forms a riposte to the "remote and islanded" psychic landscape of Shell-heap.[1] The most astute scholarly responses to such scenes have recognized the relevance of islands to women's lives. In *Writing out of Place* the authors place Thaxter's *Isles* at the very center of their enterprise. It (along with Mary Austin's *The Land of Little Rain* [1903]) "best illustrate what the representation of place means for regionalist writers."[2] The Isles' landscape of "deprivation and blankness" makes it possible to read them as "emblematic of the situation of women in patriarchal culture," yet they also epitomize the symbolic possibilities of writing "out of place" by virtue of the fact that the "more remote, the more marginalized, the more written off as a blank space . . . the more likely a region is to provide a space for the construction of meaning" for women.[3] Leaving Maine and the mainland United States behind means abandoning a socioeconomic realm dominated by white men and accepting instead new aesthetic and interpretive approaches conducive to a world "apart" from a "dominant (male) society."[4]

The notion that islands can speak with a special pertinence to the plight of women and to their propensities for fomenting a critique of the mainland is illuminating. There are few more caustic critiques of property rights than "The King of Folly Island." After a dispute with his neighbors, King George purchases an island and resolves never to set foot on another man's property. Sharing his island, and sacrificed to his ambition, are his wife (dead) and daughter (dying), a fact that at least one denizen of John's Island manages to miss with his chillingly wrong-headed assessment of King George's actions: "Don' know who he's spitin' but himself."[5] In the story's denouement King George's only remedy for his daughter is to offer her in marriage to Frankfort, a wealthy visitor from the mainland—a compound irony given the fact that, while her father can only imagine a future for her as property in a marriage market defined by his "hard cash" (44) and the visitor's "means" (44), his penchant for "look[ing] out for number one" (32) has already ruined her health and marriageability. The destructive self-contradictions of masculinist property rights have rarely been exposed with such harrowing force. Phebe's islanded life contains one symbolic space that is not reducible to property. She gives to Frankfort, the wealthy mainlander, her cardboard model of a meeting house, adorned with shells. That "legacy" (49), an image of sociality, of things that are of "use in the world" (48), but perhaps too of women's lives reduced to shells of what they might have been, means little to Frankfort. But perhaps the "much-crushed bundle" (46) looking "sadly trivial and astray" (46) on the financier's desk offers a more hopeful meeting-place for the presumably more empathetic (female?) readers capable of greater "critical and reflective distance."[6]

The challenge that northeastern female regionalist island-spaces pose to mainland thinking forms an important part of my analysis in this chapter. But the fuller meanings of these island fictions—including their more critical aspects—lack definition without positioning them within the very complex intellectual, cultural, and political play of meanings associated with nineteenth century island discourses in the United States. Works such as *The Pearl of Orr's Island* and "The King of Folly Island" appeared in journals that, at times, evinced a near-obsession with island travelogues. Visits to South Sea and in particular Caribbean islands featured heavily; so did accounts of trips to islands off the New England coast. These travelogues frequently set out to offer a psychic restorative to those beset by "fretting incidents and crushing cares"; they invite readers, at least symbolically, to an especially remote site "where we might forget all the toil and turmoil and multiplied burdens of the great bustling world in which we lived and struggled the rest of the year."[7] The common argument that female regionalism promotes touristy, get-away fictions designed to entertain urban audiences with tales of the remote, the islanded, and the idiosyncratic, draws on such articles.[8] My analysis of Stowe and Jewett in this chapter and the next does not reprise such an argument. "The King of Folly Island" demonstrates an awareness of the lure and danger of island tourist fiction and rebuts it convincingly. It satirizes Frankfort, who is looking specifically, and aimlessly, for local color in the "strange population" that "clung to these isolated bits of the world" (19) in hopes that it will rejuvenate his "very tired" (41) existence—which it does until, in a neat reversal, Frankfort finds that "business cares began to fret this holiday-maker" (41) on the island idyll he sought as escape.[9]

But island travelogues served more functions in nineteenth-century American culture than amusement for urban populations. They shared in and helped underwrite what the United States considered to be its political and commercial interests in the Caribbean. Haiti, Cuba, Santo Domingo (now the Dominican Republic), and other Caribbean islands were a powerful source of interest and anxiety for the United States throughout the nineteenth century.[10] The issue of slavery was an important motivating factor in the antebellum era. Haitian independence, for example, posed an obvious challenge to antebellum paternalist rhetoric that slaves were incapable of living autonomously. About the time Stowe was beginning to write *Pearl* (in 1852), contributors to the so-called Ostend Manifesto (in 1854) proposed annexing Cuba in order to expand US slaveholding territory. US interest in the Caribbean continued under other auspices in post–Civil War days. From 1867 to 1871 the United States considered annexing Santo Domingo.[11] Accounts of the Caribbean constantly fostered discourses of emerging nationhood and even imperialism in the United States. *Country* appeared amid talk of annexing Hawaii and as the possibility of US military intervention in Cuba loomed after attempts to secure the largest island in the Caribbean as a US dependency or even state. Throughout the nineteenth century, the extension of US political power into the Caribbean was underwritten by appraisals of islands as potential markets and as sources of raw materials. In chapter 6 I examine one aspect of this discourse: the connection between John Quincy Adams's theory that Cuba was a low-hanging fruit ready for US plucking, the tropical fruit trade, and Alice Dunbar-Nelson's remarkable rewriting of that trade in ideas and foodstuffs in "Mr. Baptiste."

Contributing to these wide-ranging US political and commercial interests, US visitors to the Caribbean began to flood the market with travelogues around the middle of the nineteenth century. They were motivated by what Edward Said describes as a "flexible *positional* superiority, which puts the Westerner in a whole series of possible relationships with the Orient [here, the Caribbean] without ever losing him the relative upper hand."[12] Writers persistently exploited the islands to define what they thought of as the superiority of (Anglo)American identities, political beliefs, and economic principles. As George Black argues, the "entire modern history" of Central

America and the Caribbean has been "held hostage to the demands of the American imagination."[13] That cultural imagining of US superiority was frequently deployed along a broad New England–Caribbean axis. A common and calculated feature of magazine features was the juxtaposition of Caribbean and New England scenes, comparing, as one writer put it, the "rugged and intellectual character of New England with the luscious, indolent life of . . . Cuba."[14] Nineteenth-century island discourses in the United States relied heavily on a symbolic structure in which New England self-discipline and orderly markets came to stand for the United States. Cuba and other Caribbean islands represented its abject other: a noneconomy, a nonfunctioning polity, luscious isles populated by indolent people. The Caribbean–New England discourse on islands also disparaged the economies of tropical islands by gendering them female—as a symbolic realm of lush, fecund nature or as a place where men, of a distinctly noneconomic variety, do nothing—and where male travelers from the United States consequently found legitimation for their status as economic man.[15]

Island discourses in the United States also tapped a rich tradition of political economic thought that had long employed island fables to examine principles of commonwealth and of economic man. Early theoretical works such as Thomas More's *Utopia* (1516) and Francis Bacon's *New Atlantis* (1627) provided influential models of how to stage an island as an imaginary commonwealth and thereby grasp the nature of human beings, good government, a wise management of resources, and the orderly development of civilized societies. Indeed, islands could be thought of not just as a model of human sociality but also as its arche. For John Locke the act of "supposing an island" underwrites *the* crucial step in theorizing how property rights, money, and relations of exchange emerged to structure human societies anew. Jean-Jacques Rousseau (1762) argued that language and society itself must have originated on islands. "Portions of the continent were by revolutions of the globe torn off and split into islands," Rousseau conjectured, adding that it is "obvious that among men thus collected, and forced to live together, a common idiom must have started up much sooner, than among those who freely wandered through the forests of the mainland," so that "it is very probable that society and languages commenced in islands and even were highly developed there, before the inhabitants of the continent knew anything of either."[16] Thought of this way, "The King of Folly Island" stages a contest between competing political economic models—Rousseau's notion that islands compel sociality colliding with King George's ad absurdum evocation of Locke's proprietary individual.

This centuries-long tradition in which the island became a paradigmatic space for elucidating principles of political economic thought certainly comported well with the history of British colonialism. John Locke's foundational act of supposing an island piggybacked on European accounts of the abundance and ease to be found on Caribbean isles at the moment of colonial contact—and provided a rationale for the unavoidable introduction there of proprietary individualism and markets.[17] The reciprocal of the model island commonwealth was the colonial domination of tropical islands for their material wealth. One vector for the substantial ideological investment Britain made in powerful cultural fables about its island imperium was Daniel Defoe's *Robinson Crusoe* (1719) and the popular genre that later built on its plot and ideological meanings: the robinsonade. The robinsonade carries with it a vast array of suppositions about colonial prerogatives, property rights, and human nature as it appeared in contradistinction to the colonized other. It foregrounds the "colonial alibi": a "man alone, on a desert island, constructing a simple and moral economy which becomes the basis of a commonwealth presided over by a benevolent sovereign."[18] The "closed space of the island" constitutes it as an exemplary imperial space since it "supplies the perfect model for a nonrelational outlook on life."[19] It transforms the "messiness of imperial expansion into a simplified story of a man successfully defending his legitimately earned space."[20] That could mean reimagining the island as an *empty* space. In order to constitute the island as a site of "reflections on origins," it had to be reconstructed as an "uninhabited territory upon which the conditions for a rebirth or a genesis are made possible."[21] At such points, imperial power and bedrock political economic principles dovetail neatly, providing mutual support to each other as they define the grounds—the state of nature, the inevitable emergence of law and property rights, a rational use of resources—upon which other islands might fall to European nations or, in Britain's cultural imaginary, to *the* island, Britain, which makes other islands around the globe meaningful in relationship to it.

US Caribbeanism in the nineteenth century invested heavily in what was already a compelling cultural fable about island economies, archived in a vast variety of robinsonades, travelogues, fictions, fantasies, political economic treatises, histories, and ethnographies of all sorts. The trope of the empty island yielded easily to a sense that island cultures were representative of preeconomic or early economic life, empty of, or at least struggling to attain, the kind of substantive, disciplined economic knowledge US visitors claimed to bring with them. The disorderly marketplace, which functioned by barter or other forms of crude, premodern trading and was typically inhabited by women, was a persistent topos. Travelogues of visits to the Caribbean leveraged stadialist narratives. A command of political economic principles allowed US visitors to grasp the backwardness of island "economies" from the privileged perspective of homo economicus, the one whose end-of-history perspective laid bare the underlying processes of history, economic transformation, and civilization.

This multifaceted discourse provides an important framework for northeastern female regionalist fiction. The remote and islanded aspect of this fiction occurs in close proximity to accounts that situate the northeastern United States against Caribbean/deserted/tropical islands and use that opposition in order to signify mainland/national identities. Jewett's "The King of Folly Island" hints at this by way of its status as an ironic robinsonade. Claiming "I wanted to be by myself" (34), King George is an "island potentate" (18) who insists "I ain't stepped foot on any man's land but my own these twenty-six years" (22). (Crusoe was island-bound for twenty-eight years before his rescue.[22]) Frankfort also realizes that he is a "lonelier and a more selfish man" (43) than King George himself; a "kind of solitary creatur'" (43), King George calls him. Frankfort's "good for nothing but money-making" (38) anomie turns out to be every bit as indebted to Crusoe's economy-for-one as King George's manic proprietary individualism: imperial manhood exists on Maine's island and on the US mainland. But neither man is as castaway as Phebe. Since there was "no actual exile in [King George's] lot after all; he met his old acquaintances almost daily on the fishing grounds" (25), it was "upon the women of the household that an unmistakable burden of isolation had fallen" (25), and upon them that Crusoe's mandate to build an orderly household descends. Phebe must suffer the desert(ed)-island fantasy that the men avow.

Stowe's *Pearl* is a cornerstone of this female regionalist cultural formation. Chapter 26, "Dolores," and chapter 27, "Hidden Things," transport the reader back in time and down South, nominally to Florida. But Dolores and her husband hail from the West Indies and Cuba. Incorporating aspects of a New England–Caribbean island discourse, the Dolores chapters are crucial for establishing and guiding readers into comprehending the political economic registers of the narrative. Stowe's analysis reproduces a familiar dynamic in which the disorderly economies of the Caribbean-South are opposed by the frugality, industriousness, and domestic order of Orr's Island, which is theorized by Minister Sewell, enacted by women's kitchen work, and affirmed by the novel's more-or-less conventional denouement that weds Moses's masculine entrepreneurship to Sally's domestic prowess. Sewell's Florida chapters contextualize the commonwealth of northeastern islands in contradistinction to "backward" economic relations drawn from Caribbean markets.

This dynamic has its complicating aspects. Though Sewell goes to Florida purporting to set the South's "neglected accounts into order," the narrative grapples with the fact and meaning of his neglected account: a story deferred for two decades and for two-thirds of the novel, revealing origins buried deep in the past yet pointing to the historical moment of 1862.[23] One consequence is that kitchen work quietly speaks to and for the political economic principles that Sewell enunciates but cannot authentically represent. At its most unsettling, the novel introduces the figure of femina economica to operate as a surrogate for Sewell. This analysis challenges the common notion that Stowe fails to think beyond ideologies that make the domestic space a "refuge from marketplace activities"[24]—that the author resists principles of laissez-faire capitalism along with slave economies.[25] Yet Orr's Island trades materially and symbolically with Caribbean islands. The novel maps out a tentative role for femina economica that is not entirely at odds with the discourse of disorderly (and feminized) Caribbean economies. It is not that Stowe resists the pronounced discursive tendency to denigrate the economies of Caribbean islands by gendering them female. But by implicating the domestic work on Orr's Island in a southern domain of "neglected accounts" and by making Dolores in the South an unexpected locus of economic probity, Stowe opens a heterotopian space within which relationships between the North, South, and the Caribbean on the one hand, and between men's work and domestic order on the other, can be scrutinized anew.

BRINGING "NEGLECTED ACCOUNTS INTO ORDER" IN HARRIET BEECHER STOWE'S *THE PEARL OF ORR'S ISLAND*

To hear the now-diffident minister Sewell tell it, his job as a young tutor in Saint Augustine, Florida, was nothing less than playing homo economicus to the "disorderly household" (252) of the South. As he recalls in his letter to Moses, bringing the Mendoza family's "neglected accounts into order" meant trying to restore damaged economies on multiple levels: financial "difficulties" (251) brought on by "disorder and neglect" (251); an uncivil society ruled by the "worse vices of despots" (249); "ill-regulated" (251) family life where children are brought up by "ungoverned" (249) mothers and "half-barbarized negroes" (251); "undisciplined" (251) family members whose moral economies harbor "expressions and actions which would seem incredible in civilized society" (252); subverted pedagogies, where the "teacher has to contend constantly with a savage element in the children" (251); dislocated geographies, making it seem as if each child had "formed its manners in Dahomey or on the coast of Guinea" (252); fractious relations leading to faction, where Dolores, the one "orderly" (253) member of the family, is the object of the "petty tyrannies of both parties" (252), picked on by "one party or the other" (253); and wrecked marital relations, where "Dolores was in her father's hands, to be disposed of for life according to his pleasure, as absolutely as if she had been one of his slaves" (254).

Published in 1862, *The Pearl of Orr's Island* clearly situates this devastating indictment of the disrupted economies of the Mendoza household within a broader narrative about the moral, political, and economic values the North might bring to heal the nation when the United States faced fracture, unleashed passions, and a threat to lawful government. Sewell represents the "simplicity and order of New England" (250); he possesses a "command of temper which is the common attribute of well-trained persons in the Northern states" (252) that allows him to model an orderly civil society for a family in which "such a variety of elements" could only be harmonized by the "most judicious care" (249). Orr's Island is Sewell's appropriate home—a commonwealth full of "material good . . . wholesome thrift and prosperity" (122), even a utopia, given the narrator's avowal that a "more healthful and desirable state of society never existed" (122). The main plot concerns the rearing of two orphaned children on Orr's Island, which suggests another contrast with Saint Augustine families: Mara and Moses are reared in a civilized society by white people. If *Pearl* is a novel of passing, as Cheli Reutter argues—Moses in particular seems to be quietly coded as a child of mixed-race heritage—then it might be thought to fabricate a myth of commonwealth where a "variety of elements" can best, or only, be harmonized under the disciplined "judicious care" of Anglo-Americans.[26] There is an ominous ring to that. Prominent among the Mendozas' sins is the suspicion that they have toppled the orderly plot of savagery-to-civilization on which readers depend to recognize and privilege "American" characteristics over those from Dahomey and the coast of Guinea.

Sewell's two-chapter account of the Mendoza household is crucial to construing the other forty-two chapters. It brings the entirety of the time spent on Orr's Island into play as a legitimate counterweight to the passionate disorder of the South. It also reconstructs, by inviting us to extend, the geopolitical boundaries of the South. The narrative urges us to chart the desirability of Orr's Island in proportion to its distance not just from Florida but from Dahomey, the coast of Guinea, and the Caribbean. Captain Kittridge's surmise that Moses "may be from the West Indies" (81) turns out to be more or less correct; his mother was from the "Spanish West Indies" (249), his father from Cuba. That Caribbean connection suggests that the Dolores chapters serve an important function by activating a discourse on southern islands and northern socioeconomic ways and embedding Orr's Island within it. In a sense it is only after the Dolores chapters that Orr's Island begins to signify *as an island*. Islands, by virtue of the sea that isolates them from a mainland, at once "produce difference" and draw special attention to the fact of, and the vulnerability of, boundaries and lines of demarcation.[27] A sea-passage separates island from mainland and marks it as a space that can be, and in most island fictions has to be, traversed. To recognize the distinctiveness of an island is to put it into relation with the mainland—to make mainland identity and island difference constitutive of each other. The Dolores chapters allow Orr's Island to reach its full potential as a signifying vehicle. It is now an island in relation to the difference of other mainland/island/slave societies; it is capable of elucidating alterity. Its characters, events, and values suddenly become relevant in the context of a debate, and a war, between North and South, while issues of economy and marriage in the South turn out to be metonymically relevant to islands in the Caribbean.

Perhaps *suddenly* is not quite the word. Encountering the backstory near the end of the narrative certainly does have the force of revelation; but one effect of reading it is to be aware that a story from the deep past has been active and potent every step of the way. Reading the Dolores chapters virtually forces us to begin the novel again. This is not exactly, or not only, an act of retrospection. The backstory has been neglected but not absent: all along, we have been reading part of a larger story and part of a larger discourse on slavery, marriage, and gendered economies extending from the Caribbean to Florida to Orr's Island. The story's strategy, or conceit, is to withhold information from readers in order to prevent them from knowing the full scope of that discourse until the Dolores chapters. On reaching those chapters, one of the things we come to know is that we already know its full scope. The revelation that the slovenly Mendozas hail from the Caribbean hardly comes as a shock. The news seems of a piece with their disorderly economies. The question worth asking, then, is not why Stowe withholds the information about Moses's parentage so long, but by means of what cultural order that information, once it is revealed, can seem so unexceptional and persuasive.

The depth and the richness of the discourse on Caribbean and New England islands, which remained relatively intact over the course of the second half of the nineteenth century, begins to explain why Stowe need barely hint at Moses's origins, and why Captain Pennel supposes, correctly, that Moses comes from the West Indies even though "nobody knows" (81). The ill-regulated, disorderly economies of the Mendozas' neglected accounts are inscribed everywhere in the attention travelogues in the second half of the nineteenth century paid to the economic malaise of Caribbean islands. Such accounts were inflected by the question of whether the island was still slave-holding. It is important to note that Stowe's narrative traces the Mendozas' egregious lack of proper governance back to Cuba, still holding slaves as she writes, and the Spanish West Indies. She deemphasizes islands such as British-held Jamaica, where slaves had been emancipated in 1838. Nonetheless, the discourse on Caribbean economies insisted upon the islands' lack of a free market economy: it is what slave-holding plantation owners actively resist, and what the colonized inhabitants of "free" islands have little or no conception of. These works provide an important context for understanding political economic discourses in *Pearl* and later female regionalist island fictions.

The American Civil War brought intense attention to Caribbean islands. Five years after the publication of *Pearl*, during the early years of Reconstruction, the annexation of Santo Domingo resurfaced as a pressing topic. Under threat of invasion by Haiti, President Buenaventura Báez asked President Andrew Johnson to consider annexing the nascent Dominican Republic as a US territory, and possibly a state. In 1869 President Ulysses S. Grant formally initiated the process to annex Santo Domingo. His goals were military (to build a base on the island) and strategic (to secure for the United States the large island at the mouth of the Caribbean). In private letters, Grant admitted that the politics of race was another compelling reason: eventual statehood for the Dominican Republic was a provision of the bill, and one reason was that a new island state might offer a way to usher freed African Americans off the US mainland. The bill failed in 1870 after a tied vote in the Senate.

Subsequently, Grant formed an investigative commission to complete a thorough survey of Santo Domingo and keep the annexation issue alive. Frederick Douglass was sent. Samuel Hazard was another appointee, perhaps on the strength of *Cuba with Pen and Pencil* (1871). His account of the investigative trip, *Santo Domingo: Past and Present, with a Glance at Hayti* (1873), is exemplary of nineteenth-century Caribbeanism. His forthrightness regarding the potential benefits accruing to US commerce, the marketability of various crops, the value of island property, and the potential for new markets for the United States, jibes with the subtler orientation of so many travelogues toward Caribbean islands in the decades preceding and following his account. All are customarily shaped by an "imperialist-colonial economy of wealth-extraction and exploitation." Travelogues play their part in a long-standing Caribbeanism: picturesque tourist encounters join hands with more overt exercises of imperial power to justify the "metropolitan nations' running Caribbeans' affairs for them."[28]

The opening pages of Hazard's book introduce us to the conundrum that, in many ways, governs the entire book: it is an "almost forgotten yet historic isle." In one sense Hazard is merely borrowing from a familiar playbook of travel writing. "Almost forgotten" avows the topicality of his insights to his readers, with a further nod here to a specific audience, a foot-dragging Congress. "How little was really known" about the island of Santo Domingo both indicts and excuses that body for its lack of foresight.[29] But Hazard's strategy is as much to problematize Santo Domingo's history as it is to bemoan his readers' ignorance of it. The island once "played such an important part in the history of the world," for Columbus first landed here, making it the "cradle of the New World."[30] Now the island has "almost lost its existence in the political world."[31] Hazard tasks the United States with helping this "historic isle" remember history by providing it with political stability and commercial prowess; it is "waiting only the assistance of law and sound government, accompanied by intelligence, industry, and enterprise, to take its place in the political arena as one of the most favoured of states."[32] An American exceptionalism clearly governs his approach. The epochal advent of the US republic seems to have transformed the very meaning of history. To the extent that sound government and intelligent enterprise emerge with, and only with, the republic—newly secured and guaranteed by the Civil War and Reconstruction—accounts of Santo Domingo's indigenous and colonial history are reduced to little more than interesting stories. Hazard's epochal shift also dovetails with stadialist logic: history has produced its capstone society, a republic worthy of the modifier "civilized."

Hazard's interpretation of history helps explain what appears to be the complete illogic of so many moments in his account where contradictory assessments of historical "fact" compete. While describing the island's peoples he asks "why an island so attractive and valuable in every way as St Domingo certainly is, should remain for so long a time unsettled and uncivilised"; sailing along the coast and noting that "no habitations are seen in the entire extent of the coast," he states that it "presents to-day to our eyes undoubtedly the same appearance" it did to the "grand Colon [Columbus]" on first arriving at the island—even though he has just stated that four hundred years ago this same coast featured the "abodes of over a million of the native Indians."[33] This pronounced strobing effect, whereby peoples and histories appear and just as suddenly vanish, is a version of the imperialist strategy Diana Loxley investigates in the context of *Robinson Crusoe*. The deserted island becomes a tabula rasa upon which Europeans and Americans "can erect their own story."[34] Hazard's history seems to be the direct consequence of his privileging of an American-inspired revolution in the meaning of history. The Arawaks and colonial settlements dematerialize because they are immaterial to the new history the US epoch makes possible—or they count only insofar as they have brought about a vacuum the United States can now fill.

Hazard commands a panoply of strategies borrowed from a well-developed discourse on Caribbean islands to smooth over this rhetorical vanishing of settlements and history. One is to represent the islanders as being replaced by spectacularly fecund vegetation. Hazard celebrates the "magnificent earth" of the islands.[35] Since the days of the Spanish adventurers in the sixteenth century, there has been "no hand of progress on these old hills, which Nature has changed more than man."[36] Fecund nature, before which humans are supernumerary, is a partial solution to the puzzle of a somehow "unsettled" historic isle. W. E. Sewell offers corroboration: The "soil of Jamaica is so rich, that two years after an estate is thrown out of cultivation it is covered with bush, and scarcely to be distinguished from wild land."[37] So does Lafcadio Hearn, decades later, pondering (in Grenada) the fate of "any West Indian port" when "the resources of the island had been exhausted, and its commerce ruined. . . . Nature would soon so veil the place as to obliterate every outward visible sign of the past."[38] History and people on these islands are erased by Nature, swamped by a fantastic, luxuriant flood of vegetation.

For many writers, descriptions of the astonishing raw resources of Caribbean islands expose a problematic in political economic theory: reminding visitors of Locke's supposed-island state of nature, island laborers need not labor in order to survive. The main cause of Jamaica's "unprosperous condition" following the emancipation of slaves, argues "Oran" in his 1858 travelogue, is that since the "wants of the negro were few and easily supplied, he was content, and could not be induced to work for a hire," preferring "days of idle ease."[39] Indolence seems a perfectly logical "economic" strategy when there is no need for a market economy. Such fables about people living in a state of nature were, however, untenable if political economic knowledge was to be thought pertinent to the islands rather than wholly immaterial to a situation that was supposed to exist before economic transactions came to matter. Of what use is homo economicus and his privileged knowledge if the islanders do not need an economy?

One solution, in the spirit of Hazard's perplexing appraisal of Santo Domingo as an "almost forgotten yet historic isle," was to argue that the islanders were merely mimicking the origins of human society: Their "state of nature" was the consequence of a fall into history. Hazard links "magnificent earth" to the "terrible mill in which the island has been ground up." The author known by the pseudonym "An Artist" links a "soil of marvelous fertility" to a "crushing despotism, civil and religious." Oran links a "wild, luxuriant productiveness" to "deserted grounds and dilapidated tenements."[40] What looked like a discourse on an abundant state of nature was in fact the effect of, and a cover for, disastrously run economies. Authors adapted the terms of stages theory to new purposes. Premarket life amid fecund nature was read as disorderly barter and peddling; subsisting without labor was read as indolence; the luxury of total abundance was read as lack. On these islands, the supposedly universal attributes of homo economicus—rational decision-making, intelligent industry, energy, sound governance, a functioning civil society, and efficient markets—are not absent so much as calamitously performed. Politically and economically, Caribbean islands aspire to the condition not of Locke's supposed island, but of Haiti as Foster Crowell indicted it in 1893: a "make-believe republic."[41]

Arrivals at island wharves offer travelers the first opportunity to register a range of economic inefficiencies. One is somnolence—the "normal condition of every body in waiting"; cab drivers are "actually asleep upon the tops of their coaches" near the wharf.[42] Disorderly wharf-life extends into one of the most prominent and privileged topoi of Caribbean travel literature: the visit to the marketplace. "The market-place is a feature of Kingston—let no visitor fail to see it," admonishes W. E. Sewell.[43] Three decades later Howard Pyle felt obliged to transport the reader thither: "to understand and appreciate Jamaica, one must see Kingston market upon a Saturday." What US travel writers typically understand in these visits is a form of rudimentary or make-believe economic activity consistent with societies that have experienced "no hand of progress" (as Hazard said) for hundreds of years. For Pyle, Kingston's markets now represent the "very essence of Jamaica life, picturesque, shiftless, dirty, aimlessly busy."[44] Hazard observes that "a more ridiculous sight cannot be imagined" than the tiny market square of Puerto Plata with its "few rude booths."[45] Nearly two decades later, Hearn follows his example: On Santa Cruz (Saint Croix, US Virgin Islands) there are piles of fruit but "no benches, no stalls, no booths."[46] Not surprisingly, marketplace babble—a "confusion of tongues," a "chatter, gabble, clatter!"[47]—obstructs efficient exchange (for US visitors) and precludes a functional language of commerce.

Crude economic encounters at wharves and marketplaces ramify through Caribbean travel literature, and in endlessly varied ways. The islands are perceived to have no stable banking system. Julia Ward Howe writes that she had heard "very strange stories . . . about the trade in lottery-tickets" among Cubans, noting that "for them, the lottery replaces the savings-bank, with entire uncertainty of any return." Howe had already observed that the Bahamas Banks—a wrecking ground for ships—had taken the place of banks; the islanders want a "desirable wreck" most of all since wreckers and pirates are the only ones making money.[48] Buccaneers are the picturesque focus of an extraordinary number of Caribbean travelogues, representatives of a predatory commerce that fascinates and appalls the US visitor. Without stable means of banking or circulating money, familiar and orderly processes of commerce grind to a halt. The peddler replaces the seller; thievery and bribery are common; and there are no fixed prices because marketing goods means bartering and haggling. Value is negotiable and unstable; it is subject to coercion and set by persuasion. It can even be seduced. Hearn observes "colored girls" coming on board the ship trying to "coax us with all sort of endearing words to purchase bay-rum, fruits, Florida-water."[49]

A quiet but persistent feature of this discourse on disorderly markets is the replacement of economic man with women. Oran argues that "nothing can give a better idea of the low estate to which these people have fallen than a coaling [carrying coal to refuel a ship] scene—while the females are bearing the heat and burden of the day, their lazy and dissolute husbands and brothers lie sunning themselves on the wharf, occasionally worrying a dime from the passer-by."[50] "All the venders of fruit and produce are women," notes Howard Pyle as he "stands in the market square bewildered."[51] W. E. Sewell's insouciant and contemptuous account of a trip to Jamaica disparages the "class of good-for-nothing idlers that loiter in the streets of Kingston and other Jamaica towns," but follows up with the countervailing observation that at the market women importune passers-by in a far from idle fashion. "Fifty or sixty women squat upon the ground, with piles of fruit and vegetables before them. They do not wait patiently for purchasers, but address themselves vehemently to the throng, and extol the superior quality of their merchandise." Sewell does not recognize the marketers' energy as labor. "How they [the piles of fruit] are all sold is a mystery that I could not fathom,"[52] he marvels. The activities of women here are not exactly illegible to Sewell, Oran, and Pyle. But within a construction of "the economic" as the prerogative of economic man, they do not quite signify as market activities. Disregard for women's market labor helps preserve two almost universal perceptions: (1) lazy islanders who are in need of Yankee order and entrepreneurship and (2) fertile islands troped as passively feminine.

Allowing islanders into the margins of economic discourse grants US visitors the ability to play homo economicus to the nominal humans living in the Caribbean. W. E. Sewell's posture in "Cast-away in Jamaica" is to play the island's lone rational economic agent, its castaway Crusoe. His superior grasp of economic principle and conditions governs his critique of the wrecked Jamaican economy and society. The island is commercially and socially a "shattered hulk," and he the island's one authentic human being. His castaway's orderly and ordering gaze always places the island in relationship to the United States. He veers from descriptions of Jamaica's polyglot society into its primordial resources—its "soil [that] yields every variety of tropical fruit and vegetable"—and then reaches out again to restate the hegemony of the market. "Such quantities of cocoas, pines, oranges, mangoes, granadillas, sapodilloes, and vegetables of all descriptions—comparatively valueless in Kingston, but worth a mint if they could be taken to a Northern market," he insists.[53] The trope of the northern market underscores a potent sense of discursive exchange; at stake here is not merely the monetary value of Jamaican crops but the value of cultural signifiers premised on the privilege accorded economic man. The strength of US ideals of social order and self-discipline—its "intelligence, industry, and enterprise," as Hazard puts it—depends on accounts of the economic malfeasance and disorderly market regimes of the Caribbean.

This construction of the US visitor as homo economicus from a "happy Republic" was always vexed by the issue of slavery, particularly in travelogues written before and during the Civil War when the capacity of Caribbean discourses to exemplify economic disorder began to seem more precarious.[54] The possibility that the United States might itself become a "make-believe republic"—that the nation is about to apply a "match to the keg of gunpowder which is to blow up the Union"—made commonplace political economic principles consequential and weighty.[55] Such narratives create an anxious Caribbeanism. Writers in the *Atlantic* looked consciously to the "horrors" of slavery in Haiti, Santo Domingo, and the British West Indies in order to reflect on how to cure the "national malady" of slavery through the virtues of free market labor.[56] One writer began with a compendium of values drawn from homo economicus—forethought, self-dependence, self-control—all of which might pertain to slaves once freed from the "inherited and constantly strengthening tendencies toward irresponsibility and idleness" under coercive regimes.[57]

Attempts to contextualize Caribbean islands within colonial histories constantly butted up against racist and racialist assumptions. What prompts Julia Ward Howe to think of a keg of gunpowder that will blow up the Union is her first glimpse of black non-Americans—"lazy as the laziest of brutes," as opposed to the "ideal negro" of the northern United States who has been "refined by white culture, elevated by white blood."[58] One writer who lamented the "crushing despotism" of hundreds of years of Spanish military and colonial rule could also dismiss the "extremely indolent" African slaves on sugar plantations, who are "less intellectual in appearance than those of the United States where the African blood has a large portion of European alloy."[59] This fabrication of an "ideal negro" of the North suggests that the Caribbean discourse on race and slavery was inflected differently even among visitors who were otherwise committed to abolition. Stadial narratives had to be redrawn: African-Caribbeans were often seen as prehuman, the precursors of those who would properly begin the first stages of human history, and therefore expelled from *any* political economic understanding of history.

The counterpart to this strident animus toward African-Caribbean slaves was an often-muted disapproval of slave-holding plantations from which visitors typically received hospitality. Observing with opprobrium that ruins of plantations on Cuba "preached sadly to us of misrule," An Artist devotes one paragraph to details about African slaves who "suffer much from being overtasked" during the cane harvests. But misrule gets quickly overlooked on the "fine estate" where he receives a "substantial meal of chickens, eggs, cakes, and bananas." Critiques often appear tangentially through a rhetoric of excess. Helen S. Conant's description of a Cuban planter with his "unbounded" hospitality—"we look back to that visit as to a dream of some golden age in a land flowing with milk and honey"—is deliberately ironic, given her later references to the "other side of plantation life," "dark, weary faces" of laborers with "no present and no future." But her quiet emphasis on "idle abundance," which stands in for a more overt criticism of her host, is in keeping with earlier representations of richly excessive plantation owner life.[60] Julia Ward Howe describes in tremendous detail the "great dinner" at the plantation of Cuban slave-owning friends, where the number of dishes is so vast that they must merely sample them if they do not want to "die before the end."[61]

A discourse on excess on Caribbean islands bracketed slaves and slave owners, turpitude and "idle abundance," laziness and extreme coercion, dissipation and overconsumption, rich resources and barely functional or mimic markets. Its consistent counterpoise was "New England comfort and enterprise and thrift."[62] Indeed, Caribbean economic disorder was so often pointed up by New England orderliness that such contrasts became endemic, a privileged figure in the discourse. N. H. Eggleston's "New England Village" lauds the "marks of care and culture" (816) he finds in Stockbridge, Massachusetts.[63] Careful readers are prepared to respond with the correct sense of opprobrium to "multitudes of people who are doing nothing" in Port of Spain.[64] Authors returned to that topos over and over, and across decades. An account of a trip to Martha's Vineyard promises that the island will "repay the tourist better for his time and labor than any jaded, glaring, seaside watering-place, with its barrack of white hotel, and its crowd of idle people."[65] The "rugged necessity" of life on the Elizabeth Islands brings about "quiet, good order, and cheerfulness."[66] Wealthy people summering from the West Indies bring "riches and gaiety" but also "an evil," a "high stile of living" to Newport, Rhode Island.[67]

This is not to say that the discourse on New England political economy was uniform. As early as the antebellum period, writers were capable of impugning the "primitiveness" of New England rural life; the islands often functioned as an extreme case. Yet Caribbeanism provided firm limits to whatever critiques might be made. Primitive rural folk were not to be confused with aboriginal Africans. The "proud, self-reliant, and untiring nature" of the New Englander and the "simple virtues and the healthful pleasures of his social life" were not to be confused with the passive "Southron" who is "content to dream away his days."[68] New Englanders might lack luxury, but this was quite different from the Caribbean, where luxuriant vegetation and a "luscious, indolent life" *represented* lack: the lack of self-discipline, of a work ethic, of orderly markets.[69] The excess and luxuriance of the Caribbean functioned as a line drawn in the sand: They represented what New England could never be.

Over the course of the nineteenth century, the idea of and ideal values of New England were constituted within an island discourse that was thoroughly imbricated with a Caribbeanist political economic idiom. It was secured by the economic transgressions of island-others: excess, disorderly markets, colonial misrule, non- or mimic-economic man, and a disorganized or ambiguously organized stadialism. One conclusion can be drawn immediately about *Pearl*. Although the fact that the wild and wealthy Mendozas hail from Cuba and the West Indies comprises a small part of the story, the Caribbean political economic contexts they represent, rooted deep in the cultural imagination of the United States, are powerfully invoked in a narrative that positions the "wholesome thrift and prosperity" (122) of New England against the "hot, stifling luxury" (118) of the Caribbean/South. This helps to explain aspects of *Pearl* that have puzzled scholars, such as the fact that Stowe seems to abandon in this novel what she thinks of as the redemptive qualities of black people (good humor, a childlike innocence, and so on).[70] In a powerful inversion of abolitionist and republican rhetoric, Stowe emphasizes the peculiarly *unregenerate* nature of Senor Mendoza's slaves. They are "half-barbarized negroes" who, far from harboring any propensity for good or for self-improvement, leave the mark of their Dahomey and Guinea cultures on the Mendozas' children. It is hard to avoid the conclusion that Stowe taps into the racial and racist coding common among visitors to the Caribbean from the United States. The Mendozas and their slaves make most sense when positioned within that volatile Caribbeanist mix of colonial misrule, economic disorder, and racial essentialism in which aboriginal Africans are so often read as that which preexists the progress of human civilizations—that which grounds, because it counters, the most minimal concept of "economy."

Stowe's Caribbeanism might be read as a ruse to deflect the worst of the (white) South's sins. She employs the Mendozas to depict slavery as a corrupt institution, to be sure, but does so as if slavery were rooted in Spanish colonial history and then exported from the Caribbean to the United States. From that perspective, the novel addresses the South less as the political entity that seceded from the North than as a repository of sociopolitical disorders whose center of gravity has been shifted toward the Caribbean. It might thus be understood as a way for Stowe to simplify the issue of race. One effect of a Caribbean-accented construction of race, in which there is no "ideal negro" from the northern United States to complicate racial distinctions, is to put the entirety of Orr's Island to the service of underwriting the ideal values represented by (northern US) homo economicus. Reconstituting the values of Orr's Island requires the oppositional values embodied by the irrational Mendozas *and* their half-barbarized slaves. One important effect—and this jibes with the opinion of most scholars—is that this strategy transforms Orr's Island into Stowe's attempt at utopia.[71] It becomes an island purified of the politics of race, a refuge for white people who model harmonious family life for a ruptured Union, and who may choose to accept as their ward the racial Other, at least when the Other is as ambiguously coded as Moses.

This quiet offshoring of the discourse of slavery changes the way in which the narrative interpellates the "simplicity and order of New England," as Minister Sewell puts it, but not in terms of a utopian retreat from the logic and ideologies of markets. Quite the opposite. Sewell's two-chapter sojourn with the Mendozas is enough to recuperate a familiar logic of homo economicus and transfer it North because a Caribbean island discourse already exists to construct the Mendozas as the locus of neglected accounts. In the novel, and in a broader Caribbeanist context, they stand for an array of shattered economies, financial, psychic, and political. These two chapters instantly imbue the Mendoza household with political economic meaning and set up what a New England–Caribbean discourse should recognize as the obvious difference of Orr's Island economies. Sewell's letter to Moses, revealing the boy's heritage, speaks clearly to that larger island-discourse. Had Moses come into his (slave master) father's estate, he might have found himself "heir to wealth and pleasure without labor or exertion" (267), which would have favored "luxury and idleness and the too early possession of irresponsible power" (267). Instead, Sewell recommends to the young man the role of an "energetic, intelligent, self-controlled man, capable of guiding the affairs of life" (267). It is clearly Moses's apotheosis as homo economicus—captaining his ship (of state) with the same disciplined self-government that Sewell displayed in Florida—that transforms him into a "fully developed man" (405). And it secures an ideal of New England, allowing the "romance," the "wonder," the "unconscious poetry" (295) of American sea-faring communities and their trade with the world to shine forth.

But *Pearl* complicates its Caribbeanism. Above all, Sewell reneges on, or fails to complete, what should be his functional role as homo economicus. There are two vectors for this unsettling development in the novel: the northern marriage market and its corollary, a struggle to impose a logical sequence leading from market disorder among the Mendozas to orderly socioeconomic conditions in the North. In Sewell's story about Florida, the plot crisis that sends him back north and leads to his long silence is Dolores's arranged marriage to a wealthy and vile Cuban plantation owner.[72] Her forced entry into the marriage market in Florida performs several complex roles in symbolizing the violence of the southern economy. Her anguished cry to Sewell, "why do you let them sell me?" (263), allows her pending marriage to represent slavery. It is therefore a cry on behalf of slaves for northerners to lend a hand. This should not be difficult if, as Dolores says, they "let" this state of affairs exist. And it defines the "being" of being a slave differently, though problematically. Her dilemma drives home powerfully what it means to sell a free person: the fact that she can be sold even though legally free matches the corrupt logic of a system that enslaves people who are, by nature, born free. At the same time, the dramatic sleight of hand whereby Dolores's beautiful white face comes to represent the plight of enslaved people on the plantation implies a symbolic erasure of the half-barbarized negroes in favor of one who can represent them better. Lydia Maria Child's argument that slavery was at heart a "Patriarchal Institution" influenced Stowe's post–*Uncle Tom's Cabin* work.[73] The story of Sewell and Dolores suggests the complexity of the author's new analytic perspective. It grants a spectrum of power differentials in society the capacity to represent the issue of slavery, but in so doing potentially erases it as a transaction between power and race.

This same move allows Stowe to extend the violence of the marriage market north. Dolores herself dies on the shore of Orr's Island while accompanying her husband, the Cuban slave owner, to Boston. If (in 1862) the North is making it impossible to "let them sell" a slave, the disposition of "pearls"— marriageable young women—on Orr's island makes it possible to see that Dolores's fate may represent them too. Stowe has to invent an array of plot convolutions, including Moses's disappearance for years on sea voyages, and perhaps even Mara's death, in order to rescue a marriage from the forthright competition between the three young potential lovers.[74] And she has to work even harder to free young Moses from fetishizing money ("wealth he saw to be the lamp of Aladdin" [233]) and, what is worse, considering it a means to purchase women. Shortly after reading Sewell's account of Dolores's plaintive "why do you let them sell me?" Moses answers Mara's tart question about his future wife—"And how much would you pay for her?"—by explaining "I'd buy her with all the rest" (271). Not until the final chapter do Moses and Sally, "fully developed man and woman" (405) at last, achieve a companionate marriage. Even here the narrator shows a decided lack of enthusiasm, merely recording that the wedding was "voted without dissent to be just the thing" (407).

Moses's statement about buying a wife might represent a sort of genetic disposition toward owning others—he is after all the offspring of Dolores and a plantation owner from the Caribbean so ruthless that he inspires a slave revolt. But Moses is also a discursive child of Caribbeanism. His marriage profiteering can be linked to an extensive cultural fable about taking dominion over tropical islands. Moses has a predilection for deserted islands. When

Moses is a callow boy, Defoe's *Robinson Crusoe* "never departs from under his pillow" (124). The tale launches him into fantasies of heroic derring-do and proud individualism: he "fancies he could command" (124) the schooner *Brilliant* "as well as 'father' himself'" (124). Less clearly marked, but with many serious consequences for understanding the political economic registers of the novel, Moses is the conduit for Caribbeanist discourses associating islands with theft-based economies. A long sequence in *Pearl* has Moses falling in with a gang of buccaneer-like smugglers—Atkinson, the leader, makes "propositions of piracy and robbery" (207) to him—who cajole him to join them with stories of "piratical adventures in the West Indies" (205). Though written for the most part as a boy's fanciful misadventure, the episode is one of the few in the novel where actual political events overtly intrude. The narrator informs us that smuggling with "the West Indies and other places" (194) in Maine grew out of the "celebrated embargo of Jefferson [in 1807, preventing the export of American goods in an effort to hurt the trade of European foes]," which "stopped at once the whole trade of New England" (194). This "weak and unworthy legislation" (194) results in a "contempt of law" among Maine citizens, for "illegal stores of merchandise" and "contraband goods" find their way "into houses for miles around" (194)—though "no one knew or cared to say how," the narrator insouciantly adds.

What makes the buccaneer sequence so perplexing is that it offers multiple, and contradictory, contexts for the contraband from the West Indies that ended up in "lonely haunts of islands off the coast of Maine" (194) after the trade embargo. Appropriate to a "community peculiar for its rigid morality" (194), the scene may reference New England attempts to succor runaway slaves, who would indeed be "illegal" in Stowe's time after the 1850 Fugitive Slave Act. Appropriate for acts "demoralizing to the community" (194), it may refer to yet another 1807 embargo: Jefferson's ending of the slave trade, an act of legislature that made a morally reprehensible activity illegal—an activity that had contributed greatly to the wealth of Rhode Island. This was one of the topics of Stowe's *The Minister's Wooing* (1859). The question of which set of New England values—slave trading or slave freeing—might be in the ascendancy is consequential to this scene because it concerns the potential rupture of the structural relationship between Caribbean islands and New England. Atkinson's avowed intent is to bring the West Indies to Orr's Island. By introducing Moses to smuggling and establishing "one of their depositories on Orr's Island" (195), Atkinson hopes to smear his adoptive father, Captain Pennel, one of the few "uncompromising" (195) men who actively resist "violations of the laws of the land" (195). Moses's fall would "implicate the family of Pennel himself in the trade" (195). Moses's crisis—he must "awake from the fun and frolic of unlawful enterprises" (207)—is therefore also a potential discursive crisis. A wrong choice on his part, which is to say abetting Atkinson in setting up a depository of the West Indies on Orr's Island, could precipitate the collapse of the entire apparatus of significations separating New England from the Caribbean, whose piracy, wrecks, and wrecked economies were supposed to affirm the difference of New England economic order and its orderly interpreters.

The novel's immediate solution is to resurrect Moses as homo economicus. Captains Kittredge and Pennel break Moses from the clutches of the dissolute smugglers by introducing him to the legalities of trade and finance. Their "liberality" (237) stakes the ship he builds, which he uses to trade on their investment "in foreign parts with a skill and energy that brought a very fair return" (237). Against the smugglers' "secret depositories" (194) and violated laws, a fair return seems to reinstitute a virtuous republicanism, enhancing Moses's "energy and enterprise" and "self-reliant" (243) ways. It puts him into accord with Sewell's economic and moral schemas for men, so that ultimately his commercial dealings jibe with theory and his newly masculine accomplishments comport with the ideal figure of homo economicus. Overcoming the "piratical" economics of trading with the West Indies seems to consolidate the superiority of Orr's Island against the temporary threats to it by reminding us of the familiar codes of a Caribbeanist discourse.

Yet illicit dealings with the West Indies are not merely an active wrong Moses must learn to resist. As befits the suddenly Gothic imagery during the smuggling episode—"violations," "haunts of islands. . . . visited only in the darkness of the night" (194)—those "unlawful depositories" are already on Maine islands, already an ominously substantive feature of the islands' black market economies. Muddling codes of legality and morality, cargoes from the West Indies imply a cultural unconscious at odds with Mainers' articulated task of shaping enterprising and self-reliant men. We could read this as Stowe's refusal to countenance any market system—the Caribbean setting up shop, as it were, on Orr's Island in order to represent a site where heinous slave economies meet the potential for capitalist excess. Investing his restless energies into the free market certainly holds dangers for Moses. He carries an exaggerated sense of self-worth into his early trading expeditions, fancying himself a "sea-king" (283) soon after promising to buy his wife with all the rest. This for Moses is an adolescent posture, however, and one that he seems to move beyond by the time he and Sally enter into marriage on the last page of the novel. The romance of trade, Moses's emergence into manhood, and a symbolic marriage seem of a piece in the novel.

Much more problematic for the novel's account of Orr's Island as a "desirable state" is Sewell's status as northern economic man. Despite the fact that his orderly and rational economic ideologies are forged in the South as a counter to a slave-owner's excesses and repeated in the North to a would-be "sea-king" as a hedge against indiscipline, his "accounts" are in fact full of odd inconsistencies. Sewell finds his growing passion for Dolores to be a "dangerous thing" (255)—dangerous enough that, during an "hour of delirium" (264) when he contemplates eloping with her, it so completely oversets his internal moral economy that he "forgot everything" (264). This may explain Sewell's response to Dolores's plea to save her from being sold into marriage, which is, strangely, to trope her request. He cannot come to her aid because "You have been so accustomed to abundant wealth and all it can give, that you cannot form an idea of what the hardships and discomforts of marrying a poor man would be. You are unused to having the least care, or making the least exertion for yourself. All the world would say that I acted a very dishonorable part to take you from a position which offers you wealth, splendor, and ease" (263). Sewell cannot save Dolores from the marriage market, he avers, because she belongs there: she has been thoroughly formed by economic excess. His argument is worth considering at some length because it is so completely illogical. First, Dolores's suffering as the plaything of a disrupted family makes his comment about her being "unused to having the least care" self-evidently untrue. Second, the pedagogical principles he brings to Saint Augustine are supposed to combat the destructive consequences of "wealth, splendor, and ease." Why northern opinion would join "all the world" in castigating his actions is unclear. Third, Sewell has already specified that Dolores (alone of the family) "had one of those simple and unworldly natures which wealth and splendor could not satisfy, and whose life would lie entirely in her affections" (258). Indeed, the "sort of order" Sewell's Yankee virtues bring—he is the "only intelligent, cultivated person she had ever seen" (254)—is what compels Dolores to fall for him in the first place (254, 256). Dolores, in short, seems a stellar candidate for the stern northern economic discipline Sewell represents and tries to teach to the wild Mendozas.

The possibility that we are meant to read Sewell's letter dramatically, holding his character, or at least his youthful immaturity, responsible for his illogic, holds promise for explaining why our emotional investment in Dolores's plight surely outweighs his dour response. Perhaps, like the young Moses, whose early capacity for love was "tyrannical, and capricious" (199), Sewell can explicate the ways of northern homo economicus but has yet to fully live them. But we cannot simply write off Sewell's rejection, which is clearly consonant with, and indeed required by, one potent symbolic political plot of the story: Dolores needs to be sacrificed to the Cuban owner in order to have her progeny, the progeny of the South, rescued in and by the North. Moreover, the republican virtues Sewell articulates for Moses twenty years on are the same ones he teaches in Saint Augustine. To think of Sewell as a poor spokesman for them to Dolores would seem to undermine their relevance to Dolores's son. Sewell, too, seems to take his own capricious nature northward. His sister thinks that he "concealed . . . all the thriftless and pernicious inconsiderateness of the male nature, ready at any moment to break out into unheard-of improprieties" (91).

His sister's opinion suggests that a persuasive alternative explanation for Sewell's failure lies in thinking through the logic of homo economicus in distinctly gendered terms. Sewell proceeds in his relationship to Dolores on the hidden assumption that the sort of northern economic discipline offered to the passionate Moses to make him a man would not befit a woman. He is not trying to inculcate northern disciplines in the South so much as recuperating the economic prerogatives of northern men. Yet Dolores, a paragon in her resistance to wealth and splendor, epitomizes republican virtue. Suddenly revealed in the confusion of a southern woman threatening to vacate her appropriate ideological role is an important link between the economies of emotion and money within hegemonic masculine ideologies. Sewell's absurd accusation that Dolores only has a desire for abundant wealth barely covers what would seem a deeper underlying anxiety about forgetting his self-control in a disturbingly excessive emotional liaison with her. The northern male response to southern excess seems not to be orderly self-government but anxiety about excess. The orderly, rational, and self-controlled principles pertinent to northern economic man operate here as a powerful fiction. In Sewell's letter they are rolled smoothly into place not only to articulate Moses's preferred role within the moral and emotional economy of northern manhood-fashioning but also to cut short the question of why Dolores, with what seems an instinctive aversion to wealth and splendor, cannot be included.

These fragmentary attempts to instantiate a powerful figure of economic man on Orr's Island as an ideological buttress against southern excesses are unsettled further by the novel's disturbing temporal displacements. Young Moses's financial stake would have been considered an auspicious beginning "in those simple times and regions" (237). But the "factious wants and aspirations" (122) of "our modern times" (122) have brought such simple times to an end. In terms of Stowe's plot, Moses succeeds in following Sewell's advice about how to fashion himself as a disciplined entrepreneur. Yet the insistent hints that his story belongs to the irretrievable past—that it cannot be repeated today—curtails the importance of his success. This might seem to do little more than acknowledge Orr's Island as the once-and-future storehouse of republican value, to which modern times should look if men and women are to reach the fullness of their capacities. But the pastness of Orr's

Island—the fact that it stages an antebellum society—plays havoc with the plot of civilization that allows Sewell to recognize in the Mendoza family "expressions and actions which would seem incredible in civilized society" (252). Northern discipline is clearly superior to southern ill-management on account of Sewell's well-trained and orderly mind. But his well-trained mind is produced by a desirable state of society that countenances slavery in the South. Somehow, buying and selling people is compatible with the utopia of Orr's Island as it used to be, and nothing demonstrates that better than Sewell fleeing from the southern scene of bride-selling and slavery and then neglecting to tell his account of it, even when Dolores washes up on his doorstep. The knowledge he withholds is one more of those unlawful depositories smuggled onto the island.

The conundrum the novel poses is not that the ship of state runs the risk of replaying the events of the first chapter of the novel—running aground and sinking. It is that the very visible, benevolent plot of redemption subsequently set in motion—disciplined, warm-hearted northerners raising the orphaned child of the South in accordance with civilized practices and ideologies—falls apart entirely upon the recognition that "bringing up a child in this [antebellum] state of society was a far more simple enterprise than in our modern times" (122). The novel's barely enunciated trajectory leading from a northern idyll to the "factious wants and aspirations" of the 1860s makes the trajectory of barbarism to civilization that Sewell displays in his story of his role in the Mendoza family look facile. What Sewell neglects to say is that his plot of civilization, faithfully transmitted to Moses and poetically enhanced in virtually every scene of the novel thereafter, has to be wrecked. Breaking apart the United States, the import of the novel's virtually silent history suggests, is the only way to bring slavery to an end. The fully developed man and the fully resolved plot in the final chapter of *Pearl* through the complex metaphor of marriage—the now well-cultivated child of the South [Moses] marrying the exemplary "housewifery" (405) of the North [Sally], a marriage locking together energy and abstract principles of disciplined management—is always and already a beautiful fable.

Both Sewell and Moses fail to secure a political economic discourse that had, across the course of the nineteenth century, guaranteed the difference between New England and Florida/the Caribbean. But that failure opens a different space for the domestic activities of women, who have a natural predilection for order and frugality, "saving every possible snip" (90). As a response to his "thriftless" ways, Sewell's sister, Emily, fills her head with "endless calculations to keep . . . his housekeeping comfortable and easy, on very limited means" (239). Early in the novel we find Mrs. Kittridge "busily engaged in ripping up a dress, which Miss Roxy had engaged to come and make into a new one" (33). Later, Sally mocks Mara's impecunious ways by revealing how she finds so many "wonderful bargains" (185), buying old or imperfect dress fabrics "half-price" (186) in order to make "exactly as good a dress" (186). These are the kinds of moments that scholars have recognized as endemic to Stowe and to female regionalist writing more generally. But *economizing* has not generally been considered *economic*. To make middle-class domestic orderliness into a moral privilege and a source of articulate resistance to a brutally competitive masculine world, Lora Romero's "idiom of social housekeeping" suggests, women cannot enter the market.[75] The frugality of Stowe's northern women—saving scraps and darning men's socks—is a virtuous alternative to a capitalist economy and to a slave economy because it occurs off-market. And that position might be thought to squander, or severely constrain, the critical potential of their domestic activities.[76]

Sewell's Dolores chapters pose a challenge to that approach. To begin with, they compel us to recognize households North and South as being imbricated with political and economic meaning. Because economic mismanagement in Florida is the master trope of the "disorderly household," ramifying through every other economy, domestic, psychic, familial, pedagogical, and more, orderly households on Orr's Island are positioned to exemplify the principles of a well-managed economy. Second, the more Sewell's claim to economic man becomes emptily rhetorical, the more it becomes apparent that the female household managers of Orr's Island reclaim the principles that Sewell tries, and fails, to impart to the disorderly South: self-government, industry, frugality. For example, Sally's economizing, her bargain-hunting, and repurposing of flawed materials, take on a specific and abstract economic significance—they model better economic principles—because she steps into the space vacated by Sewell's many neglected accounts. Orderly domesticities on Orr's Island participate in a political economic discourse that men articulate but women put into practice. Proper household management constitutes a counterknowledge to the extent that they represent a more rational exercise of economic principles than men seem capable of achieving.

On this basis it would be possible to argue that the women of Orr's Island complete the novel's Caribbeanist discourse. They seem to effect what men cannot—a stable and consistent underwriting of the difference of Orr's Island economic systems—by virtue of their orderly household management, a symbolic practice that dovetails theoretical principles of political economy with the material good of a northern island economy. In that sense they are the orderly counterparts of the female vendors in Caribbean travelogues whose slovenly marketing helped to consolidate the discursive position of US homo economicus. The household becomes the locus of attempts not to evade the machinations of the marketplace but to bring about a truly desirable state—a politicized and nation-building aeconomia—improving relations and bringing about a renaissance of the South and of the Union. From this point of view, women backstop men's inadequacies as ideological agents. They mobilize the domestic space in order to ensure that Caribbean island disorder remains, as it were, far offshore—a move that enlists their newly functional economic practices in the service of the national imaginary.

Yet the difference between Orr's Island kitchen economics and the disorganized markets of the Caribbean is always subject to an unsettling confusion. Orr's Island never achieves the "closed space" that Chris Bongie perceives as a key sign of imperialist island strategies. Aeconomia cannot be said to function in exactly the same way as masculinist market ideologies in the construction of the New England island discourse, partly because women, young women in particular, are prey to slave- and women-exploiting markets, and partly because men such as Sewell and Moses, controlling the public conversation on economic matters, present the household as a subaltern discourse. But there is a more pressing reason why female household managers on Orr's Island cannot simply step into the symbolic position Sewell vacates. Contraband goods from the West Indies have made their way into households on New England islands, which reap their benefits despite the fact that no one cared to say how they arrived there. The utopia of Orr's Island households thereby becomes heterotopia, a site conjoining economic principle to illegal stores, articulated ideals to secret depositories—and femina economica to a Caribbean trade. To the extent that women's kitchen economizing on Orr's Island thrives off an illicit trade, it becomes impossible to sunder it completely from what US Caribbean discourses disparage as the economically unsound activities of women in island markets. This is not to say that the narrative incorporates actual histories of Caribbean islands, but neither does it accede to the common Caribbeanist strategy of making those islands vanish from history. *Pearl* represents the relationship between Orr's Island and Caribbean islands as unlawful but also discursive. They are terms that require each other and are mutually constitutive of each other within a particular set of historical conditions.

The same heterotopian logic leads to another unexpected outcome: the disorderly household cannot be securely consigned to the South. Dolores, who lives the life of a "lonely" (252) exile among the Mendozas' disrupted economies, somehow manages to be "orderly in all the little arrangements of life" (253) even before Sewell arrives to try to set things right. If the plot contrives to have Dolores voyage North in search of what seems a more appropriate home, Sewell arrives in Florida to find that a concept of the orderly household precedes him, and is waiting for him, in the shape of femina economica. Her quest clearly continues after he succumbs to the dangerous excesses of passion. Her presence in Saint Augustine has two key effects. First, like the women in Caribbean travelogues who exchange goods in the market without ever being seen as economic agents, Dolores's orderly mind challenges Sewell's claim on, and articulation of, economic man. She is a potential economic agent, hidden, like Sewell's sister and Sally on Orr's Island, in plain sight.

Second, Dolores inverts the logic of the secret depositories of the West Indies trade in the North. The overt victim of a Caribbean slave trade in the South, a child of Cuba and the Spanish West Indies, she somehow turns out to be a representative of Orr's Island aeconomia at its best. She confuses and disrupts the role of women in the Caribbeanist discourse of the novel. The figure of femina economica on Orr's Island cannot merely substitute for northern homo economicus in this narrative so long as Dolores exists in the South as a sign of incompletion. It is possible to think of Dolores as an eccentric center of the entire discourse on aeconomia—the figure to whom Orr's Island women might look to exemplify their tarnished ideals, a utopian instance of what progressive economic principles might one day effect both North and South. If so, she cannot represent femina economica fully. Wholly isolated in Florida, washed up on Orr's Island after the shipwreck as a mysterious corpse, she is uncompromisingly liminal, a signifier of heterotopia, a troubler and exposer of neglected accounts rather than their resolution. Moving this daughter of the Caribbean to the discursive center, moreover, would be to threaten the entire structure of Caribbeanism. Perhaps that is why Dolores's voice sounds through Sewell's account of her, and then only after twenty years.

4

THE KITCHEN ECONOMICS OF GREEN ISLAND
IN JEWETT'S *THE COUNTRY OF THE POINTED FIRS*

In "The King of Folly Island" Sarah Orne Jewett constructs an ironic robinsonade—ironic because the King claims to be the sole proprietor of his island without realizing that another human is living there with him. Or perhaps he simply reduces his own daughter to property. In *The Country of the Pointed Firs* (1896) Jewett seems intent on wresting back an island discourse—and the political economic principles islands have always helped to illustrate—from the follies of such men. Accompanying Mrs. Todd on a visit to her mother on Green Island, the narrator participates in the serene activities of the "old kitchen" where Mrs. Blackett performs something of a latter-day loaves-and-fishes miracle for three unexpected guests.[1] She creates a satisfying chowder from the sea's bounty (a haddock), one onion (a gift from her daughter), and her own potatoes, aided by the narrator who labors happily without remuneration to dig them up. "There is all the pleasure that one can have in gold-digging in finding one's hopes satisfied in the riches of a good hill of potatoes" (73) enthuses the narrator, seeming to discover a form of pure use-value in her substitution of potatoes for gold. Her sense of plenitude in the potato patch passes to the kitchen where communal acts of cooking and eating prepare them for the moment when she and Mrs. Blackett "understood each other without speaking" (81). It is not until returning to Dunnet Landing that Mrs. Todd "had to make business arrangements" to cart away a keg of mackerel and a "generous freight of lobsters" (81). Quietly marked, that "had to" recognizes psychic demands that communing with and digging potatoes for Mrs. Blackett never inspired.[2]

It is tempting to argue that Jewett invokes strategies of utopian representation. According to Jean-Joseph Goux, utopian republics seek to overthrow the "tyranny of the symbolic," all that is a "parasite upon . . . healthy use-values."[3] They have to be societies without money since money establishes the jurisdiction of a symbolic general equivalent, setting up what seems to be an independent measure of value into which, and for which, everything can exchange and thus realize its value. Money alienates the labor of individuals, transforming actual work into what it is not—what symbolically represents and values it. Without money, labor attains its ontological purity; without money, things become the things themselves, self-identical and nonexchangeable; without money, healthy use-values and social relations are revealed in all their plenitude. Utopian republics rupture—or set out on a quixotic quest to rupture—the modality of the sign, since the sign points inexorably toward the logic of exchange, and exchange, in a capitalist economy, points inexorably toward the hegemony of money. As they near Green Island, the travelers experience exactly that challenge to the sign/exchange. The "tyranny of the symbolic" has the narrator asking, mystified, what a flag on Green Island's shore represents. The answer, unsurprisingly, is commerce: "That's the sign for herrin'" (67), Mrs. Todd observes, explaining that the flag is raised when "they get enough [of a catch]' for the schooners." The narrator's puzzlement testifies to the work that must be done to supply what cultural systems organized around the sign of a market economy withhold—and withhold, young Johnny Bowden's "contemptuous surprise" (67) at the narrator's ignorance emphasizes, from women in particular. But on Green Island the narrator's world becomes "one" (75) with Mrs. Blackett's; so does Mrs. Todd's when she communicates with her mother uncannily by means of a "quicker signal" from the "heart on shore to the heart on the sea" (67).

Lives diverge around the gendered sign of the herring flag. Johnny will spend the visit, Mrs. Todd predicts, "down to the herrin' weirs all the time we're there" (64); the narrator's route to utopia passes through the potato patch, where, under Mrs. Blackett's presiding influence as a principle, perhaps *the* principle, of nonexchangeability, she produces potatoes that have no value in exchange, on an island that disdains general equivalents, and for a woman—the "Great Mother"—with whom she becomes "one."[4] Green Island's break from male-dominated capitalist relations has made it a touchstone of the swirling debates about female regionalism. Feminist scholars have celebrated it as a quintessential "location, space, and place that is disconnected from ownership."[5] Green Island is where Julia Bader finds a "timeless and ahistorical" paradise.[6] It exemplifies what Josephine Donovan considers the female regionalist desire to create a "matriarchal community" that exists as a "counter to the urban, upper-class, capitalist, industrial, male-dominated civilization" of the late nineteenth century.[7] More commonly, scholars have read such domestic idylls in terms of a counterworld—an emptily utopian turn from the era's actual economic tribulations.

One can see why. It would be hard to guess from the tranquility of the four-chapter trip to Green Island that Jewett composed *Country* during the

1893–96 depression, when, as one popular commentator wrote, in agitated counterpoint, the "cry of distress is heard on every hand; business is paralyzed; commerce is at a standstill; riots and strikes prevail throughout the land."[8] Douglas Steeples and David O. Whitten place the disastrous business contraction at the very "center of events," the "crucial force" shaping the United States during this "tumultuous decade."[9] The real history of the 1890s, from this perspective, appears as a negative imprint of all Green Island's utopian representations. The rise of urbanism gets thrust behind its small-island agrarian life; angry and often violent disputes between labor and capital behind free labor in a potato patch; debates about the gold standard behind the narrator's dismissal of "gold-digging"; the rise of consumerism and corporate capitalism behind its premarket, preindustrial idyll; the restructuring of the US economy under monopoly power behind the narrator's longing to become "one" with another human; the national and even imperial concerns of the United States behind this "tiny continent . . . of fisher folk" (69); the looming issue of invading or annexing Cuba behind the timeless serenity of Green Island. Amid these debates, Green Island seems to retreat from history into nostalgic domesticity and myth.

It comes as a scandal for all of these approaches that Mrs. Todd is on Green Island to do business. One reason for her visit is her desire to "settle an account" (74) with William: she brings him forty-two cents "for them last lobsters he brought in" (72), a quotidian piece of "business" (72) she announces in the very kitchen where Mrs. Blackett is about to assemble her miraculous chowder. Trade has been taking place on Green Island all along—money for the lobsters Mrs. Todd has sold, lobsters returned with her to the mainland to be marketed—a commerce that seems in retrospect all the more pervasive since the narrative does not identify the moment when the exchange of island lobsters for mainland money takes place. Contributing to a feast that requires no money, she nonetheless traffics in lobsters and mackerel; she carries mainland currency and interprets mainland signs (she is the one to explain the herring flag); she enters into a business arrangement on the return to Dunnet Landing—all these the inevitable consequence of her business on Green Island. The excursion to Green Island neither wholly erases relations of exchange nor makes them the exclusive preserve of men. Jewett's representation of kitchen economics demands negotiation amid the circulation of commodities and signs back and forth across the sea-gap between continental Maine and the tiny continent of Green Island.

I contend that Jewett's relationship to late nineteenth-century socioeconomic conditions is far more entangled than the counterworld hypotheses suggest.[10] I challenge the common feminist assertion that Jewett's narrative order opposes the hegemony of white male market relations—but also the new historicist assumption that she sets out to construct a tranquil rural hinterland too removed from exchange relations to allow a productive critique of them. Jewett roots the events of the excursion to Green Island—the lading of the boat, the assessments of the various island communities they pass in the bay, the digging of potatoes, the preparation of the feast—in traditions of political economic thought. Trading on a long history of imaginary island commonwealths—in particular Thomas More's *Utopia* (1516)—the Green Island chapters urge us to consider broad principles about how a healthy polity might organize a productive distribution of resources and wealth. They engage the sort of questions about the nature of commonwealth that thinkers such as Plato and More had made the domain of pre-Enlightenment political economy. Like so many representations of supposedly archetypal human behavior in economic discourse, the fablelike scene where the narrator ponders how best to dig and carry potatoes for the chowder entails abstract principles governing the human management of natural resources. What is the nature of human desire and choice? How should one use resources wisely? What underpins concepts of value? What are the stages humans move through in developing their propensity toward exchange?

Operating under the ambiguous sign of femina economica, Green Island economies certainly contest the presumption of mainstream economics that rational economic behavior *must* manifest in self-interest, market exchange, and a desire for profit and capital accumulation; and they complicate the stadial logic that conjoins civilization to the arrival of market behaviors. But they also renew the logic that humans faced with scarce resources make rational decisions, maximize their utility, and obey laws such as the division of labor. Jewett's appropriation of political economy sits uneasily with accounts premised on a complete disengagement from male capitalist social relations. Her economic reasoning implies the very positions and logic it seems to critique. Moreover, this orientation toward political economy affords new ways to consider Jewett's engagement with her historical moment. On Green Island, abstract principles of political economy are informed by late nineteenth-century debates about how best to create and distribute national wealth amid increasing class conflict and economic turmoil. By the 1890s those debates "dominated the political imagination of all social classes and strata."[11] They are evident in the narrator's gold-bug potato digging: the way in which her harvesting of potatoes calls on late nineteenth-century discourses about gold as an immutable locus of value, only to rethink them from the vantage point of the kitchen.

From Thomas More's *Utopia* (1516) to classical and neoclassical elaborations of Robinson Crusoe as the quintessential economic man, political economic thought has compulsively exploited the topos of the island.[12] Jewett embraces that tradition, in part by strategically aligning Green Island with More's signature early-modern work of political economy. Mariners could not approach Utopia safely, says Raphael, More's "traveler, or rather a philosopher" from fabled lands, if "some marks that are on their Coast did not direct their way" to this ambiguously situated island, which lacks coordinates and was not even an "Island at first, but a part of the Continent."[13] Jewett's voyagers to the complete and tiny continent of Green Island require similar guidance from Mrs. Todd, traveler and "rustic philosopher" (65), who engineers the trip and interprets the relevant signs—the herring flag and her mother's quicker signal—before landing. During the trip to Green Island and on it, the economic implications of the narrator's excursion begin to take full force. The signs pointing to Utopia lead directly to a series of fluid speculations on the nature of commonwealths as well as back to the historical and socioeconomic conditions of the late nineteenth century.

Utopia allows us to rethink, for example, the economic significances of the "eager little flock" of sheep on the first island Mrs. Todd and the narrator pass who "bleated at us so affectingly that I would willingly have stopped" (66), though Mrs. Todd sails on with hard words for the "sheep's mean owner . . . who grudged the little salt and still less care which the patient creatures needed" (66). In book 1 of Utopia, Raphael contemplates and elaborates on a similar circumstance: "a Prince ought to take more care of his Peoples Happiness, than of his own, as a Shepherd is to take more care of his Flock than of himself." It "were certainly better for him to quit his Kingdom," Raphael states, "than to retain it by such Methods." Later, the narrator's "gold-digging" in the "riches of a good hill of potatoes," in which task she "longed to go on" were it not that "it did not seem frugal to dig any longer after my basket was full" (73), recalls still more pertinently Raphael's thoughts on the value of kingly restraint. He remarks that an "excellent King" of the Macarians refrained from having more than one thousand pounds of gold in his treasury lest he might "impoverish the People." Raphael continues, "He thought that moderate sum might be sufficient for any Accident. . . . He also thought, that it was a good Provision for a free circulation of Mony, that is necessary for the course of Commerce and Exchange: And when a king must distribute all those extraordinary Accessions that encrease Treasure beyond the due pitch, it makes him less disposed to oppress his Subjects."[14]

Routed intertextually through Utopia, the trip to Green Island raises important questions about the nature of economic well-being in a miniature commonwealth. The narrator delights in the imperatives of subsistence economies: she must not over-dig Mrs. Blackett's "riches" and the latter must "make . . . do" (72). But the narrator is not exactly frugal; she says it did not seem "frugal to dig any longer after my basket was full." Like the Macarian king's thousand pounds, her goal is not frugality but sufficiency. Her sufficiency certainly differs from the mean owner's. His diminishes the sheep's well-being: his investment of accrued wealth in the form of a moderate sum of salt would make him less disposed to oppress his subject sheep. A moderate sum contributes to productive relations. Moderation marks the point in More's narrative where to "encrease Treasure beyond the due pitch" is to "impoverish [the king's] People," but where a sufficient amount provides for the "free circulation of Mony." It marks the point in Jewett's where to dig too many "riches" from the potato field might lead eventually to an impoverished larder and an immovable basket, but where a full basket (and a full measure of salt) takes care of appetites (and sheep) while leaving more for later.

The general principles of commonwealth that concern More's *Utopia* also surface in Jewett's extended meditation on principles of productive distribution. Raphael argues that "how plentiful soever a Nation may be, yet a few dividing the wealth of it among themselves, the rest must fall under Poverty."[15] The voyage to Green Island extends this critique of economic imbalance in numerous ways. Asa, a surly onlooker, places the weight distribution of Mrs. Todd's boat under scrutiny as they set sail—"she's lo'ded bad, your bo't is,—she's heavy behind's she is now!" (65). His accusation is unfair; Mrs. Todd's boat sails beautifully. But it makes perfect sense when transferred to the second island they encounter where two feuding farmers whose families have "shared the island" for generations refuse to have any dealings with each other at all, to their mutual impoverishment. On an island where "plenty [of people] likes to hear and tell again" the imagined "wrongs" of the two families, poor ideas in circulation turn "plenty" into its opposite. Mrs. Todd notes particularly that their houses are "small" (66). The feuders' mean moral economy matches up with their poor grasp of economic principles: Neither party wishes to exchange profitably. As Mrs. Todd says, "them as fetch a bone'll carry one" (66). Adam Smith provides another useful context. What defines humans, Smith argues, is their propensity to enter into exchange, for "nobody ever saw a dog make a fair and deliberate exchange of one bone for another with another dog."[16] From that point of view, the bone-exchangers on the feuders' island are barely economic—and minimally human.

In contrast, a proper distribution allows Mrs. Todd's little ship of state to carry even her heavyset body. And the narrator's frugal-but-full basket of potatoes provides several other potential bioeconomic answers to the problem of balanced and just distribution. The food supply and the body (politic) that is dependent on it are at the center of the potato-digging scene. First, the narrator digs only the amount she can carry. Next, she accepts William's offer to distribute the weight of the basket between them, an act of sharing that resonates with the properly laden boat as well as with the cooking practices of Mrs. Blackett's kitchen, where several contributions combine to make the chowder that Mrs. Blackett assembles by slicing potatoes "layer after layer, with the fish" (73). The broader meanings of one haddock and some potatoes feeding five people (and a kitten) now begin to become clear in economic terms: sustainable amounts, just distribution, and forces in equilibrium. Production on the principle of sustainability and mutual aid opposes the mean owner who grudges his sheep a little salt while noting that sustainability implies a minimum—not zero—investment of resources. Jewett does not pin production to the lower limit; the narrator derives all the pleasure from having a full basket. A basket too heavy to move and a stomach unable to consume potatoes indefinitely implies an upper limit to fullness: plenitude should not be confused with limitless increase. Plenitude, moreover, is constrained by the interaction of forces of production and distribution. An economy pinned to appetite, like the Macarian king's thousand pounds of gold devoted to the task of keeping money in circulation, would have to grow in response to the pressure of an increasing population and thus eventually run afoul of an inexorable Malthusian logic: health leads to population increase, which in turn compels ever more money in circulation, ever more potatoes. The narrator's basket begins to answer this dilemma. Five people require more potatoes than two, but demand is ultimately envisaged here not in terms of what five people can eat but the amount they can eat in conjunction with the narrator's physical ability to carry it. The full basket poses the question of what sort of production a body politic can sustainably carry as well as ingest. Addressing sustainable production through a logic of the moderate sum, the basket of potatoes advocates for a rational husbandry of land and resources conjoined with the advantages of equitable distribution.

It is possible to situate the narrator's potato digging in what has been, to date, the most useful context for understanding this sort of economic reasoning: the withdrawal from market capitalism Nancy Glazener finds characteristic of female regionalism and the "stalled" critique it implies.[17] From this perspective, digging for potatoes—and provocatively contrasting the "riches of a good hill of potatoes" to the pleasure of gold-digging—seeks a symbolic resurrection of an idealized republic of small freeholds at a moment when its possibility had all but vanished, or taps a populist idiom that frequently foregrounded agrarian metaphors in its critique of a northeastern, urban money power. One writer in the *Arena*, a populist magazine, observed that "there would be very few rich men if the real production of each was all that he could hold," suggesting that the narrator's deliberations about how best to fill and carry a basket of potatoes can signify as a riposte to the threat of individuals who inequitably derive an unearned increment from other people's productivity.[18] That same logic leads to what seems stalled about this form of economic analysis. The notion that holding one's real production as if it were a basket of potatoes could be envisaged as a practical solution to an industrialized and corporatizing economy seems ludicrously out of synch with the conditions of modernity. To embrace a populist political rhetoric seems to solve all manner of economic ills by, essentially, ignoring them.

Jewett's play with *Utopia* suggests that a populist agrarianism, vaguely privileging the edible products of the soil over filthy lucre, is not the only and perhaps not even the most obvious intellectual context for exploring her political economy. The narrator's equivocal reference to potatoes delivering "all the pleasure that one can have in gold-digging" makes it possible to read potatoes and precious metal as equivalent to one another. Contextualized by the narrative's covert nod to the Macarian king's thousand pounds of gold, the scene begins to perform a different sort of cultural work. It leads directly to consequential late nineteenth-century debates about national prosperity in which the nature, value, and supply of money became the idiom for articulating the most highly charged social issues of the day. Becoming prominent after the Civil War, and reaching a climax as Jewett was publishing *Country*, conflicts between goldbugs and silverites became a prominent locus for negotiating labor-capital unrest, antimonopolist struggle, and arguments for the necessity of a secure financial system. Financial conservatives favoring the gold standard squared off against populist proponents of free silver who, opposing the massive accumulation of capital in the hands of a wealthy elite associated mainly with the great financial center of New York, advocated increasing the supply of specie. In *Coin's Financial School* (1894), Coin, the author's spokesman, observes that all the gold in the world would fit into a cube with sides of twenty-two feet.[19] He dramatizes on the one hand the ease with which gold and the standard of value it represents could be cornered by a wealthy elite and on the other the need for a more robust supply of specie (i.e., silver) to redeem paper. Pinning the circulation of money to a moderate sum of gold is for silverites what has curtailed economic growth and fostered social inequity.

As fears for the security of the gold standard stoked financial uncertainty through 1896, financial conservatives spoke in favor of (1) a controlled money supply, (2) the virtue of stable economic values, and (3) the concentration of capital in the hands of urban financiers. The trope of gold in late nineteenth-century discourses undergirded a concept of value that seems absolute because it is one with itself. Goldbugs argued that the only way to guarantee the "full amount of the value which it [money] professes on its face to possess" is to resist the logic of fiat money freed from its "intrinsic" value in gold, the one substance that remains self-identical.[20] Gold, in other words, is its own general equivalent: The value of potatoes can be expressed in gold; the value of gold can only be expressed in gold. What seemed the self-evidently enduring properties of gold, moreover, could be parlayed into a powerful rhetoric of republican virtue. Gold was celebrated by financial conservatives as "moral money that went along with thrift, savings, and economic progress through honest labor. Unlike an inflated currency, gold did not lend itself to speculation, unearned increments, and lazy debt accumulation."[21] As part of this same cultural idiom, all hard money proponents in the currency debates constructed their arguments around a fear of excess. Goldbugs condemned the inflationary prospect of free silver, and goldbugs and bimetallists touted the perils of "greenbackers"—those favoring fiat money unbacked by specie, or what James Garfield denounced in 1876 as the "delirium" of "large issues of currency."[22]

Contextualized in the currency debates, the narrator's sentiments reveal her to be something of a potato-digging goldbug. Her full but not overfull basket of potatoes/gold, which is to be distributed among a finite number of people with limited appetites, places natural constraints on the potato/ money supply. Inflating the potato supply—taking a silverite stance, as it were—would overwhelm the body (politic). Moreover, Jewett's potatoes under nonmarket conditions function, like gold under market conditions, to remind us of the importance of secure and inalienable value. The value of the potato to the health of the body derives, like gold from the intrinsic allure of a precious metal, from the value it professes—it cannot be transferred to its representations. At the very least, the economic logic of Green Island counters greenbacker delirium. Potatoes cannot be created by fiat or consumed in the shape of the paper signs (money or credit) for which they exchange in the marketplace. And large issues of them—emptying the potato field too quickly—would invite future shortages in Jewett's model commonwealth. From this point of view, Jewett's bioeconomics derives its discursive power from narratives about gold, drawn partly from More's Macarian fable of what makes for a tranquil commonwealth and partly from late nineteenth-century arguments in favor of the gold standard, the legitimacy of which was particularly compelling to northeastern urban elites. Potatoes have to be potatoes to sustain the body, just as gold has to remain gold, the gold standard a standard, in order to guarantee both economic well-being (a secure fiscal foundation and a free circulation of money) and political tranquility (freer subjects).

The narrator's investment in goldbug potato digging returns us to the conflict over class that has so energized Jewett studies over the past couple of decades. Debates over fiscal value worked in the late nineteenth century across multiple cultural registers to express imbricated anxieties about class, nation, identity, immigration, and (as Michaels argues) representation.[23] In the "Paper Money Craze of 1786," for example, John Fiske skillfully sutures the centenary of Shays's Rebellion to contemporary labor/capital disputes. Haymarket (May 1886) looms over Fiske's article; so do silverite and Greenbacker calls for an inflated money supply. The crisis of post–Revolutionary War scarcity and debt was exacerbated by the "hopeless confusion due to an inconvertible paper currency," which brought on an "era of wild speculation and extravagance in living." Fiske builds his analysis, in part, around a deep-rooted unease among cultural elites over the capital-holding classes of the United States: wealthy speculators are far from blameless. But it is the poorest people who "earn their bread by the sweat of their brows and have no margin of accumulated capital [who] always suffer the most. Above all men, it is the laboring man who needs sound money and steady values."[24]

Other commentators on the money question were still more forthright about employing the currency debates to articulate class differences. The journalist Jonathan Baxter Harrison calls for working men to practice the "most rigid economy" instead of succumbing to the "delusion" of fiat money and to the Populist fiction—his specific adversary here is the National Party—that "there is already sufficient wealth in existence in our country to give the working people good times, if it were only rightly distributed."[25] Skeptical that the "earth contains materials for unlimited wealth," Harrison concludes (through his mouthpiece, a misunderstood capitalist friend) that the only solution to depressed economic times is for "workmen to live on as little as possible. . . . And the capitalists be content with small profits."[26] But the financial system plays a crucial role in motivating workers toward economy. In a subtle move, Harrison attributes workers' extravagance to the failure of the banking system to sustain the value of savings amid compromises over the gold standard and the "madness of the workingmen in demanding irredeemable paper money."[27] By guaranteeing financial value, he contends, a secure gold standard ensures that workers will avoid the delusion of fictitious values, unjust redistributions of wealth, and misguided calls for social activism.

For both Harrison and Fiske, the currency question engages an array of class ideologies. A rhetoric of excess plays a key role. Valorizing a careful husbandry of resources results in what seems a counterintuitive explication of class differences. Most rich people live "more carefully and economically than most of the working-people."[28] The laboring classes are by contrast wasteful, succumbing intellectually to the "madness" of paper money; physically to poor food and excessive drink;[29] culturally to the "opiate" of bad reading materials;[30] and demographically to an influx of a "great number of people from other countries" which prevents a "real unity or homogeneous character by the population of our local communities."[31] Urging laborers to shun extravagance and the empty values founded on silver and paper therefore dismisses labor's claims for a fairer distribution of capital on the basis of workers' supposed disposition toward excess. The specter of the rich speculator also haunts Harrison's account in the shape of the "multitudes" of businessmen who succumbed to a "passionate greed for riches" after the Civil War.[32] Fiske and Harrison seek not only to contain anxieties about working-class agitation but also to reclaim for laborers an important symbolic role in assuaging the anxieties experienced by upper-class urban elites amid the turmoil of an emergent consumer market society. Laborers should know their symbolic place representing foundational American values of frugality and self-sufficiency, a cultural role that does not sit well on the rich.

From this perspective, Jewett's kitchen economics represents class anxieties in which the narrator's potato/gold standard hedges against fears of eroding traditional values by way of a powerful link between fiscal probity, moral rectitude, stable class boundaries, and the produce of the American soil. That same logic translates it into a set of free-ranging recommendations to the most divisive questions of the late nineteenth century. Like the feuding farmers, the feuding parties most commonly referenced in the late nineteenth century—labor and capital—require a conversation. Like the narrator, labor must delight in the joy of laboring. Like the mean sheep owner, capital needs to learn the principle of the moderate sum. Like the sheep, perhaps, workers need to be content with just a little more salt. Like the basket, its weight easier to carry when shared, and like Mrs. Todd's boat, fully laden but afloat because of a careful distribution of weight, the ship of state requires all stakeholders in the American economy to learn how to distribute resources more equitably if it is to sail on. Again the chowder is exemplary, its interleaved layers suggesting a metaphorical social reconstitution in which producers and consumers, laborers and leaders of the process of labor, not only collaborate harmoniously but actually are one and the same. Yet its stratified composition can also imply the sort of recipe for economic health Harrison puts forward, where moderation does not mean an equal distribution, but instead workingmen living frugally and capitalists making do with smaller profits. Green Island's kitchen economics invokes related though differently inflected historical contexts, suggesting a nostalgic and phantasmal commonwealth of agrarian producers on the one hand, and on the other, an uncommon commonwealth where Anglo-Americans operating a metaphoric gold standard seem to speak, like Harrison and Fiske, for the virtues of social order.

Yet Jewett's possible goldbug proclivities—a desire to harness disorderly social forces through a political economic trope of the moderate sum—sit uneasily with her emphasis on practices of production and distribution within a model commonwealth centered on the activities of women. The gender of the body in Jewett's body politic makes a profound difference to the way we comprehend its ideological resonances, especially when it comes to her representation of homo economicus, the supposedly rational agent characterizing "man's" economic identity within market society. The Green Island chapters frequently dwell on the scandal of male appetites and the economic imbalances they can produce. Though the frugal-but-full basket argues for the possibilities of economy built around the natural limitations of human appetite, young Johnny Bowden, "hungry enough to eat his size" (72), possesses, like Jack in "Miss Beulah's Bonnet," a preternatural appetite, an appetite out of all proportion to the natural size of his stomach. And he is not the only man to exemplify disproportion. The mean sheep owner refuses to provide a small measure of salt; the two feuding farmers pass between them a "bone." Asa, who so badly misreads Mrs. Todd's command over the lading of the boat as to recommend "let the boy. . . . steer" (65), is another man of imbalance "too ready with his criticism . . . on every possible subject" (65). Mrs. Todd trims her boat while drawing attention to the voracity of men. "We don't want to carry no men folks . . . takin' up all our time" (64). Jewett's narrative here conceives the male body politic in terms of disproportionate appetites and systems of exchange.

Green Island's commonwealth must instead be read in conjunction with an implied femina economica. Aspects of political economic schemas appear everywhere on Green Island, but defamiliarized, made strange on this island heterotopia. The chowder requires a division of labor: the narrator digs potatoes, Mrs. Todd provides the fish, Mrs. Blackett cooks, while William and the narrator together facilitate the task of carrying the basket. The narrator exhibits self-interest and even a measure of insatiability: she "longed to go on" in her pleasurable task. But she never thinks to truck, barter, or exchange; nor does she consider that her free labor grants her a property in its fruits. Moreover, the narrator reverses the assumption of classical political economic thought from Smith to Mill that humans desire to accumulate riches at the expense of others while avoiding the pain or disutility of labor. She longs for the pleasure of digging potatoes rather than the joy of amassing them. And if there is a sense in which she digs potatoes for her own consumption then it is nonetheless the communal nature of the enterprise that motivates her to dig and, crucially—because her restraint benefits Mrs. Blackett's later consumption—to refrain from digging. It must also be noted that her cool-headed resolution to constrain her immediate pleasure in order to sustain future consumption is an exemplary moment of rational economic decision-making, given the conditions of a common stock that cannot be increased by circulating it through the market. Making chowder on Green Island observes the necessity of allocating resources rationally, welcomes a division of labor, and even contemplates a construction of human nature driven by desire. If it is possible to make dinner benevolently without a market, if disinterested motives can master self-interested desire, and if labor for the sake of laboring might be pleasurable, then the supposition that human beings are motivated to compete with others by the urges of self-interest, acquisitiveness, and infinite wants comes into question. Green Island's kitchen commonwealth emphasizes a balanced distribution of sufficient resources in conjunction with limited (or at least satiable) wants.[33]

This does not imply that potato digging and chowder making resolve into an economic imaginary, as Mrs. Todd's business on Green Island—the forty-two cents she carries to "settle an account" with William—reminds us. Green Island's heterotopian commonwealth does not function in the same way as Goux's utopian republic. The cultural work undertaken by this tiny sum of money in fact turns out to be immense given that it resurrects property as a problematic. Mrs. Todd carries the profits from the sale of lobsters to Green Island. A new freight of lobsters induces her to establish a business arrangement at Dunnet Landing. Commerce traverses the sea-gap between the mainland and the tiny continent of Green Island. A more compelling context for Green Island kitchen economics might therefore be Lawson's "political economy of the freehold" or what Timothy Sweet calls an American Georgic: a "discourse of rural virtue," the marks of which were "sedentary farming . . . and embeddedness in [simple] market relations."[34] From that point of view, what seems a radical conception of a nonmarket civil society, a utopian republic standing outside market relations, yields instead to an evocation of precapitalist social relations: local exchange, micromarkets, relatively trivial sums (forty-two cents), renewable resources (potatoes and lobsters), and age-old technologies (a wheelbarrow), all of it offering space for off-market or small-market practices of production and distribution. That vision would seem inexorably nostalgic.

But neither proposition—that Green Island is disconnected from ownership or that it stages a fading Jeffersonian dream—accounts for the there-and-back-again narrative structure of these chapters, a structure that destabilizes any notion that Green Island functions as an ideological terminus. Green Island, like Orr's Island, ultimately makes hazardous the security of the distinction between mainland identity and island difference. A number of interwoven sequences suggest that the kitchen economics of Green Island builds on the propensity of classical political economic thought to favor narratives about how economies develop—but in confusingly mismatched plots of polity. Mrs. Blackett's chowder, for example, caps a long-running debate in these chapters about how a division of labor benefits economies. The two feuding farmers "divide" the island to their economic and moral ruin rather than dividing their labor for their mutual benefit. Subsequently, more generous divisions of labor offer an antidote. William offers to divide and thus ease the weight of the basket. Later he cleans the fish for the communal chowder—a fish caught on the lines he set, and transported to the feast by his sister. And the chowder, as Adam Smith's theory of efficient production predicts, is in excess of requirements. It is enough to feed five people, including Johnny Bowden with his gargantuan appetite, and still have some left over for Mrs. Blackett's kitten. One way to read the trope of division over these four chapters is to trace in its elaborations a history of civilization: the feuding farmers, stupidly refusing in their Hobbesian animus to lend each other a hand, yield later to more productive nonmarket practices—numerous people dividing their labor to assemble diverse materials into a meal—and then, potentially, to necessary market practices as the complexity of the tasks increase.

Jewett's analysis of resource distribution can accord with the virtually unanimous assumption among late nineteenth-century thinkers that civilization evolves in lockstep with increasingly complex capital-intensive systems. The narrator digging potatoes emulates Smith's "rude state of society." An efficient division of labor has the predictable effect of easing her task and plunging the solitary William—as Henry George's laborer on the once-empty savannah eventually found—into deeper, enriching social ties. A larger load of lobsters inaugurates exchange relations and property rights: A wheelbarrow cannot be hired until all parties recognize the legitimacy of William's claim over his lobsters (and, indeed, the wheelbarrow owner's over the wheelbarrow). The Green Island chapters describe progressively intensifying investments of capital as the amount of goods to be distributed increases, from producing potatoes with a hoe to using a basket to having two people carry the basket to employing four people to make the chowder to using a wheelbarrow. Far from defining Green Island as either a marketless utopia or a small market utopia, the narrative frames a nonmarket economy as one stage of a process. Producing small amounts permits free labor; producing and distributing larger amounts introduces the need for manufactured goods, hired labor, a more sophisticated division of labor, and a general equivalent. Nor is Dunnet Landing necessarily the end of the process. Mrs. Todd's business arrangements seem to position the wheelbarrow as the pinnacle of technological achievement consistent with a mandate that markets remain small. The issue is complicated, however, by the narrator's return to Dunnet Landing to find it "large and noisy and oppressive" (81). The logic of the "power of contrast" (81) implies that the return from Green Island ghost-writes yet another trip: Dunnet is symbolically aligned with the noisy and oppressive environs of the metropolis. This analogical chain implies still further transitions to still more intensive capitalist relations, such as gold standards and general equivalents.

The general directives of stages theory establish the underlying logic. Though it would be possible for one person to perform all necessary tasks—running a farm on an empty savannah, singlehandedly dragging boats and digging potatoes, refusing to exchange anything with another—maturing societies require more complex social interactions, more developed technologies, more highly evolved systems of exchange, and more capital. In one reconstruction of the ideological order in Jewett's narrative, the step from simple market conditions to oppressive social relations in the metropolis seems (perhaps tragically) inevitable if swelling populations are to survive, so that immature technologies (a hoe, a wheelbarrow, interest-free financial transactions) represent an earlier, now fading, stage in the life of human societies. In another, quietly iterating Henry George's position, the judicious and restrained investments of capital on Green Island and at Dunnet Landing represent the stage at which capital accumulation has advanced far enough to inspire human proclivities toward equilibrium and the "necessaries." In short, the "power of contrast" linking the city to Green Island and Dunnet Landing can forebode the excessive appetites to come or presage the moment when the oppressive relations of a new social form, the metropolis, will yield to a more mature form of social organization.[35]

The travelers traversing between mainland and island, however, plays havoc with sequence.[36] Like Freeman's "A Mistaken Charity," this narrative urges us to consider how we orchestrate its elements, and what those configurations signify for its schemas of history and polity. Does Green Island chowder represent a liberation from exchange value at the utopian end of history, toward which market relations (should) trend? Does the narrative invite us to read from an oppressive technological regime in the city to the wheelbarrows and simple exchange relations of Dunnet Landing, thence to an idyllic society downsized to what the human body can carry and consume? Or—given that the travelers return to large and oppressive environs—does nonmarket production represent merely the rude state of society, the stage whence exchange relations necessarily emerge and whence civilization evolves, so that wheelbarrows are an inevitable consequence of the progress of civilization? Should we then read up an evolutionary chain from the pleasurable but limited exercise of carrying baskets in a (more or less) state of nature to wheelbarrows and thence to the capital-intensive technologies that Dunnet Landing/the metropolis must eventually compel? These questions are confused further by the fact that the travelers can hardly return to business arrangements when business gets transacted in Mrs. Blackett's kitchen.

As the difference of Green Island as a site of pure nonmarket relations decomposes, so the question of where and how capital accumulation, the emergence of property rights, commerce and markets figure in an unfolding plot of polity becomes more and more problematic. What is the necessary condition of a leap to civilization: technology, capital, a gold standard, property rights—or their abandonment?

Green Island is no island apart. In these chapters Jewett stages a sophisticated debate about constructions of commonwealth and sustainable economic practices that is positioned among the historical, material, and ideological concerns of the late nineteenth century and thoroughly imbued with political economic principles. Jewett's kitchen economics encompass the practical (how much salt do sheep need? how best to shift a load of lobsters?); the monetary (how much gold is required to support a free circulation of currency?); the cultural (how should labor and capital resolve their differences about their share of GDP?); and the gendered (are men creatures of inordinate appetite? what is the difference of femina economica?). She constantly invokes the theoretical concerns of political economy: Is nature miserly? Do Malthusian laws prevail? What are the laws of production and distribution? What measures value? What is the relationship of appetite to production, particularly when some men's appetites are outsized? How should one distribute resources and wealth so that the ship of state sails? Do societies evolving from simple to complex forms require general equivalents, markets, and capital accumulation? If so, what is the nature of that sequence?

The cumulative effect of these questions is to challenge late nineteenth-century conceptions about the insatiability of human wants and (neo)classical assumptions about the mandatory role of efficient markets, competition, capital accumulation, and property rights in the development of progressive societies, and to replace them with a political economy that privileges balanced distributions, moderate sums, and stable measures of value. But the there-and-back-again structure of the sojourn at Green Island resists the imposition of static models. It resists the imputation that nonmarket conditions as they exist ephemerally on Green Island are the endpoint of Jewett's economic reasoning, or that the chapters recommend digging potatoes and making chowder as a solution to late nineteenth-century economic turmoil. The island's curious economic properties are heterotopian and speculative. That they are also informed by abstract principles poses a formidable challenge to counterworld thinking and makes Jewett's work of special concern to twenty-first century reconstructions of history and of economics.

5

TALKING TURKEY

The Political Economy of Thanksgiving in Cooke and Stowe

To contribute toward her niece's wedding, Miss Beulah has to institute draconian household economies, which include plenty of cheap "pudding and johnny-cake."[1] This food/wedding relationship is a familiar topos of female regionalist fiction. In Rose Terry Cooke's "Mrs. Flint's Married Experience," the "plum-colored silk" the Widow Gold wears for her second marriage to Deacon Flint is soon supplanted by a starving time as he begins to feed her on "sloppy gruel and hard bread."[2] Over her "birthright" of marriage, Louisa Ellis in Freeman's "A New England Nun" favors the "pottage" of freedom—more precisely, the narrator informs us, a "glass dish full of sugared currants, a plate of little cakes, and one of light white biscuits."[3] To preserve her "maiden independence," Louisa in Freeman's "Louisa" carries a lot of food back from her uncle's, tripling the seven-mile journey because she has to divide the load in two.[4] Cooke's "An Old-Fashioned Thanksgiving" (1892) begins with Hannah and John, newly married, journeying to a tiny log cabin, where Hannah provides the bread and cheese for "their supper at home for the first time," thus creating that "joyful sense of home so instinctive in every true man and woman."[5] It ends with their daughter's wedding and a Thanksgiving feast comprising a "mighty turkey, the crisp roast pig, the cold ham, the chicken pie, and the piles of smoking vegetables, with a long vista of various pastries, apples, nuts, and pitchers of cider" (151). Then the fiancée's father and two brothers return from fighting in the Revolutionary War just in time to celebrate. No wonder the story concludes with "Amen!" (151).

Metaphors of food speak to and represent an astonishing variety of cultural phenomena. To subsist, we must eat; but to eat is to plunge into symbolic realms. In myriad ways, cultures invest with meaning the taste of food, its mode of preparation and site of consumption, its preparers and consumers, its lack or plenitude, its provenance, taboos, and traditions. Food is associated with important political and spiritual practices. It constructs and perpetuates gender roles; it is central to family and communal life and important rites of passage. In "An Old-Fashioned Thanksgiving" the huge feast, sign of a forthcoming commonwealth of prosperity, affirms a family reunited; a family split through marriage; a family uniting with another through marriage; a new nation splitting away from the old (Britain); and a new nation uniting ("all said Amen!"). The story develops a familiar plot of polity. As if intent upon mapping the history of the American republic onto a stadial schema of emerging civilizations, the story takes us in short order from Hannah and John's "log hut" (123), where they share their first scanty supper, to the "good-sized frame house" (127) John builds for his growing family, where Hannah and her children survive the "sodden and monotonous diet" (134) of war time and work hard to lay in a "good store of apples, pork, and potatoes" (139) before its end, and finally to the superabundant banquet that concludes the story. That hint of a Communion supper when the feast begins with a shared Amen! serves several complex political purposes. It bestows a blessing on a history of settlement (from the seventeenth century) and nation-building (in the eighteenth), while presaging a new and ever-more prosperous US republic (under God).

More wittily, it rewrites that history in terms of fowls consumed. During the winter that tries the family's body and soul—"their hearts failed, as their flesh did" (134)—it is Hannah's "savory stew" (134) made from two "fat and fine" (134) chickens that gives them renewed strength and courage. The next year they raise "brood after brood of chickens" (138) in a new chicken-yard, growing more corn to feed them. In return, "many a dollar was brought home about Thanksgiving time for the fat fowls" (138). The "mighty turkey" presiding over the feast is therefore more than just a generic sign of Thanksgiving and the prospect of sated bodies. It signifies the fat and fine resources of what has already become a mighty body politic. Possibly it picks up Ben Franklin's legendary preference for the turkey over the eagle as an icon of mighty American power. Certainly it traces the roots of the coming American republic back to Hannah's kitchen. Her work and her struggle to subsist keep her family alive and together, and then branch out into market exchange as the family transitions from eating chickens to raising and selling them. When the "ragged" (149) and "ravenous" (151) soldiers appear, they return to a well-dressed family and well-stocked table provided in great measure by femina economica—by Hannah's economies and economic successes. Cooke employs a language of chickens and mighty turkey to enact a woman-centered history of the United States. The kitchen concenters a discourse on political and economic progress; the men's contributions take place offstage.

The broader context to this discussion is what Catherine Gallagher calls "bioeconomics": a pronounced tendency in the nineteenth century to inscribe political economic knowledge in terms of "interconnections among populations, the food supply, modes of production and exchange, and their impact on life forms," so that "issues of bodily well-being and of economic circulation are frequently articulated both through and against each other."[6] Food and drink represent more than mere subsistence. To eat a mighty turkey is to construct a multitude of implied narratives about production and consumption, about the socioeconomic relations that shape them, and about the reproduction of social ties to which they contribute. Gallagher traces this political economic mode to Thomas Malthus's "Essay on the Principle of Population" (1798). The brief inquiry into the food/wedding nexus in female regionalism that began this chapter gestures toward the postulates that generate his argument. First, "food is necessary to the existence of man." Second, the "passion between the sexes is necessary and will remain nearly in its present state."[7] From these postulates Malthus derives his theorem that the "power of population is indefinitely greater than the power in the earth to produce subsistence for men": population increases in a geometrical ratio, subsistence in an arithmetical ratio.[8] The human predilection for procreation will eventually exhaust the earth. This is not to say that these stories owe a debt to Malthus's ideas in particular. Mrs. Flint's starving body implies the opposite. As Gallagher observes, one of Malthus's great challenges to prior political economic thought was to what seemed the most obvious of correlations between a healthy body and a healthy body politic.[9] For Malthus, misery awaits the body politic not to the extent that it is diseased or unclean but to the extent that it is healthy and thus capable of producing more and more children. "Mrs. Flint's Married Experience" restores an older political economic logic. It affirms an underlying relationship between more and better food for Mrs. Flint—and the Flint household does not lack for resources— and the improved health of the body politic.

Thinking about Cooke's and Stowe's stories in the context of bioeconomic reasoning restores the kitchen directly to political economy via metaphoric connections between the feeding of the body and the health of the body politic. There are good reasons not to trust that connection. The urge to construct an idealized body politic around a notion of a "'true' human body"— the Aryan body, for example—is "notorious for its complicity in some of the more heinous exercises of power and violence of the modern age."[10] And late nineteenth-century discourses in the United States constantly worked to enshrine the hegemonic figure of the clean, healthy, powerful white male body—and by derivation the robust white mother—as the interpretive key to questions about race, class, and nation. Female regionalist kitchen economics accommodate the logic and power of those bioeconomic discourses. But these stories do not necessarily arrange the American body around the

Thanksgiving table in conventional ways. The ragged, unkempt soldiers attending the feast in "An Old-Fashioned Thanksgiving" do so with femina economica as the symbolic provider of the feast. Though the enchanting, untroubled conclusion goes some way toward mystifying the fact that the feast was in significant ways paid for by women, a kitchen commonwealth has the capacity to stage a heterotopian body politic—to make it signify through alterity, as an unsettling version of the hegemonic (male) social body.

The stories by Stowe and Cooke (chapter 5), Dunbar-Nelson (chapter 6), and Jewett (chapter 7) that I examine in the following pages demonstrate a range of symbolic bodies politic. In this chapter I trace them through the very common trope of the Thanksgiving feast, beginning with the complex primer of kitchen (bio)economics Harriet Beecher Stowe puts forth in the Thanksgiving chapter of *Oldtown Folks* (1869) in order to signify the limits to a newly reconstructed United States. Cooke's Thanksgiving stories present a still more complicated situation. "An Old-Fashioned Thanksgiving" shows Cooke tapping a mythos of family reunited/polity united—as does, more subtly, "My Thanksgiving" (1863), a story published during the Civil War. The collection in which "An Old-Fashioned Thanksgiving" appears, *Huckleberries: Gathered from New England Hills* (1892), includes no fewer than four Thanksgiving stories: "An Old-Fashioned Thanksgiving," "A Double Thanksgiving," "Home Again," and "How Celia Changed Her Mind." Reading across story boundaries from feast to feast poses the bioeconomic idiom of Thanksgiving as a problematic. As if to upend the first story's fidelity to a political myth of (coming) US prosperity and comity, Celia, having suffered Mrs. Flint's married experience of being physically starved and emotionally abused when she marries Deacon Everts, ends up throwing a Thanksgiving feast for the abjected of the village—"every old maid in town" (314). From that perspective, the fairy-tale piling-on of coincidence at the end of "An Old-Fashioned Thanksgiving," where a wedding, Thanksgiving, and the soldiers' return all transpire in one afternoon, suggests that Cooke may not be wholly transparent in this otherwise celebratory story. At the very least, *Huckleberries* spreads a heterotopian table for the characters who keep doubling for each other across its many Thanksgiving tales.

Not talking turkey can be aligned with the fabulist implications of these kitchen commonwealths. As Annabel Patterson demonstrates convincingly in *Fables of Power* (1991), fables can possess substantial political content. Patterson's "historicized poetics of the fable" shows that the fable-form provided a symbolic grammar that was deployed in a variety of ways from the Renaissance to the nineteenth century as a "medium of political analysis and communication, especially in the form of a communication from or on behalf of the politically powerless." In Aesop's fable "The Belly and the Members," the hands, mouth, and teeth rebel against the belly until it "consented to take its proper share of the work." Finding that they begin to lose energy, the members ultimately realize that "even the Belly in its dull quiet way was doing necessary work for the Body, and that all must work together or the Body will go to pieces." The fable provided a "symbol of the distribution of wealth in the body politic" that favored the claims of centralized power, however indolent or ungrateful it might appear, but which could also be used to affirm the demands made by the rebellious members.[11] Fables can disassemble and reconstruct representations of the body politic, even when they carry the hegemonic weight of Thanksgiving—and even when the subject is the extended family/clan of the Bowden reunion (in Jewett's *The Country of the Pointed Firs*) and the "great national anniversaries which our country has lately kept" that accompany it.[12]

In this chapter I address the sorts of bodies politic that families assembled around the body of a turkey construct and symbolize. Turkeys signify. And representations of the family (re)united around the ubiquitous turkey—plus pies, puddings, and a multitude of other foods—constantly invoke an imaginary body politic situated within diverse economic relations and real or fabulous histories. That Thanksgiving body is typically gendered. The parson, for example, presides over the final feast in "An Old-Fashioned Thanksgiving," which commences with his "long grace" (151) and an invitation to "eat and be glad" (151). This story and many others pay lip service to the social power of patriarchal figures. As even this relatively conventional story shows, however, female regionalist fictions may shape an unruly body politic and map a different account of history. The story comically interrupts the parson's attempts to impose his authority on the proceedings, Madam Everett's spectacular feast overcoming his usual struggle with a "tangle of texts" (133). Afterward, John says that he "shortened up so 'mazin' quick on that prayer" because he "smelt the turkey" (151)—as if to remind us that the feast could not have taken place at all without Hannah's dedicated hen-farming. The fact that the story ends with "all said Amen!" ringingly endorses a well-fed body and body politic. But it is a body politic constructed and celebrated under the aegis of aeconomia.

When Stowe published *Oldtown Folks* in 1869, Thanksgiving was a more contested expression of national unity than in the halcyon-seeming post-Revolutionary period she chooses as the timeframe of the novel. Abraham Lincoln's 1863 proclamation that all Americans, North and South, would celebrate Thanksgiving on the same day, and thus transform a day symbolizing amity and community into a gesture of political reconciliation, was still not in effect. Sarah Josepha Hale, the editor of *Godey's Lady's Book* and campaigner for a national Thanksgiving Day, was still proselytizing for it in an 1871 editorial. Antebellum sentiment in the South often thought of it as a "Yankee abolitionist holiday."[13] Reconstruction would come to an end before southern states fully embraced the Thanksgiving holiday.[14] That fact helps us recognize the ironic play of Stowe's always-complex time signatures in one of her keynote chapters, "How We Kept Thanksgiving at Oldtown." Thrust resolutely into the deep past, the harmonies of the feast nonetheless seem designed to address the fractures of a post–Civil War United States. A body politic emerging out of a community of happy, sated revelers points to what has not, in 1869, come to pass, but should. Yet Stowe's old-fashioned Thanksgiving belies the simple virtues of feasting together that it otherwise seems to espouse. While "all the tribes of the Badger family" have been carousing, kidnappers have sneaked into the village to steal Aunt Nancy Prime's children across the state line to become slaves.[15] The body politic that Horace Holyoke, the narrator, idealizes at the Thanksgiving celebration turns out to be missing some bodies. The fact that the Oldtowners spring into action to save them presages future historical events, not the "United" States as it is constituted in Horace's fond memory. And not until we have moved deeper into the narrative can we look back to know what that hazily utopian old-timey Thanksgiving was missing all along. These quiet time shifts bring into question what appear to be a once-upon-a-time unity and prosperity from which a post–Civil War United States might conceive a new polity—and along with it the symbolic nationalizing function that the kitchen commonwealth tentatively embraces.

As if to celebrate the contributions an undivided nation could or should make to prosperity, Horace admires the "endless variety of vegetables which the American soil and climate have contributed to the table" and which were "all piled together in jovial abundance upon the smoking board" (398). Horace's paean testifies not only to an abundant harvest but also to the rich national enterprise that has made it possible, for he salutes an iconic e pluribus unum: one soil, endless variety. The idea of the American soil is crucial to Horace's vision of commonwealth. Ineluctably natural and self-evidently productive, the soil celebrates a common bond beyond the reach of division, state lines, and free or slave-holding territories. This loaded table to which all are bidden is an ideological counterpart to, and material proof of, the governor's Thanksgiving proclamation: "God save the Commonwealth of Massachusetts" (389). And the Badgers' Thanksgiving takes the notion of a commonwealth for all its tribes seriously. The feasters are entertained by the "jollity" (400) and fiddling of "black Caesar, full of turkey and pumpkin pie" (400). In a salute to the mythos of the first American Thanksgiving, the narrator notes that "all the poor, loafing tribes, Indian and half-Indian, who at other times wandered, selling baskets and other light wares, were sure to come back to Oldtown a little before Thanksgiving time" (392–93) to partake of the "Indian Hogshead" (393) of cider. Aunt Lois observes that the "whole tribe" will be there "till we give 'em something" (393). The peripatetic and "shiftless" (395) white Sam Lawson is given a turkey because his children "ought to have something good to eat Thanksgiving day" (395). Quietly, Stowe sketches in a paternalistic, but recognizably political, message. Though small, Oldtown functions as an ideological center; its generous sharing caters for the whole tribe, for the "whole generation" (393), including the "softly shiftless class" (393) to which the Indians and Sam Lawson belong.

Grandmother's household is the epicenter of this extensive cultural work. According to Aunt Lois, the whole tribe arrives at the Badgers' door because of grandmother: "That's just mother's way," she says; "she always keeps a whole generation at her heels" (393). The biblical text that follows Aunt Lois's statement puts a conventionally Christian stamp on grandmother's ideologically centering role—"If there be among you a poor man . . . thou shalt not harden thy heart," quotes grandmother among the "pounding and chopping in the kitchen" (393). Grandmother suits her actions to her words. Even shiftless Sam Lawson receives a turkey from her. But the backstory to that gift suggests that her household economies might extend into the more unconventionally political terrain of the Thanksgiving Day kidnappings. Admonishing him after hearing his story about getting his "old tom-turkey froze as stiff as a stake" (395) because he forgets to bring it inside, grandmother observes "you oughter 'ave been at home that night to fasten up your own barn and look after your own creeturs" (395). For all that Sam Lawson is played for laughs—and for all that grandmother gives him a free turkey anyway—his reneging on domestic duties symbolizes a broader lack of attention to political responsibilities. In pre–Civil War days where slavery still exists, grandmother hints, all of the white denizens of Oldtown sink to the level of Sam Lawson in failing to look after their fellow "creeturs." The rescue that follows—during which Sam makes up for his shiftless ways by going along—augurs a heroic future for men. But the last word in the episode is grandmother's, who busies herself "in comforting the hearts of Aunt Nancy and the children with more than they could eat of the relics of the Thanksgiving feast, and bidding them not to be down-hearted" (411–12). Arguably, the relics here turn out to be the true embodiment—the heart, reached through the stomach—of Thanksgiving's political meaning. As Aunt Nancy and her children consume them, the relics extend the feast to include for the first time the bodies of the stolen and (nearly) enslaved. It is also a neat riposte to the southern states who refused to accept a national day of Thanksgiving. In grandmother's book, the day after Thanksgiving proves to be a truer

Thanksgiving than the one designated in the governor's official proclamation.

This sense that grandmother rather than the religiopolitical authority of Massachusetts and the United States speaks for its central political and moral values is richly elaborated through the productions of the kitchen. The "endless variety of vegetables which the American soil and climate have contributed to the table" overwhelms Horace, but they are not eaten raw. The smoking board acknowledges the endless labor of cooks and their helpers. A commonwealth where "all [are] piled together in jovial abundance" turns out to have been put together in the kitchen. At the heart of this important kitchen work is a political economy of the pie. In his longest meditation on the "sublime" (389) and "sacred" (390) mysteries of pie-making, Horace observes that the "pie is an English institution, which, planted on American soil, forthwith ran rampant and burst forth into an untold variety of genera and species. Not merely the old traditional mince pie, but a thousand strictly American seedlings from that main stock, evinced the power of American housewives to adapt old institutions to new uses" (390). The oven "brooded over successive generations of pies and cakes, which went in raw and came out cooked, till butteries and dressers and shelves and pantries were literally crowded with a jostling abundance" (391). That abundance is specified in great detail: "Pumpkin pies, cranberry pies, huckleberry pies, cherry pies, green-currant pies, peach, pear, and plum pies, custard pies, apple pies" (390), and more. Placed in a "cold northern chamber," moreover, the frozen pies "formed a great repository for all the winter months; and the pies baked at Thanksgiving often came out fresh and good with the violets of April" (391–92).

Horace's later celebration of the Thanksgiving feast resides rhetorically in this meditation on American pies. The "untold variety" (390) of the "American soil" leads to "jostling abundance" (391), its abundance this time being overtly multihued: dark-skinned (plum, huckleberry), light-skinned (peach), and red (cherry). Once more Horace implies an enduring national enterprise. Northern climes preserve the spirit of Thanksgiving through the politically frozen antebellum years—through "successive generations" in fact—and into the more auspicious days of postbellum spring (and probably Easter). In other ways Horace's account of pie-making does not jibe well with his later more conventional paean to the American soil. Pies signify quite differently from vegetables. In the oven, pies properly "went in raw and came out cooked"; but if they can be "planted on American soil," act like "seedlings" and run rampant into a "variety of genera and species" (390), then the cooked pies function as if they were a raw product of the soil rather than the vehicle for transforming raw produce into something cooked. Horace's conflation of the two collapses what appears to be the priority of the raw products of the soil. Put in political terms: when Horace uses the metaphor of the American soil at the feast, he extols that which precedes and supersedes political division. The American soil could not otherwise metaphorize a common bond persisting from the era when Horace is supposed to be writing (after the Revolutionary War) to the era when Stowe writes (after the Civil War). But pies planted in the American soil represent republican ideals in ways that are unambiguously cultural. They, and the soil they grow in, are "cooked" in Lévi-Strauss's sense of the term.[16] These pies have a history; they are in the lineage of English pies but have adapted "old institutions to new uses" (390). And they are unambiguously gendered. This multihued abundance is the province of "American housewives," the product of the "boundless fertility of the feminine mind" (390).

One of the old institutions American pies adapt and demystify is an iconic slogan such as the American soil. To imagine pies planted so strangely in the soil is no longer to conceive of the soil as a universal ground of shared American values, or even as dirt, but wholly as metaphor. The American pie does not quite make the cooked raw. It does not transform women's work in the kitchen into the true political ground from which a male-dominated iconography of shared ideals and prosperity faultily derives. The meanings of the pie-sublime are heterotopian rather than oppositional. An untold variety of pies and an endless variety of vegetables out of the American soil incorporate each other rhetorically and in the oven. Cooks depend on an endless variety of produce for their "ecstasies of creative inspiration" (390), but the raw produce of the soil depends on cooks to make it palatable. When grandmother serves Aunt Nancy and her children the relics from the Thanksgiving table, there is a compelling sense in which her enlargement of the body politic adds to and completes the governor's official proclamation and the minister's Thanksgiving day sermon, which, "freely concerning the politics of the country" (396), hints that he takes on the issue of slavery. The governor and minister speak in the abstract. Grandmother, comforting the hearts of the Prime family with generous portions puts the body—stomach, heart, and brain—into the body politic.

This is a tenuous achievement. The multihued pies cannot save Aunt Nancy's children from being stolen. And if the relics upon which they feast do in fact extend the meanings of Thanksgiving beyond its designated day, grandmother's new body (politic) hovers somewhere between the spiritual and the macabre. The powerful symbolic meanings accruing to sacred relics do so because the people are dead. That can be parsed in several ways. Relics allow for the resurrection of a spiritual body in the sense that they betoken a new Communion, the symbolic body of Christ reanimating the bodies and spirits of the once-stolen and lost. But sustaining the lost by ingesting the (dead) relics of the feast makes for a decidedly ambiguous body politic. A momentary foray into the Gothic has the Primes attending the Thanksgiving feast as abjects, fed on dead remains. This would be the other, less savory interpretation of extending the feast to the day after Thanksgiving: It functions as a faded substitute, where the Primes receive the crumbs off the table. They have more than they could eat but lack the full presence of "black Caesar" at the actual feast, who is at once "full of turkey" and fully embodied as a participant in the celebration. The absent Primes ghost the full body of Caesar. This is not to absolve Stowe of the imputation that, for her, the fullest presence in a polity the black body can achieve is in terms of eating turkey, playing the fiddle, providing "jollity," and giggling with "joy and exultation" (401) at being acknowledged by Lady Lothrop and her husband. His "awe-struck obeisance" (401) here does not seem ironized. Nonetheless, the substitute feast, for all that it provides plenty of food, implies a serious deficit on grandmother's part. She sets out to rescue the Prime family's belly and heart by telling them the members would come to their aid: "the neighbors would all stand up for them" (412). This turns out to be wrong—in fact egregiously wrong, because one of the kidnappers, Eph Miller, *is* a neighbor, and grandmother is the one who has just named him (411). So while she approves of Sam Lawson's sentiment that "a woman's a woman, an' child'en's child'en, ef they be black" (407), giving the Prime family relics seems of a piece with the fallaciousness of the symbolic "all" she blithely puts forward as her own day-after-Thanksgiving proclamation. Aeconomia and political economy in pre–Civil War days operate in tandem to place under suspicion the very idea of the common good.

The substitute feast is as close as Stowe gets to admitting the limits to Badger largesse—not because they are not generous enough, but because they possess enough of the Commonwealth of Massachusetts to make commonwealth imaginable only on their terms. Grandmother and her helpers create multihued pies good for a multihued commonwealth. As the recipient of the relics of the feast, however, Aunt Nancy Prime is not herself a contributor. The sustenance of her body and her children's bodies depends on others. In the time frame of the novel, this paternalistic sense that the Badgers are in charge of feeding up the body politic does not necessarily pose a moral or political dilemma for Stowe. Pre–Civil War the Primes cannot unilaterally create a free commonwealth by themselves. This is no longer the case in 1869. To imagine the Thanksgiving chapter as some sort of solution to a fractured body politic during Reconstruction is to affirm the Badgers' continued legitimacy as moral and material guardians of commonwealth. Part of the narrative's ideological work here is to universalize the Badgers' generosity—to take it out of history altogether. As one of grandmother's pious Bible texts observes, the "poor shall never cease from out of the land" (393); there will always be a shiftless class, so there will always be a need for Badger open-handedness. This can also be stated the other way round. If shiftless people are to keep pestering the Badgers for turkey, cider, pies, and relics from the feast, and thus to keep alive their dominant role in the body politic, then the Badgers cannot bring about the commonwealth their actions seem aimed at accomplishing. The poor may not cease from out of the land.

Though an untold variety of pies get fed to the tribes, to the Primes, to the shiftless class, and to the cultural elites (Lady Lothrop, the minister), and though grandmother's kitchen work provides an important reconfiguration of the body politic as conceived by the male religiopolitical authority of the day, there cannot be an untold variety of kitchen workers. Aunt Nancy and Sam Lawson's wife and "Betty Poganut and Sally Wonsamug" (393) from the whole tribe require feeding if grandmother and Aunt Lois are to remain feeders. The relics given to the Prime family invoke a subterranean sense that the body politic would be better fed if Aunt Nancy's pies could contribute to a Thanksgiving commonwealth. But the narrative—and perhaps this is Stowe's Thanksgiving aporia—has already shut down that possibility in its extended meditation on the political economy of pies. The lineage of the pies, after all, is indisputably Anglo-Saxon: the "main stock" (390) which produces the untold variety of American pies is an English institution. Were those "thousand strictly American seedlings" thought numerous enough to include potential contributions from Aunt Nancy and Betty Poganut, that would still be to obey, rather than transform, this passage's logic of history, since it refers all diversity to variations on an English institution. The "boundless fertility of the feminine mind" seems to reach its limit at the question of whether the history of pie-making in America could accept Africanist or Native American roots—or berries. If the Badgers are to perform their task as the heart of the body politic, the untold variety of pies out of grandmother's kitchen requires a history centered on her lineage.

In April 1863, a few months before the tides of the Civil War turned at Gettysburg, Rose Terry Cooke published "My Thanksgiving." Like "An Old-Fashioned Thanksgiving" three decades later, it exploits the pathos of a soldier's unexpected return from war just in time to reaffirm and intensify the spirit of Thanksgiving. Joe, missing and presumed dead, turns up to find Thanksgiving dinner on the table; a wedding joins him and Annie, the narrator, a week later. The story is in part a call-to-arms: its first words are Joe's "I must go" (to war), followed by Granny's wits-wandering but of course benedictory "who died for us!"[17] The story dispatches Joe to war as a type of Christ, a relationship later underscored by the severe injuries he sustains at

Antietam—pierced by bullets, his leg badly broken—and in his unlooked-for return/resurrection. No matter "how battered or broken, no matter how wan and thin," says Annie, "he was back again!" (645).

But the story's more compelling, if subtler, aspect is its call to imagine a broken body politic through the symbolic female body and then, like Stowe's grandmother, to attempt to repair it at the Thanksgiving table. Annie's romantic history—her relationship with Joe and with the nameless man she foolishly loved before him—maps a political history of the United States. With her first beau, she adopts the "girl's idea that constancy is a virtue" (637), but it is an "ill-placed . . . love" (637) for a bad prospective union. "I threw myself away on a hard, cool, selfish, imperious nature" (637), Annie admits. It left "frightful scars on heart and mind" (637). After being abandoned, she is "broken in health and spirit down to the very dust" (637). From that perspective, her ill-placed love and compromised body has to be associated with "myriads of us all over this struggling, bleeding country" (637)—"us" being women who, like Annie, are suffering from the loss of loved ones. The antebellum Union is figured as a cruel romantic liaison in which the South's perfidious and imperious nature pulls the wool over the eyes of the "eager, faithful passion of youth" (637). The "bitter herb of knowledge" (637) comes too late to prevent separation/secession and the emotional, physical, and geopolitical scars it causes. The final restorative union with Joe, her "heart's desire" (645), extends a symbolic resolution: The "house" where she was taken in after her parents died is now "home" (645).

The house and its inhabitants play a complex role in representing the antebellum United States. Though adopted into a loving household—Cousin Martha, Joe's mother, is a "loving woman" (637) who acts as surrogate mother to the orphan (637)—Annie shuns the opportunity for a more perfect union with Joe, giving it up for the "wasted" (637) love for, and "dread" (637) of, union with the attractive but treacherous other. Even Cousin Martha mothers her only in a "certain imperfect sense" (637). Despite possessing all the "homely flavor of a New England farm life" (637), Martha, like Annie, is subject to waste—the "wasting consumption" (637) in this case. Her grave illness allows Cooke to align her dying body with the "bleeding country." "Three long years" of suffering in that "racked frame" (638) bring "pains like the torture of rack and wheel in every wasted limb, the dreadful gush of scarlet blood, the utter prostration of arterial life" (638). Three years of war are writ bloodily on Cousin Martha's body. Consumption is a "mock" (638): it constantly deceives by giving fits of "sudden but false strength" (638). A failing body (politic) that from time to time mimics life implies three years of turbulent conflict, and perhaps too the many efforts to repair the Union that preceded it. Cousin Martha cannot make the household whole. The story is perhaps at its most remarkable in intimating the diseased nightmare hidden behind the homely walls of antebellum New England farm life. In an odd moment, Annie shrieks when she looks into Joe's face as he sets off to war and sees a "dead face" (636) that becomes "cold, rigid, ghastly" (636).

The Thanksgiving dinner that ends the story is necessarily transformational. Several major plot threads weave together here. First, Annie, making sure that "no poor soul I knew of, within our township, should go without a good dinner to-day" (644), has a "big basket of pies, and chickens, and tongues" (644) delivered to the needy. This conventionally charitable action takes on special emphasis in the story since Joe has charged her with making sure that her grief does not interfere with the "usual routine of home" (640). Indeed, Joe's charges to her—keeping the farm going, looking after the poor, and not omitting to keep Thanksgiving—seem intended to address several of her problems. Domesticity will help to heal her earlier "frightful scars," steady her in her grief at losing Joe, and counter the "unconscious egotism" (638) of her "self-absorbed" (637) character. Taking over the farm's dairy business and maintaining its "reputation for the best butter sent to Boston" (641) effects a transposition in which Annie steps into (the now dead) Cousin Martha's caring role. Joe's return seems to reorganize the Thanksgiving table. His "manly" (645) self, which, ghostlike, Annie had imagined seated at the table, reappears in the flesh to preside over the changes he has wrought in her—a restoration of conventional gender roles ratified by his Christ-like return from the dead, which collapses the ghost supper and brings four living bodies into a new Communion around the table.

But the Thanksgiving dinner unexpectedly transforms Annie's role. She begins to symbolize possibilities of national and political reconciliation as a counterweight to Joe's spiritual function, which is projected entirely outside the political schema of the story. He fights for, but cannot represent, a polity in flux, because he is wholly constant. His "unflagging service" to Annie never varies. "Blessed is the woman who loves a man better than she is!" (639), Annie remarks, making it plain in the next sentence that Joe's Christ-like "self-denying love" gives to her "even as He gave Himself" (639). Annie is the one who needs to awaken to new responsibilities and recognize the flawed would-be union that left such frightful scars. She can represent change. Responsible for healing Joe's broken body and entering into a loving union with him, Annie now becomes the fabricator of a new and stronger body politic made from her experience of how to recover from loss. That body extends to the South. Her newfound love for Joe and then separation from him is what allows her to feel "that even at this deadly crisis we could hold open arms to rebel women, and weep with them in the divine reconciliation of a mutual sorrow" (637). Those open arms offer some hope of re-membering the "racked frame" of this "bleeding" country in which, at a time when "rebellion was higher-handed than ever" (640), individuals such as Joe are "broken," regiments "cut to pieces" (641), and women such as Annie hold "bleeding hands" (643) against heaven. This rebellion of the hands against the body (politic) is what makes the "big basket of pies" she makes for the town's poor, with its metaphoric sense of feeding a commonwealth, into a belly-and-its-members-type fable about restoring the cooperative functions necessary to a healthy body.

Opening arms to rebel women is an oddly destabilizing moment in the story. It confuses Joe's symbolic role. Though Annie witnesses Joe's resurrection, and in one ecstatic moment at the Thanksgiving table "knew nothing" until she finds "both his arms round [her]" (645), she and the "myriads" of women like her who suffer loss seem more capable of performing Christ's loving role by reaching across to their enemies. The fact that "now was the time for men" (640) to protect the Union makes it difficult for the story to extend Joe's Christ-like function very far. He cannot fight high-handed (male) rebels and use his arms to embrace them at the same time. Annie's ability to do so grants her and other women what the story appears to tout as their profound political responsibility to regenerate a polity torn up by men. In fact her loving arms *upset* the story's attempts to align her with a nation's history as she, and it, move from self-delusion to a new commonwealth. The problem is that the rebel women she symbolically embraces are not really rebels; women from the North and South suffer from war but they are not *at* war. Nowhere is this clearer than in the fact that all of them suffer identically; their experience has no political or even moral vector. Suffering when one's love is fighting for "the good cause" (64) is no different from suffering when one's love is fighting in the service of treachery. Putting arms around rebel women could never underwrite the restoration of a body politic because there is nothing political about the suffering of women.

To put this another way, at the end of the story the Thanksgiving table opens a space for a new and whole body politic figured by lovers reunited and by the anguished women around the nation that Annie symbolically embraces. But there would appear to be no way for rebel men to appear at this feast. They have been expunged along with the deceitful lover whose absence is the only way for Annie to heal from her frightful scars. It is possible that Joe's putting "both his arms" round Annie at the Thanksgiving table is meant to resolve this dilemma by virtue of inviting rebel women to look beyond their own perfidious lovers to the faithfulness displayed by northern men. Joe waits for years for Annie to come to her senses. If so, it is difficult to see why the suffering of southern women for their treacherous men would be equivalent to that of northern women. The Thanksgiving table stages what seems to be an irreconcilable conflict in Cooke's symbolic schema. Suffering women who share, as it were, a common body all appear to be welcome at this table. But in order to construct a common body politic, the story would have to acknowledge and confront the fact that rebel women are complicit in the rebellion that is raging as Cooke writes—that southern women have actively seceded from the table she wishes to set.

Of all the stories collected in Cooke's *Huckleberries*, "How Celia Changed Her Mind," ending with its "old maids' Thanksgivin'" (315), has deservedly received the most acclaim.[18] Like "My Thanksgiving," it enacts a feast for suffering women. But its effectiveness has much to do with the fact that it caps a series of Thanksgiving stories in *Huckleberries*—"An Old-Fashioned Thanksgiving" is the first—which set up expectations that "Celia" almost entirely collapses. By the time "Celia" begins, the topos of Thanksgiving is overdetermined. Indeed, these first stories iterate the same plots and ideas so many times that the topos of Thanksgiving seems to *become* overdetermination. As though recycling the much earlier "My Thanksgiving," "An Old-Fashioned Thanksgiving" ends with a feast, a wedding, and a soldier's return. In "A Double Thanksgiving," Joe (Hazard), like John in "An Old-Fashioned Thanksgiving" (and therefore like the Joe of "My Thanksgiving"), returns on Thanksgiving Day after being thought lost (at sea). His story of shipwreck and restoration "proved to be the old story."[19] The Thanksgiving blessing given by his wife, Sally, is thereby doubled; his is tripled, since he returns to find twins awaiting him. This multiplying effect continues into the last words of the story. When children "leaned against his knees, there was no story they liked to hear or he loved to tell so well as the story of his 'Double Thanksgiving'" (258). Here an array of repetitions (story/story, liked/loved) and internal rhymes (tell/well, leaned/knees) sets the stage for the self-reflexive gesture that concludes the story: it states its own title, capitals and all, as if he doubles for Cooke and we double for the children. No wonder Joe, turning from his first sight of the twins, laughs "'T aint fair to double up things on a feller so" (258).

The next story, "Home Again," replays this away-and-back plot. Joe (Gillett) goes to New York, gives "every power of his life to the acquisition of money."[20] He becomes a rich banker, enters into a "heartless union" (274), loses all his money (as well as his wife and two babies, a tragic counterpart to Joe Hazard's twins), realizes that his money was but "fairy gold" (276), and finally returns, a prodigal son, poorer but newly blest in spirit. The story builds Joe's growing infatuation with wealth around Thanksgivings missed. It was his mother's "one hope and thought that Joe should come home to Thanksgiving the first time" (266)—to the "one home-day" (267) of New

England—but "year after year passed by, and still he did not come" (269). The ensuing wreck of his finances—yet another "old story" (275) of riches to rags—leads at last to a Thanksgiving return to his mother at the old farm and, a year later, another "double celebration" (282): Thanksgiving and the seemingly inevitable wedding, this time to his childhood sweetheart. The story ends with yet another Thanksgiving, this time experienced by Tommy, the village fool, whose function is (like Granny's in "My Thanksgiving") to speak elliptical truths and serve as "chorus" (262) to the village. In fact no one defines the story's iterative underpinnings better. Tommy performs his "daily duties" (265) well, asks Mrs. Gillett a "daily question" (265) about when Joe will return, and sings hymns so often that Joe likens him mockingly to "an old cracked hurdy-gurdy, morning,' noon, an' night" (264). His death, which concludes the tale, has Cooke's title "Home Again" once more echoing through the story's last words. Tommy is "goin' hum [home]" (282) to the Lord; he is "a-goin' to keep Thanksgivin' 'long o' Him" (283).

The first three Thanksgiving stories of *Huckleberries* (as well as the earlier "My Thanksgiving") represent the celebration in terms of permutations on an "old story." Joe and John are lost to battle; Joe Hazard is lost at sea; Joe Gillett loses himself to the pursuit of wealth before enduring the "losses" (278) that finally set him right. The first three put themselves on the line for the good of country and family. Joe Gillett has to learn not to put himself first. All of them return on Thanksgiving to an overabundance of blessings, to old farms, loved ones, and weddings. "Home Again," as its title suggests, typifies this iterative strategy. It begins as if determined to tell a different story—the Joe who does not come home for Thanksgiving, the Joe who thinks that he does not have to, as his mother says, "work the farm just as father done before ye" (259)—only to find that the "old story," the Thanksgiving message and plot, draws him inexorably back. The self-reflexive endings of "A Double Thanksgiving" and "Home Again" acknowledge that invoking Thanksgiving comes with a mandate: to tell the same story, either because a writer could hardly forego the pathos and drama of an unexpected Thanksgiving return, or because returning to the old farm satisfies a late nineteenth-century nostalgia for rural retreats where money has supposedly not "built up a wall of separation" (278) between human beings. "Home Again" makes that latter interpretation more or less explicit. In New York, Joe finds "his money returned to him again and again, doubled and redoubled, till he was almost a rich man" (270). But those doublings are mere "speculations" (274) and fairy gold. To go "home again," to iterate the old Thanksgiving story, is to break through the wall of separation. Tommy's Thanksgiving suggests one more possibility: that plot permutations demonstrate the incompleteness of earthly Thanksgivings, which are all doubled, or ghosted, by the final "goin' hum" to the Lord. The earthly home is never quite home; New England's "one home-day," coming around every year, reminds us in the end of the one eternal Thanksgiving. That would be the only day that truly changes the plot of going home. All else is a substitute.

This reading comports with a widespread sense among scholars that Cooke is a committed Christian whose "evangelical thought . . . informs [her] fiction."[21] Consequently she believes that the "divinely ordained nature of woman required the shelter of a home where, as wife and mother, a woman can undertake the 'legitimate business of a married,' a 'genuine,' woman."[22] The main problem Cooke's female characters face is not "their lack of political power, their economic dependence, or their limited access to education," but the evil of individual men like Joe Gillett or the treacherous lover of "My Thanksgiving."[23] Cooke's Protestant ideology allows her to shape a strategy of "literary housekeeping": It offers a way for women's domestic work to take part in debates about the "moral health and civic welfare of the nation."[24] Moments such as Joe's resurrection from the dead or Tommy's eternal Thanksgiving with the Lord, however, would seem to inscribe clear limits to the sort of political work literary housekeeping could hope to achieve. There could be no earthly way to repair a broken body or stage a perfect Thanksgiving if the body and grace of Christ signifies the only true power. Whatever political symbolism the domestic sphere accrued would always be circumscribed by a desire to return women to the divine sanctum of home, and ideologies of home would always find a more comfortable (and comforting) symbolic fit with a heavenly home.

"My Thanksgiving" and the first three Thanksgiving stories of *Huckleberries* do not fit smoothly into such a conception. To begin with, taking charge of the political economy of the household while their men are away at war allows Annie and Hannah to transform their domestic obligations. To the extent that feeding the body (of the family, of the poor) demands their partnership with the marketplace—trading butter in Boston, raising and marketing chickens—they move beyond a merely moral concern with civic welfare to enact a body politic and aeconomia. Participating in the marketplace becomes women's moral concern. Nonetheless, the very logic of the unexpected and joyful return—Joe and John from war, Joe Hazard and Joe Gillett from trade—curtails the space available for an enduring kitchen commonwealth. It is not so much that the men's homecoming terminates the women's activities. It is that the unbridled joy of a man's return constitutes aeconomia in terms of incompletion, loss, and even despair. In emotional and dramatic terms, the plots of these stories create a fairly unambiguous yearning for the reappearance of the male body that will make the domestic space—however radically reconfigured—whole again. Mrs. Gillett's and

Cornelia's decades-long patience in waiting for their prodigal son and lover in "Home Again" is exemplary in this regard. Cornelia is a "superb and serious woman," one of those who can "make even a poor and dreary house into a real home by their presence" (280). But the real home cannot be realized until Joe returns. The story bends all of its considerable powers toward insisting on what does *not* happen over twenty years of missed Thanksgivings. One year Mrs. Gillett even "sold her turkey and her squash" because there was "no Thanksgiving story or song in her lonely heart" (268). His return marks the first time in twenty years that there would "indeed be a Thanksgiving at the Gillett farm" (279).

The shift away from aeconomia is underscored in this story by Tommy's appearance on the evening before Thanksgiving, when Cornelia sits, sewing, across the hearth from Joe. Tommy supplies the requisite material to transform Joe's homecoming into a parable of the wandering soul returning to Christ. Joe is the prodigal son, for whom Mrs. Gillett has "ben an' killed the fatted calf,—thet is to say, the turkey" (281). Here the parable of the prodigal son and Cooke's plot of Thanksgiving double for each other. Joe's completion of the secular plot completes the spiritual plot of return and redemption. To grasp this is to understand that the story of the unexpected Thanksgiving return is not so much a formula as the compelling requirement of an underlying spiritual narrative. By the time "Home Again" draws to its end on the heels of two prior emotionally satisfying Thanksgiving homecomings, the massing of references to Joe's many missed Thanksgivings exerts an undeniable pressure for the story to resolve correctly, which is to say, expectedly. The constant drumbeat of references to what Joe is failing to do surely persuades us that his return is being deferred so that it will generate a still greater emotional power when his homecoming, our desire for a plot resolution, and the completion of the spiritual story of redemption all occur at the same moment. Whatever women's role is in the political economy of the household while the men are away, it could only ever be temporary, a placeholder, while we await the resolution of the plot, which drives us forward in "Home Again" through an emotionally fraught experience of deferral and omission to the eve before Thanksgiving when Cornelia sits by the hearth, sewing, and to the next Thanksgiving, when she gave her heart "openly into his keeping" (281)—and when she and Joe and presumably readers can proclaim: "Now I *am* at home again" (282).

"How Celia Changed Her Mind" is at its most extraordinary in taking the plot of Thanksgiving and its associated cultural fables about (men) coming home to turkeys, family, nation, and God, and letting them run amok. If there is nothing more predictable than Joe's "unexpected" Thanksgiving return in "Home Again," "Celia" is wholly unexpected insofar as it ends up as a Thanksgiving story at all. Along with the village of Bassett whose astounded inhabitants "opened eyes and mouth both" (314) at the prospect of an old maids' Thanksgiving, readers might be shocked by the fact that the story misses so many of the appropriate cues. Previous Cooke stories set up their Thanksgiving plots early. Joe in "My Thanksgiving" tells Annie "don't omit to keep Thanksgiving" (640) before he goes off to war. "A Double Thanksgiving" informs us that "by November Sally began to make ready for Joe; but the month went on and on without him" (253–54). A full year passes before her expectation is fulfilled. And "Home Again" structures its entire narrative around skipped Thanksgivings. A Thanksgiving denouement therefore ghosts the development of these earlier stories; we anticipate (and maybe long for) the drama its arrival will bring. The one moment of anticipation in "Celia"—"I'd hold a Thanksgiving Day all to myself ef I'd escaped" (299) being an old maid, announces Celia early in the story—works in an entirely different way because her marriage to Deacon Everts seems to erase the conditions under which such a feast could take place. Married, and under her new husband's starvation regime, she can no longer "get such viands as would satisfy a healthy appetite" (305), let alone prepare a feast "all to myself." Thanksgiving in this story arrives apropos of very few textual cues and therefore exerts extra pressure on whatever interpretive structures readers have fashioned to this point. When the "old maids' Thanksgivin'" (315) does take place in the final scene of the story, it occurs contrariwise. Celia throws it to celebrate escaping marriage, not being an old maid. Moreover, it sabotages the expected plot of unexpected return. It only takes place at all because the male figure who looms largest in Celia's life cannot possibly come back. The ending therefore poses its resolution of the narrative as a problematic. Up to this point in *Huckleberries*—really, from the time of Cooke's Civil War story—the unexpected Thanksgiving return has functioned as an anticipated and hoped-for resolution to a well-understood schema. Here the issue seems reversed: What is the plot that this wholly unexpected return to the Thanksgiving motif resolves?

The beginnings of an answer to that question can be found in this story's rescripting of the bioeconomic value of food in constituting a body politic. In Cooke's prior Thanksgiving stories, the appearance of the turkey at the table accomplishes gendered cultural work, positioning men in powerful relationships to the food being served and to its cultural meanings. Kitchen work produces food that is not for men alone, but it cannot seem to forgo the pressing attention of men. "How Celia Changed Her Mind" upsets this formula. For one thing, men occupy the symbolic realm of food much more forcefully than in any previous story. When, at the beginning of the story, Parson Stearns arrives home "tired and hungry and cross" (287), his wife not only has the "kettle boiling to make him a cup of tea on the spot" (287), she almost force-feeds him in her rush to "assuage his irritation" (287). She "replenished his plate with stew, and cut for him more than one segment of the crisp, fresh apple-pie, and urged upon him . . . squares of new cheese" (287). Deacon Everts bookends men's control over the kitchen in this story. "I have n't no intention to starve ye" (306), he says, but, as the double negative implies, his believing that it is "hullsome to get up from your victuals hungry" (306) creates what Celia calls a "poor-house [of] home." Like other "intemperate brutes" to whom most married women entrust their "whole existence" (308), Stearns and Everts overset a "healthy appetite" (305). Their appetites for food and for denying food go to extremes.

One of the oddest resonances of Celia's final joyful directive, "let's go to work at the victuals" (315), is that it restores to her a symbolic realm that she was supposed to have had anyway. If "My Thanksgiving" and "An Old-Fashioned Thanksgiving" extend women's kitchen work into the marketplace, this story seems to do little more than recoup the kitchen. Its ending might even be read as a fairy-tale conclusion to a cruel but still comic plot of disorderly overthrow made right, as if the feast merely redeems the problems that arise when a man mismanages the household economy. It is a woman's task to make a poor-house back into a home. Celia's feast, however, takes place on defamiliarizing terms. It restores her to the culturally powerful female-domestic realm of food, nutrition, and nurturance, but it does so now in full knowledge of the fact that this realm is alienable. In the body politic this story shapes prior to the feast, men control food as a material resource and as a source of cultural power: women hurry to feed them and/ or starve. We can think of this as a jaundiced version of "The Belly and the Members." Occupying the belly, as it were, men coerce what should be a harmonious interrelationship between the various members of a healthy body (politic). From this perspective, the story quietly reinstates the rebellion of the members against the belly as a legitimate aspiration. It enacts the same fable on a wholly different premise, resurrecting abstract principles of harmonious relationships between contributing members, but doing so on the basis of reassigned roles. Displacing men, the final feast positions Celia and seven "old maids" as a communal belly waiting to go to work at the victuals. Stated in more conventional terms: Familiar kitchen functions take on unfamiliar meanings when no longer performed in relationship to what men require of domesticity.

Like previous stories, "Celia" sets out to recast the symbolic properties of the Thanksgiving table. "We Yankees are conservative at Thanksgiving if nowhere else, and like to gather our own people only about the family hearth" (314), the narrator notes—which is why Celia has only "once or twice shared the turkeys of her more fortunate neighbors" (314). Plots of Thanksgiving typically ground the concept of "our own people" in heteronormativity and in kinship ties while seeking to reconstruct the idea of the family in order to model a broader body politic. Under the benevolent aegis of a male-female pairing, for example, "My Thanksgiving" quietly opens a space for rebel women, while the grandmother in Stowe's story extends the Thanksgiving feast to include the newly rescued Primes. But "Celia" is nowhere more striking than in making the symbolic body (politic) assembled around the Thanksgiving table all women—and, what is more, abject, or at least once-abject, women. Celia argues that there "ain't one of the hull [whole] caboodle [of men] but what despises an onmarried woman!" (287), a position with which, at the beginning of the story, she agrees. She hates old maids "worse than p'ison" (284) because "you might as well be a dog as an old maid" (285). Old maids in fact "ain't nothing nor nobody" (284). At the feast she embraces the "nothing" that she was—she does so deliberately by calling herself an old maid, even though, as Sally points out, she technically no longer is—and in so doing transforms "p'ison" into "victuals." She repossesses her subjecthood; she can "keep Thanksgivin' to-day with my hull soul" (315). She comes home to herself. The final feast is a Thanksgiving for once-abject women, not an abject Thanksgiving: It is joyful, vibrant, full-souled. One of the fiercest twists of this story is that these old maids who have lived on next to nothing turn out to be less abject than the married women attending their family Thanksgivings—most of them, the narrator observes, enduring lives of "sleepless exhaustion" (308) and even "constant terror" (308). In this respect, Celia's previous exclusions from her neighbors' Thanksgivings may not be so unfortunate after all. The patriarchal family enacts a distressingly violent body politic.

Fetterley and Pryse argue that Celia's Thanksgiving feast devoted entirely to women should be read as the blueprint for an "alternate institution."[25] The story's difference from Cooke's prior Thanksgiving/wedding plots makes that interpretation plausible. Celia's wedding appears in the middle of the narrative—and she throws her feast to celebrate her husband's death and her reacquisition of old-maidenhood. Rosabel, the young woman Celia helps to leave the village, weds, returns—and dies. The feast itself abandons kinship ties entirely. The appearance at this table of "Sarah Gillett" (314) and the "ancient twins" (314) who "lived together on next to nothing" (314) seem to explicitly counter the interpellating function of twin babies (Joe Hazard's, Joe Gillett's) and of Mrs. Gillett's "double celebration" as they call men back to, and into, home. And crucially, the feast discards the topos of a man presiding over the table and its common variant, awaiting the presence of a man to preside over the table. Here Celia "bloomed at the head of the board"

(314). Her newfound authority may well signify a "social reproduction of the queer."[26] Her Thanksgiving blessing—"I'm so thankful to be an old maid ag'in!"—certainly promises to disrupt heteronormative relations, which rely in part on the "abject gratitude" average women show for the "least attention" (296) from the "intemperate brutes" who dominate them. And Celia certainly looks to reproduce this queer Thanksgiving. "So long as I live," she announces, "I'm goin' to keep an old maids' Thanksgivin'" (315), something that may well continue if her plan to adopt and bring up Rosabel's two orphaned children to be "dyed-in-the-wool old maids" (315) comes to pass.

The potentially subversive force of a queer and alternate Thanksgiving is underscored by the fact that this one is billed as the very first. Bassett has never seen an old maids' Thanksgiving, and Celia has "never before . . . celebrated this old New England day of solemn revel" (314). It is a first Thanksgiving to replace, perhaps, the enduring mythos of "the first Thanksgiving," with its blithe embrace of interracial comity and shared natural resources and with its actual affirmation of patriarchal power. As a new "first Thanksgiving," this one reveals the sequence of Thanksgivings preceding Celia's feast to have evolved a generic plot formula that, as it accreted through doubled and redoubled versions of itself, seemed intent on assuring readers that it will happen this way again, that there is no room in it for "firsts." Upon reaching a true "first"—Celia at the head of the board, a queer Thanksgiving composed entirely of women—it is plausible to look back on this pattern of doubling as a careful replication of the very process of social reproduction. Patriarchal power and its attendant ideologies iterate the same plot over and over until that plot seems to compel belief in benevolent male characters; in a female desire to make and remake the domestic space, emotionally fortified and ideologically consecrated by the blessed return of a man; and in a body politic, metaphorizing the nation, rooted in the structure of the patriarchal family. Celia's first feast enables us to see how far we have been led astray, how far we might have been led into yearning for a man to reoccupy a position of power.

For Celia's feast to be truly alternate, however, it must effect a complete rupture with the past; it must be an *other* Thanksgiving, not *another* Thanksgiving. The structure of *Huckleberries* makes this approach suspect. Cooke's first Thanksgiving stories are cumulative. Plots of earlier stories underwrite Joe Gillett's attempts to get home again, and if the collection were to end here, we might think of this story as the fulfilment of a transtextual plot. As unexpected as Celia's feast is, it can legitimately be seen not as rupture but as the collection's final iteration of its Thanksgiving topos. From this perspective, the story is not a free-standing artifact, effecting its meanings from difference alone, but the collection's capstone feast, the one that the entire collection has actually been leading toward. The capstone seems askew, to be sure, but this may be because the sweet homecoming (again) in "Home Again" tempts us to foreclose the emerging plot of Thanksgiving and thus miss its full unfolding, which can only be glimpsed when Celia's final/first feast takes place. Troping itself in its final gesture, revealing itself to be part of a plot that quite suddenly acquires the capacity to end differently, *the* plot of Thanksgiving we thought we had grasped through the end of "Home Again" consequently begins to unravel into *a* plot, which may in fact be only a part of a still larger plot of Thanksgiving that also includes Celia's. Social reproduction is not inexorable; recountings of the same plot are not the same, but cumulative; and subsequent versions of preceding plots may offer room for "changing one's mind." So Joe Hazard's joy at his blessed doubles (homecoming/twins) is commensurate with and points toward the double doubles at Celia's feast (the "ancient twins," Rosabel's two children who are about to get a home, Celia finding herself). But the firsts at Celia's feast also raise in retrospect the possibility that previous depictions of joyful Thanksgiving returns, usually in the context of some form of wedded bliss, might have been outliers.

Celia's Thanksgiving is alternate or cumulative depending on how one positions it within the entire array of Thanksgiving stories in *Huckleberries* (and before). Within the context of the story, a feast of and for old maids recognizes, and prioritizes, the femaleness of the female body, thoroughly abject outside of the institution of marriage and even more particularly within. From this perspective, women stand no chance of celebrating themselves and each other—finding their "hull [whole] soul" (315) as an individual in the company of other like-minded and like-experienced individuals—unless they feast without men. Understood as the capstone of Cooke's Thanksgiving plots, the story participates in that important function of so many Thanksgiving representations, which is to move bodies into the realm of abstraction where they can signify a reimagined national body. From this perspective, Celia's Thanksgiving table makes whole a body politic that would always remain incomplete if the people reintroduced to it in an effort to compose a "hull soul" were only men such as Joe, broken from war, or Joe Gillett, "haggard, bent" (280) from a lifetime of trying to double and redouble money. That act of reorganization can still be read as woman-centered. Celia turns out to be a better household manager than the food-extremists Stearns and Everts, and her feast opens symbolic spaces that hitherto have only been implicit in scenes of joyful returns. The crucial twist is that Celia's feast makes its argument for a new body politic on the same bioeconomic ground as Stowe: It participates in a cultural realm saturated with political economic meaning rather than attempting to write the very first Thanksgiving, as if all of its precedents had to be banished rather than redeemed.

6

RECONSTRUCTING THE "FRUIT SUBLIME" IN DUNBAR-NELSON'S "MR. BAPTISTE"

Barter and the Political Economy of the Tropical Fruit Trade

"Titee" resurrects and adds a happy ending to a story Alice Dunbar-Nelson had published in *Violets and Other Tales* (1895). In the later version young Titee, having broken his arm trying to help an "old man exhausted from cold and hunger," as well as a "tramp cow, old and turned adrift, too," does not die.[1] Perhaps Dunbar-Nelson felt the need to celebrate one act of open-heartedness amid so many stories about dispossession, penury, and displacement: Tony's wife, "sent . . . forth in the world penniless" (33) after losing her livelihood and her social and legal status (for she is not Tony's wife); Little Miss Sophie, "starving herself to death" (149) for the man who probably abandoned her; Sister Josepha, one of the "scraps of French and American civilization" (157) thrown into a convent to live out her life in tedium; the "little fruit-eater" (118), Mr. Baptiste, losing his life in a dock strike; M'sieu Fortier, who loses his job playing violin at the opera when it is bought up by an American "syndicate" that wants to run it as a "guarantee business, with a strictly financial basis" (76), and who, to make ends meet, is then forced to sell his "exquisite" (73) Cremona to the wealthy Courcey. The fact that Courcey ends up returning it to M'sieu Fortier—it was a "whim with me, a passion with you" (82) he says in graceful acknowledgment of M'sieu Fortier's superior claim on the instrument—barely disguises the violinist's desperate straits. He still has no job, and the socioeconomic transformations reshaping the New Orleans landscape on a strictly financial basis run by anonymous syndicates would seem to ensure that he will continue to be overlooked.

Dunbar-Nelson's stories often exhibit a comprehensive discomfort with the arrival of modernity. Courcey's friend accuses him of being one of those "nineteenth-century vandals" (74) subject to the "sordid, mercenary spirit of the world" (81); a bayou with modern bridges and boat houses demonstrates the "ruthless vandalism of the improving idea" (86). At such moments these stories strike a note of plaintive elegy for lost or passing times and for the "small, weak folks" who suffer in them, which scholars have often dismissed in the work of northeastern regionalists as counterworld thinking—a desire to return to a nation less sordid and less mercenary, and therefore more communal, homogenous, small-market, more accepting of idiosyncrasy and residual folkways. In many ways "Mr. Baptiste" seems exemplary. At the heart of the story is a unique kitchen economy. Mr. Baptiste subsists by picking up free (spoiled) fruit at the docks and bartering it for cooked food in the kitchens of an extensive clientele of New Orleans housewives. By the end of the story, these long-lasting arrangements have been made to seem archaic. Swamped by titanic forces of history and associated acts of vandalism—the dock strike during which machinery belonging to "Negro stevedores" (120) gets sabotaged—Mr. Baptiste loses his subsistence and then his life. Scrapped by the processes of historical change, he is, like M'sieu Fortier and Sophie, an abject. He finds himself disposed of like the discards of the tropical fruit trade. The story's last sentence dispassionately and laconically consigns his body to oblivion: "It was finally dropped unnamed into Potter's Field."

But if Mr. Baptiste is one more of the thrown-away or set-adrift scraps of New Orleans, the story that bears his name shapes a strategy of retrieval—though not nostalgia—for the abject histories, discourses, and indeed economic systems his life and death implicate. It pushes us toward acts of historical reconstruction. His free enterprise—collecting unwanted fruit—ramify through histories of labor disputes and the antebellum trade in free labor, which is to say unpaid slave labor. The story also affords a remarkable rewriting of the Caribbeanist discourse at work in Stowe's *Pearl* as, from the islanded margin of the northern United States, Stowe set out to define New England economic and moral values before and during the crisis of the Civil War. "Mr. Baptiste" brings together the material history of the New Orleans fruit trade with what I term the fruit sublime: a matrix of ideas and metaphors connecting the extravagant tropical fruit-production of Caribbean lands to the orderly and disciplined procedures of US-style capitalism, as well as to long-standing projects aimed at bringing Caribbean lands under US control. The fruit sublime implies abjection in at least two ways: (1) a trade so rich that it can afford to throw nearly ripe fruit away, and (2) a richly imagined Caribbeanist discourse in the writings of US visitors to tropical lands that elides or ignores the history of US involvement in Caribbean lands in favor of fabulous islands crowded with fabulous fruits into which their populations more or less vanish. "Mr. Baptiste" recalls and resists that vanishing by making discarded people and histories an insistent part of its narrative. At the heart of that strategy are the "back door" (113) barter arrangements the title character makes with women in the kitchens of New Orleans.

"Mr. Baptiste" commences with an uneasy backpedaling. "He might have had another name; we never knew," observes the narrator. "Some one had christened him Mr. Baptiste long ago in the dim past, and it sufficed. No one had ever been known who had the temerity to ask him for another cognomen" (111). Such moments might suggest a cusp-of-modernism epistemological and narrative crisis to which Mr. Baptiste's other name falls victim. The narrator seems either culpable or muddled. The most puzzling issue is not what Mr. Baptiste's other name is or why the narrator does not know the name. It is why the narrator believes he might even have another name. The narrator avers that "no one had ever been known" to ask a question that, since no one has thought to ask it, might not be a worthwhile question in the first place. Why does the narrator want to make an issue of the unknowable? There are two obvious logical approaches to this question. One is that the story assigns its main character to metaphysical mysteries. The story is hardly reticent here. He is christened Baptiste, spending much of his time near a river; he is "like the Son of Man" (111–12); wounded on his temple and killed, he is surrounded by "fishmen" (122) and dropped unnamed into a tomb. "Oh, mon Dieu, mon Dieu!" (122) wails a woman at the moment of his death. Moreover, he is an Adamic figure, a "fruit-eater" (118), his the "first life" (124) lost in the strike along the Mississippi. It is possible to think of the narrator, having eaten like all humans of the tree of (imperfect) knowledge, shaping a spiritual narrative around Mr. Baptiste, a type of Christ—a martyr, an unknown man of sorrows. If so, the bitter codicil to the story makes his spiritual lineage sound like a jaundiced fantasy: This anonymous figure does not rise again.

Most scholars have followed a different line of inquiry when considering epistemological obstacles in Dunbar-Nelson's work. They have pinned them broadly to an issue faced by all regionalists marketing their wares to a mass urban audience—how does one explain the idiosyncratic folkways of a far-flung region to a city dweller?—and specifically to an issue faced by Dunbar-Nelson: how to convey the complex racial politics of New Orleans to an audience, largely white, that is unconversant with them. Kristina Brooks argues that Dunbar-Nelson's stories all depend on "hidden or coded local knowledge of the inter-connected relationship between race and ethnicity in Creole identity," so that a detail such as Mr. Baptiste's "wrinkled brown temple" might signify to the "perceptive—and mainly local-reader that the protagonist of her story is a Creole of color."[2] For Pamela Menke and Violet Harrington Bryan, reading Dunbar-Nelson's fiction demands "insider knowledge. . . . available only to those who share that same secret."[3] To "any reader knowledgeable about New Orleans culture" reading "Little Miss Sophie," the "words *dusky-eyed* would signify Miss Sophie was a quadroon," probably subject to the New Orleans institution of *plaçage*, wealthy white men keeping women of mixed race as mistresses.[4] The narrator's strange play with Mr. Baptiste's other name might index a complicated construction of race on the principle that having "another" name names him as Other. Perhaps he is passing. Or perhaps we are in a still more provisional situation where we cannot be sure what the racial signs we think we apprehend actually signify.[5]

The most perplexing epistemological conundrums of "Mr. Baptiste," however, arise from the narrator's confidently assertive introduction of economic history. "The Morgan steamships, as every one knows, ply between New Orleans and Central and South American ports, doing the major part of the fruit trade" (112), the narrator says. "Sometimes, you know, bananas and mangoes and oranges and citrons will half spoil . . . and the officers of the ships will give away stacks of fruit" (113). And though "many forgot afterwards whose was the first life lost in the struggle" (124) between the (white Irish American) longshoremen and the "Negro stevedores," our knowledge of the "fearsome war" itself is supposed to be faultless. "You remember, of course, how long the strike lasted" (123–24), announces the narrator. The narrative's rhetoric of certainty here opens an array of puzzling possibilities. What are the grounds, even in 1899, upon which one could confidently aver that "every one knows" about Morgan steamships? And who would know that officers on Morgan ships give away stacks of fruit? The phrase "you know" in this context might count as the sort of throwaway statement one interjects into conversation, meaning something more like "I know you do not know, but you do know this *now* because I am confiding in you." It signifies a desire for camaraderie rather than secure knowledge. Along the same lines, "as every one knows" could be construed as a friendly under-the-table narrative gesture, complimenting those who know and ensuring that those who are ignorant do know by the time they have completed the sentence. It is a familiar-enough rhetorical strategy for regionalists who have to introduce distant readers to unknown territory. Its underpinning assumption is that every one does *not* know about the unknown region but will soon know more.

"You remember, of course, how long the strike lasted" pursues a similar rhetorical strategy to very different ends. The problem here is not so much the specificity of the information we are supposed to remember but the fact that the sentence does not, with the narrator's usual spirit of congenial inclusiveness, help us out by writing something like "you remember, of course, the strike lasted two days." In the absence of such clues, "you" here could only designate a true insider and participant—someone who not only remembered the number but, because the narrator's "of course" bespeaks absolute surety, had very good cause to remember it. This form of knowing excludes virtually everyone while making uncompromisingly sure that everyone thus excluded is very much aware of it. The only logical response to that emphatic "of course" is an equally emphatic "of course we do not." That "of course" is therefore a provocation. It assumes we possess knowledge momentous enough to make ignorance of it risible. Since we do not have that knowledge, "of course" draws fresh attention to the narrative strategies that jolly along the ignorant, convincing them that they know more than they actually do. It draws attention, in short, to knowledge that has gone missing from the historical record, to the pressing question of why it has gone missing, and to the more or less comfortable "as every one knows" strategies that can be designed to circumvent the problem.

To the extent that we wish to become more like the "you" who does know the inside story, the narrative urges us toward research and investigation. But this solution is complicated by two factors (beyond the mere difficulty of pursuing such research). One is that there is no single answer to the question of "how long the strike lasted." There were multiple dock strikes in New Orleans in the 1890s. Dunbar-Nelson seems to have in mind primarily the October 1894 dockworkers' strike in which white union members responded to owners hiring nonunion black longshoremen (the "scabs," as the striking Irishmen contemptuously characterize them) by assaulting them as they stowed cotton and other cargo. Five men were shot, one drowned; six ships were involved. After a series of work stoppages, serious trouble resumed in March 1895 when white strikers assaulted black workers on two ships.[6] The fact that the story does not specify which strike, however, opens up a number of possible historical contexts. The 1892 New Orleans general strike organized under the aegis of the American Federation of Labor was better known because strikers of all races stood in solidarity despite the provocations (racial slurs and threats) of business leaders and the city's Democratic administration. The 1894–95 strikes brought to an end fifteen years of relative racial amity and cooperation in New Orleans labor movements. One correct answer to the narrator's question is therefore "three" (days in October 1894); another is "about a month" (white stevedores were on strike from mid-February to mid-March 1895). But the sort of invested and committed "you" who "of course" knows how long these strikes lasted would seem capable of recalling that it was preceded by fifteen years of complicated labor history. The knowledge we need in order to emulate that "you" does not conclude once we have sorted through the historical record of just one among many strikes.

The question of which strike "the" strike refers us to is further complicated by what appear to be deliberate misrepresentations about shipping lines. In "Mr. Baptiste," the "war" begins dockside where stevedores, or screwmen, are compressing cotton into the hold of a "White Star steamer" (120). But the White Star line—its most famous vessel was the RMS *Titanic*—plied the sealanes between Europe and *northern* American ports. In the decades around the turn of the century, it was responsible for bringing about 2 million (European) immigrants to the northern United States, mostly through New York. It is possible that the narrator is still thinking of the aforementioned Morgan Line—its flag contained a white star—rather than the actual White Star line. But Morgan Line ships were not involved in the New Orleans strikes of 1894 and 1895 either.[7] One would therefore expect the "you" who "of course" knows how long the dock strike lasted to also know that readers who trust the narrator to impart accurate information on a friendly "you know" basis are being led astray—or being led into a different *kind* of construction of historical knowledge unmoored from specific shipping lines. *This* White Star steamer, for example, has the capacity to metaphorize an unbroken American history privileging white ownership of commercial enterprises in the New Orleans region. In that sense, all of the shipping lines operated under the white flag. That was true of the international slave trade as well as the antebellum transportation of slaves down the Mississippi to New Orleans's markets after the international trade came to an end. And it was true of the fruit trade that was still booming as Dunbar-Nelson wrote. Morgan Line ships brought fruit from Havana, Cuba, under flags bearing a white star; the Boston Fruit Company's ships transporting bananas from Jamaica to Boston during the late nineteenth century was known as the Great White Fleet.

There is good reason to think of postbellum race relations and the emerging color line more generally under the sign of the White Star. In 1874 the White League of Louisiana was instrumental in rolling back Reconstruction when five thousand of its paramilitary members faced off against thirty-five hundred police and state militia at the so-called Battle of Liberty Place in New Orleans. Winning the battle, they usurped the Louisiana state government (then housed in New Orleans); the Republican administration fled. Though ended by federal troops after three days—another "tramp, tramp, tramp" (123) of armed forces on the banks of the Mississippi—the insurrection in the long run proved a successful part of the southern Redeemers' policy of restoring civil, political, and economic power to wealthy white men. The Democratic Party returned to power in Louisiana in 1876, its platform an uncompromising celebration of white supremacy. One of its main (and successful) objectives was rolling back voting rights for freedmen. Between 1890 and 1908, the number of black voters on the registry declined from about 128,000 to 2,000.[8] The "delicate poles of the costly machine" (120) collapsing on top of the cotton packed in the hold of the White Star steamer invokes, among other historical events, the destruction of fragile gains—partial ownership of the means of production, the acquisition of nascent political power—made by black people during Reconstruction.

Dunbar-Nelson could hardly help bearing witness to that during the years she lived in New Orleans (1892–96). The historical event that more than any other granted legal sanction and cultural legitimacy to Jim Crow laws—the Supreme Court's decision on *Plessy v. Ferguson*—was initiated in New Orleans when, to protest Louisiana's 1890 Separate Car Act, Homer Plessy rode a railroad car reserved for white riders only. The you who knows how long *the* strike lasted, and who would know to look twice at the White Star steamer at the dock, would be in a position to map worsening race relations among dockworkers onto the unfolding of the Plessy case. Plessy rode the car as a challenge to segregation a few months before labor solidarity during the 1892 strike raised the possibility of a broad alliance against rigid color lines. The Supreme Court handed down its verdict legitimizing segregation (in May 1896) a year after strikes, race riots, and assaults against black people indicated the collapse of such hopes.

The narrative strategy of "Mr. Baptiste" is incorporative and open-ended. It moves from singular cases to multiple instances; it insists on moving beyond discrete facts (which shipping lines were involved in *the* strike) to the broad histories and socioeconomic contexts that make them meaningful. Once the accretive strategies of *the* strike become apparent, the same logic can be employed to map other histories onto it. The labor dispute down at the docks takes place amid bales of cotton and "cargoes of molasses and sugar" (117) with the "Negro stevedores . . . steadily laboring at the cotton, with the rhythmic song swinging its cadence in the hot air" (121), listening to the "overseer's reassuring word" (121). These moments invoke other still more infamous aspects of New Orleans's history. The city was a lynchpin of the sugar-rum-slaves Atlantic triangle before the international slave trade ended in 1808. Between 1808 and the Civil War it became the largest and most prominent market for slaves in the United States. Cotton was its main export. The fearsome war that breaks out also recalls the largest slave rebellion in US history—the German Coast uprising—when hundreds of slaves marched on New Orleans from two upriver parishes, one of which was Saint John the Baptist. Now Mr. Baptiste's name, which so perplexed the narrator, urges us to recall specific historical details and invest the story with them. Then too there were "tiny blazes in the cotton" (117). The marchers from Saint John the Baptist parish, for example, fired five houses and crops along the way. And then too the tramp, tramp of the militia was heard. Around ninety-five black men lost their lives in pitched battles along the Mississippi and at ensuing executions. The point is not that nothing at all has changed— these stevedores own the "costly machines" (121) that the Irish American unionists smash—but that the racial animosities on display during *the* strike take us far back into a dim past in order to find the same elements occurring under slavery and under capitalism: black labor bought, sold, and under threat; a trade in cotton, molasses, sugar, and labor; strikes and rebellions; fearsome wars taking place on the banks of the Mississippi; the tramp of militias; black people dying.

Into this complex history of economic and political malfeasance Dunbar-Nelson inserts a unique kitchen economy in the shape of Mr. Baptiste, the "little fruit-eater" (118) as the Irish laborers call him. Mr. Baptiste subsists primarily through barter. Collecting spoiling fruit from the docks, he slips in at the "back door" (113), the "kitchen door" (114), of his clients and leaves a "load of fruit behind as madame's pay" (114) for hot meals. "Thus did he eat," we are told, "and his clients were many, and never too tired or too cross to cook his meals and get their pay in baskets of fruit" (114). It is a precarious economy, parasitic on, and at the mercy of, capitalist enterprises. The dock strike, shutting down the fruit business, brings his trade to an abrupt end. Like M'sieu Fortier who loses his job when the opera is put on a "strictly financial basis," Mr. Baptiste is the victim of the new tidal economic forces of modernity: unions, labor-capital disputes, militias, Morgan and White Star lines, all trump "small weak folks" (112) like him. His trade defines him: like the "baskets of forgotten fruit" (113) he carries away, like the too-spoiled fruit that is thrown into the river, he is "dropped unnamed into Potter's Field" (124) at the end.

But forgotten fruit does not have to stay forgotten in a story that constantly urges us to recoup knowledge that has been pushed into the interstices of history. Nowhere are these potential acts of remembering on more spectacular display than in the story's complex leveraging of the history, material and discursive, of the Caribbean–Central American tropical fruit trade. Trading in discarded fruit was common at the port of New Orleans where, after a long sea-voyage, spoiling fruit was "sold at a discount to store owners and peddlers" from the docks.[9] Lafcadio Hearn, who lived in New Orleans and wrote extensively for the *Daily City Item* in the decade before Dunbar-Nelson, published a diatribe against the "small fruit vendor [who] usually buys only damaged fruit at a nominal price, and sells it for good fruit at an imperial price," using strategies such as turning damaged fruit over to hide imperfections. Selling "rotten fruit at a prodigious and incredible profit" pays dividends. After vending fruit in "obscure side streets, like spiders waiting to catch flies," these sellers "catch so many that after a few years they can open a corner grocery; and after a few years more they become wholesale merchants."[10] Hearn predicted the career of New Orleans's most famous fruiterer, Sam Zemurray, the "Banana King." In the 1890s the young entrepreneur made his fortune by purchasing "ripes"—bananas discarded because they might not make it to market in time—straight from the docks, first in Mobile, Alabama, and then in New Orleans, loading them immediately on to trains and selling them to shopkeepers along the rail lines. At the age of twenty-one Zemurray had already banked $100,000.

Zemurray's success in profiting on nothing more than the residue of the fruit trade suggests that Hearn's narrative arc, which traces the development of shady backstreet dealer to wholesale merchant in New Orleans, occupies a mere fragment of the long history of relations between the United States and the Caribbean (and Central and South America) in which fruit as commodity and trope came to express a variety of political, economic, and cultural dominations. In 1823 John Quincy Adams memorably constructed a "ripe fruit" theory to explain the relationship between the United States and Cuba—and by extension other Caribbean lands. In a letter to Hugh Nelson, the US Minister to Spain, Adams observed that since "an apple, severed by the tempest from its native tree, cannot choose but fall to the ground, Cuba, forcibly disjoined from its own unnatural connexion with Spain, and incapable of self-support, can gravitate only towards the North American Union."[11] Fruit must fall, and falling fruit must gravitate toward the most powerful attractor. The United States made many attempts over the course of the nineteenth century to hurry along the process of Newtonian mechanics: attempts to purchase the island (Thomas Jefferson tried in 1809; the writers of the Ostend Manifesto in 1854 proposed the same); unauthorized military invasions (filibusters) in 1850 and 1851; and finally war and temporary occupation (the 1898 Spanish-American War) at a time when Cuban struggles for independence from Spain were beginning to threaten US trade in the Caribbean.[12]

By then, US fruit companies exercised tremendous power over Caribbean and South American trade—and, indeed, countries. The "Morgan-line steamships" (112), which sailed between New Orleans and Cuba, South American, and Central American ports, bringing fruit that was then loaded onto railcars at the "Texas and Pacific warehouses" (112), were by no means the only players.[13] The Boston Fruit Company's Great White Fleet shipped tropical fruit to the northern United States. Minor C. Keith shipped fruit from around the Caribbean and Central America to the railheads at New Orleans and other Gulf ports and thence to destinations north and west. Keith's Tropical Trading and Transport Company owned plantations, vast properties, railroads, shipping lines—and governments. When Zemurray, a year after founding the Cuyamel Fruit Company in 1911, helped overthrow the Honduran government, he merely followed in the footsteps of an array of US capitalists—Keith and Cornelius Vanderbilt among them—who had exerted tremendous political and economic influence over Gulf and Caribbean nations.[14] By 1884 Keith owned 5 percent of Costa Rica. By the time his company merged with Boston Fruit to form the company that was to dominate the trade and politics of Caribbean and Central American countries from 1899 through the 1960s—United Fruit—it was already, through his efforts, a "brooding presence across six lands: Costa Rica, Panama, Columbia, Cuba, Jamaica, and the Dominican Republic."[15] All of the US fruit companies—Keith's Tropical Trading and Transport Company, United Fruit (1899), and later the Cuyamel Fruit Company (1911) and Standard Fruit (1924)—imported cheap tropical fruit into the United States by dint of pressuring Caribbean and Central and South American countries into offering land concessions, low taxes, and cheap labor.

During the nineteenth century tropical fruit became a material conduit for and a visible sign of the extension of US economic and political power into the Caribbean and Gulf regions. It was the material counterpart to the metaphor of ripe fruit Adams saw as pertinent to the geopolitical status of Cuba vis-à-vis the United States. The trope of fruit, moreover, functioned in a still broader ideological fruit-trade. It was one way in which Americans "knew" the Caribbean and, by contrast, came to articulate the principles and values underpinning US hegemony there. Writers convey the rich natural bounty of Caribbean islands by means of a fruit sublime. Oran, traveling to the Caribbean in 1858, is "astonished" by the "great number, variety, and exceeding beauty" of Jamaican woods and the "groves of every kind of tropical fruit."[16] The original page in *Harper's* frames this discussion with drawings of gigantic trees whose mangoes and "poypoya [papaya]" appear much bigger than the tiny wigwam-like hut they shelter.[17] Almost without fail, writers effuse over those "marvelous piles of fruit!"[18] those "luscious . . . fruits growing in great profusion,"[19] the "most picturesque" Campo del Marto (marketplace) in Cuba where "all the products of this fruity isle hang in masses of rich confusion."[20] Lafcadio Hearn drives home the ineffable nature of these fruited isles: "Infinitely more puzzling are the astonishing varieties of green and yellow and party-colored fruits . . . out of the confusion of which you retain only a memory of calabashes and cocoas, guavas and sapotillas, barbadines and pommes-cythères, guinettes and bunches of tiny bananas."[21] The difficulty (and delight) of representing the fruit sublime is evident here. The outlandish names identify without delivering to the uninitiated any information whatsoever.

These paeans to tropical fruits certainly include a crude appraisal of islands' commercial potential. The writers' monetizing of the exotic and picturesque goes hand in hand with their sizing up of a productive but undeveloped natural resource, as W. E. Sewell rhapsodizes: "Such quantities of cocoas, pines, oranges, mangoes, granadillas, sapodilloes, and vegetables of all descriptions—comparatively valueless in Kingston, but worth a mint if they could be taken to a Northern market."[22] What Sewell sees as comparatively valueless fruit (to the inhabitants) plays an important role in ideologies of the fruit sublime. Fruit, to begin with, underwrites the colonial trope of the empty island. People constantly exchange for or disappear into fruit. In 1871 Helen S. Conant observed a "huge old black woman" guarding a "heap of oranges and green cocoa-nuts, among which roll half a dozen naked black babies, with an air of sunny contentment so delicious to behold that one forgets to inquire, how about the oranges?"[23] She implies that one need not inquire about the oranges: the delicious heaps of fruit-babies ripening in the sun make a perfectly good stand-in. Two decades later, Hearn, on his trip to the West Indies, hyperbolically intensifies the same discourse. He spends pages describing flesh that "does not look like flesh, but like fruit pulp" and the "fruit-colored populations"; indeed, it is "only with fruit-colors that many of these skin-tints can be correctly compared."[24] A major thrust of the fruit sublime is to imply that Caribbean islanders and their histories are sublimed—subject to a change in state—into astonishingly diverse and mountainously heaped-up piles of fruit. One implication is that these fruit-people have as little aptitude for subjecting the confusion of fruit to orderly cultivation as would the fruit itself. Indeed, a confusion of fruit explains the metaphoric link between it and the islanders' neglect.

Once more, the marketplace becomes a key site for travelers intent on representing the disorderly economics of Caribbean fruit selling. The fruit sublime presents the spectacle of meager commercial practices that fail to keep up with the profuse (over)production of tropical lands. Marketers sit among fantastic piles of fruit. Howard Pyle observes women sitting in "long rows with baskets of oranges in front of them and piles of oranges around them, and bananas and plantains and yams and baskets of strange fruit everywhere."[25] But Pyle, like Sewell, sees them failing to realize the fruit's potential value. Though Kingston harbor once drew the "commerce of the Western world to its wharves until it became one vast storehouse of wealth," in the current markets one is apt to "return overburdened with those odd picturesque baskets filled to overflowing with luscious fruit, buyable at so ridiculously small a sum of money."[26] Conant, too, lovingly describes a traveler feasting on marketplace fruits "too luscious to endure exportation" without mentioning any exchange of money at all; smaller amounts of fruit, she explains, can be purchased from traveling vendors for a "ridiculously low price."[27] G. O. Seilhamer sees a general principle at work: "Not only among the black and colored people of Jamaica, but also among the freed coolies in Havana, and, indeed, wherever a race is poor and labor is unremunerative, there is a strong tendency to engage in trade in a small way." And "small merchandising" is strongly associated with premodern forms of exchange.[28] Accounts of incomprehensible island jabbering are consistently linked to barter. Pyle observes that in the market are "none but gabbling negroes chaffering, haggling, buying, and selling."[29] S. B. Hynes notes that "vendors and purchasers of all ages and shades jabber together with all their might in their almost unintelligible patois."[30] Samuel Hazard adds that the "amount of chaff and compliments exchanged even in the most ordinary purchase, is somewhat astonishing to people of the Anglo-Saxon race." It becomes "quite a pleasant amusement to have a seller name some ridiculous price for an article, just to see to how much one can finally reduce it."[31]

The customary pleasant amusement of such scenes has a still more important function: it invokes the residual status political economic thought has typically assigned to barter economies. For Adam Smith, barter is crucial because it points to the natural human propensity to truck, barter, and trade; before there was money, humans were making markets and participating in exchange. But barter economies have obvious limitations, Smith argued, among them the problem of the so-called coincidence of wants. Bartered goods are not easily fungible. One can imagine swapping baskets of fruit for hot meals, but how would one swap baskets of fruit for a cow if the cow's owner disdained fruit, or required some other good, or wanted just one basket? Moreover, the value of each good—the ratio of baskets of fruit to the cow, for example—would also surely change, and keep changing, depending on need or on the skill of the individual barterer. Value is rhetorical: it depends on the quality of the argument. Barter promotes, as Smith put it, "higgling, haggling, swapping, dickering," for barterers have no choice but to engage in time-consuming debates about something (value) that is always up for grabs.

To measure and stabilize the relative value of goods that are dissimilar in size, quantity, or kind requires a standard independent of individual arguments—a general equivalent, usually money. By allowing people to compare and value goods on a like-to-like basis, a general equivalent makes processes of exchange efficient; pricing a commodity circumvents haggling debates about what its value might be. The only consequential question is whether the consumer wishes to purchase that value, not what the value *is*. As a corollary, political economists argued, money allows the rapid accumulation of capital, which is essential for the progress of human civilizations. Political economic thought therefore conceived of barter in stadialist terms. It was a necessary, but necessarily passing, stage in the evolution of human societies. It proved not only that humans were naturally drawn to exchange one commodity for another but also that they were bent on making that process more rational, logical, and efficient. To the extent that adopting a general equivalent maximizes efficiency, the shift from barter to money economies might be thought of as the critical step responsible for market society and for the very concept of homo economicus.

Selling "strange fruit" in the "chattering babel of color and noise" of the marketplace conveys a strong sense of disproportion between the astonishing fruit and the scanty commercial means brought to their selling.[32] Here, an unintelligible patois makes authors the masters of intelligible economic discourses. Unintelligible discourse in the marketplace in fact translates easily into economic terms: it implies the premodern haggling of moneyless barter, or excessive rhetoric in tandem with ridiculously small sums. Jabber, therefore, is not equivalent to mere gibberish, however much writers seem to emphasize the point. Hearn's description of a market in Frederiksted, Saint Croix, is paradigmatic. The "black dealers [who] speak no tongue comprehensible outside of the Antilles" employ a rhetoric to match the "great wealth of verdure" under which they sit: they speak in a "rolling current of vowels and consonants pouring so rapidly that no inexperienced ear can detach one solitary intelligible word." In one sense, this sublime, ungraspable speech signifies a mundane commercialism. A vendor's importuning "'Massa, youwancocknerfoobuy?' (Master, do you want to buy a cocoanut?)," translated by a passing planter, is the first reported speech in Hearn's narrative.[33] But this first attempted exchange on the island of language for fruit is incomplete. The islanders' language of exchange does not function beyond the bounds of their own marketplace. Absent a translation, the "cockner" presumably will not change hands. Their patois metaphorizes their lack of a general equivalent—a common language in which to exchange goods efficiently. Unintelligible speech and poorly functioning economies are reciprocals of each other.

Hearn's ability to translate the phrase (and to want the phrase translated) is the crux of his transactional rhetoric of fruit and fruit-people; it situates him as the exchanger of reference. The fact that the islanders in the marketplace presumably adopt some sort of general equivalent among themselves does not come into play since Hearn's description merely indexes confusion. Exchange, in other words, is not really exchange unless the islanders enter into it with *him*. The coconut seller's inability to find an adequate language of exchange sabotages her efforts to sell a coconut until Hearn takes the time to supply it. Indeed, he markets the cockner much more effectively than its owner. He profits from her picturesque but almost unintelligible patois insofar as it becomes his commercial property, sold first to *Harper's* magazine in 1888 and then republished in *Two Years in the French West Indies* (1890). Her honorific (Massa) salutes his sense that he is the master marketer. The patois "youwancocknerfoobuy?" and its translation sketches an entire history of economics. The fruit seller's rudimentary language and incipient urge to trade yields to a complete language of exchange—Hearn's—evinced first by the author's ability to render an unintelligible patois into precise, intelligible English; second, by the rational self-control necessary for intelligibility; third, by the efficiency of an intelligible economic language; fourth, by command of a (linguistic) general equivalent, a common language in which the coconut can be easily traded; and fifth, by the author's possession of what the coconut-seller most lacks, knowledge of the stage that follows barter and small merchandising.

Travelers to Caribbean and Gulf nations seem to endorse Smith and later political economists on at least two counts: (1) a desire to enter into exchange is a natural human attribute, (2) economic systems favoring more efficient and more rapid capital accumulation necessarily supersede premodern systems. Authors draw on stadial theory in order to position Caribbean fruit marketing at a moment before or during what was supposed to be *the* crucial step in the development of civilization: when people transitioning from barter to money economies begin to realize the efficiencies accruing to a general equivalent. Marketplace barter and chaffering show the drag of premodern economic systems. Ridiculously small sums of money changing hands suggests a dawning awareness that superseding stages exist, but the disparity between vast piles of fruit and small merchandising reveals that superseding stages have not yet arrived. Small merchandising in the logic of fruit-discourses is little different from barter in the sense that neither realize value as it exists in properly functioning markets. Barterers cannot conceive of the possibility of nonnegotiable, because independently determined, value; small merchandisers cannot conceive of the potential value of the vast piles of fruit.

A concept of true value cannot exist without the presence of international trade and an international visitor: the first to maximize the value of the fruit, the second to realize the value of maximizing. Only those who have known what it means to maximize value could possibly recognize the value of doing so. Only those who have passed beyond small merchandising could look back on it as a stage. The "inexperienced ear" of US travelers in the presence of the fruit sublime—their astonishment at "strange fruit and monstrous vegetables," their professed bewilderment at an unintelligible patois—turns out to be a ruse.[34] Travelogues monetize the fabulous, understand fruit and fruit-people as island produce, transform unintelligibility into haggling, and disparage the islanders' ownership of fruit by associating it with various forms of barter. The fruit producers tacitly admit they do not comprehend the value of what they own, or that they do not comprehend the value of ownership, or that they think of ownership itself as a mutable and flexible concept, subject to whoever barters most successfully. One consequence is that it affords travelers an ideological claim to the fruit they write so effusively about—anyone can claim ownership if the concept of ownership is merely rhetorical—though that logic marks the writers of travelogues as the most successful hagglers, not the repositories of true, substantial, and enduring value.

The significance of Mr. Baptiste's bartering and of the dock strike that brings it to an end ramifies though a complex history of ripe fruit activities that, in the final third of the nineteenth century, brought the Caribbean-Gulf fruit trade under US political and economic domination and were ideologically supported by a rich imaginative discourse contrasting the experienced economic eye of the US traveler with inexperienced fruit "owners" who did not know the value of their sublime fruit. This is not to say that Mr. Baptiste metaphorizes the Caribbean fruit trade; rather, the metaphoric weight of the fruit trade invests the terms of his abjection. In that investiture lies a potent critique of the discourses that contextualize him. To the Irish American dockworkers, the fruit Mr. Baptiste distributes both identifies him and signifies his otherness: he is a "fruit-eatin' Frinchman," which is to say, unlike them, a French-speaking Creole; he is the "little fruit-eater," which is to say one of the "small, weak folks," fruit-bred, unable to fight for himself. Like the islanders of the travelogues who vanish into a kaleidoscope of fruit-colors, his "wrinkled brown" (122) skin implies that he is a Creole of color, metaphorically represented by the "ripes" he gathers. Indeed, his abjection is apprehended through the eye, as McMahon insists as he lets fly with the brickbat that kills Mr. Baptiste: "Will yez look at that damned fruit-eatin' Frinchman!" Like those islanders sitting among their awe-inspiring piles of fruits without understanding how to market them properly, moreover, he is the owner of his fruit in name only.

Dispossession marks the beginning and the end of the fruit-trade. Travelogues implying that the maximal value of island fruit can be truly realized only in relation to an international trade are part of a broader Caribbeanism in which the taking away of names and lands and sovereignty has become a matter of course. Fruit arriving in the US was produced on lands purchased by US companies or deeded to them by corrupt or coerced governments, and then transported by US-owned shipping lines. In New Orleans, Mr. Baptiste also subsists precariously through barter in relation to those who own the international trade. It is another way to understand the significance of his insubstantial name, which the narrator discloses may not be his, which seems to have its genesis elsewhere and in some other time. In each arena, barter becomes a key signifier of the provisionality of ownership and the precariousness of economic systems operating in the interstices of the fruit trade.

Nonetheless, the story presents bartering—"pay in baskets of fruit" (114) for hot meals—as a productive form of kitchen economics. Mr. Baptiste's enterprise supplements the orthodox fruit-trade by revaluing what appears to be its useless residue—by redeeming that which has been debased. That which no longer possesses market value does possess use value. After she has "carefully inspected the plantains," Madame Garcia sees that "they were good and wholesome" (115). Mr. Baptiste's bartering thus challenges capitalist production on at least three counts: (1) what capitalists suppose to be useless is not; (2) what capitalists suppose to be an efficient system produces enormous waste; and (3) barter, what classical economists consider to be an economically inefficient system, satisfies Mr. Baptiste and his clients without waste or surplus. Kitchen barter arrangements fulfill many of the functions of a marketplace in commodities. Wholesome goods get distributed, payment agreed on, and exchanges transacted between Mr. Baptiste and his clients. Each party is satisfied. He departs "filled and contented" (114); his many clients are "never too tired or too cross to cook his meals" (114). This marketplace turned inside out—the vendor making numerous visits rather than consumers congregating around a cluster of vendors—works well. Indeed, the story presents Mr. Baptiste's bartering as a long-term enterprise. "Never a day passed" (112) that he was not seen taking fruit from the docks; his clients "understood and knew his ways" (113) and gave him meals. The cordial relationship he enjoys with his clients does not make them selfless. Madame Garcia's careful inspection of the plantains as a prelude to exchange implies that barter arrangements also observe the maximizing behavior political economists imputed to homo economicus. Bartering works because of its utility to all parties involved.

But back door kitchen transactions differ from market exchange relations in important ways. The story positions barter as a viable economic practice in which payment gets expressed not only as an exchange of nutritious food but also as a social exchange designed to build a cordial body politic over the long term. Its barter-members do not haggle but converse—or perhaps haggle and converse. Though in this case Madame Garcia is "inclined to agree with anything Mr. Baptiste said" (115) because the plantains are good and wholesome, she is clearly committed to future trades; she calls after him, in fact, to ask if he does not want his luncheon when he walks away in despair (116). In this sense, the more appropriate context for Mr. Baptiste's living arrangements is not political economic thought so much as anthropological investigations into barter as a means of social organization, solidarity, and reproduction. Like Marcel Mauss's analysis of the social dimensions of gift-giving in *The Gift* (1925), anthropological approaches to barter tend to emphasize the ways in which nonmonetary exchanges are conducive to making, enacting, and maintaining social relations even between people who are competitors. Because barter is conducted without external criteria of value—without a general equivalent—the value of the transaction to the respective parties must be discussed or argued for on a case-by-case basis. The invisible hand of the market yields to a negotiation traditionally performed face-to-face. And because each participant in barter counts on the other to remain invested in the process in order for the transaction to continue, barter depends on the (re)enactment of a mutually beneficial social relationship. In this instance, Madame Garcia receives a basket of wholesome fruit for nothing more than her expression of sympathy.

The productive social relations generated by Mr. Baptiste's barter-economy contrast powerfully with the conditions of the strike at the levee, which is composed of disparate and violently opposing groups—the union workers; the scabs; the cotton-packing operators who hire them; the shipowners (represented in the story by flags, and as those who do not own the costly machines used to pack the cotton aboard their ships [121–22]); the militia; "fishmen and vegetable marchands" (122); and people grouped into generic racial categories. Unlike Mr. Baptiste's satisfied customers, all involved in the dock strike are antagonistic. No one has sympathy—"killed instantly" (123) is the doctor's laconic epitaph for Mr. Baptiste—and no one talks to each other beyond Finnegan's "damn ye . . . now yez can pack yer cotton!" (121) after he has smashed the stevedores' machine. These market relations are policed at the point of a gun. But they are also mystified: as the story's ironic rhetoric of "you remember, of course" helps to reveal, historical events and their broad economic and political contexts need to be recuperated if their pertinence to Mr. Baptiste's fate is to be realized. The story develops a barter economy that works by recognizable principles of exchange to illuminate the deficits of US capitalist enterprise: its economics of exploitation and coercion, conflict, and exacerbated racism, and its mystifying discourses explaining how to possess fruit, fruit-lands, and fruit-peoples. One of the story's most provocative interpretive possibilities is that Mr. Baptiste's and his clients' kitchen economy can be more efficient than orthodox capitalism's, which here experiences a total breakdown as the cotton and fruit vessels "lay in de river, no work, no cargo" (115).

That this interruption in the commercial fruit trade also collapses Mr. Baptiste's kitchen commonwealth emphasizes its precariousness. We could hardly call Mr. Baptiste's fruit trade *alternative*. Though it is tempting to think of him as an anti-Zemurray, Mr. Baptiste's barter arrangements are as materially dependent on a preexisting trade as was the future Banana King in the

1890s on discarded ripes. The intimate link between Mr. Baptiste's kitchen trade and the broader trade in tropical fruit underwrites the story's most redoubtable symbolic challenge to the ideologies of the fruit sublime: it refutes the stadial script of classical political economy, which insists that barter occupies a premodern phase of economic and social organization. The story explains the expunging of sociality down at the docks not in terms of a metahistorical theory—that capitalist relations must eventually subsume barter on the basis of its greater efficiency—but in terms of the coercive and violent relations of capitalist trade itself. Mr. Baptiste's barter trade is a function of modernity, operating in lockstep with the trade from plantation to shipping line to the stevedores at the dock. His livelihood depends on the material profits US capitalists derived from Caribbean–Central American nations; it collapses when the effects of rationalized labor relations—one generator of that profit—make their presence felt; it points to the ideological framework that had derogated the economies of fruit-producing countries for half a century, and was still doing so as Dunbar-Nelson wrote. And because barter in the interstices of the late century capitalist fruit trade confuses any narrative touting the difference of modernity—whether as the acme of civilization or as a singularly mercenary, and therefore unique, rupture with the past— Mr. Baptiste's barter arrangements underscore the logic of our having to read back from conflicts along the levee to their multitudinous historical precedents. It is because modernity collapses back into history that, the narrator insists, we have to remember what happened long ago in the dim past.

7

ECONOMICS GINGERBREAD STYLE

Toward a Model Political Economy of the Kitchen

In 1885 an anonymous reviewer of Sarah Orne Jewett gave her stories a back-handed compliment: "because they are so fine . . . one looks for something more important to happen in them than the eating of apples or the making of pie."[1] The culinary feats produced to celebrate the end of the Bowden re-union in *The Country of the Pointed Firs* (1896)—elaborate pies, a remarkable gingerbread version of the Bowden house—suggest otherwise. An exemplary instance of the curious mixture of domestic activity, fable, and abstract eco-nomic thought that I call kitchen economics, the scene deserves particular scrutiny for its complex and important representation of economic model-ing. Nonetheless, the reviewer is in one sense correct. Scholarly appraisals of making pies and gingerbread—or digging potatoes, making chowder, or put-ting a turkey on the Thanksgiving table—have acceded as one to the propo-sition that the socioeconomic conditions of modernity must be discovered elsewhere. A persuasive political economy of the kitchen must therefore ad-dress the structure of knowledge that overlooks, or devalues, the possibility that it constitutes a legitimate discourse about economics at all. Though the economic conditions of modernity have indeed been shaped by the rise of neoclassical economic thought, the assumptions about history and human nature it entails have delimited scholars' constructions of what is meant by "the economic." In part, those constructions have been made visible by the unfortunate privilege of the early twenty-first century. The looming threat of ecocatastrophe has compelled new economic models and strategies, among them attempts to resuscitate the sort of political economic outlook that shaped the nineteenth-century kitchen commonwealth.

Like Stowe's meditation on the American pie in *Oldtown Folks*, Jewett's feast-fable in chapter 19 ("The Feast's End") conjoins practical household affairs with an abstract discourse on aeconomia. The status of food as dis-course in this scene is particularly conspicuous. Pastry, pie, and gingerbread constantly "speak." "Dates and names were wrought in lines of pastry and frosting" on the pies; there is "even more elaborate reading matter" on an apple pie "which we began to share and eat, precept upon precept."[2] The words "Bowden" and "reunion" are eaten by Mrs. Todd and the narrator, leaving an "undecipherable fragment" (123) behind. Later, the narrator comes across the "most renowned essay in cookery"—a "model of the old Bowden house made of durable gingerbread," which was baked in sections and then pieced together by an "artist," as the narrator calls her, and which "was shared by a great part of the assembly" as if it were a "pledge and token of loyalty" when it "fell into ruin at the feast's end" (123). Histories, precepts, and pledges are not the only textualities assembled at the feast. The narrator's first response to the gingerbread house is to call up "lively remembrances of a childish story" (123)—Hansel and Gretel—a reference later quickened by teasing references to the cook's witchlike "gleaming eye" (123) and to her kitchen, where resides "one of the last of the great brick ovens" (123). And fairy tale is baked together with a discourse on realist aesthetics. Thinking about her gingerbread art, the artist/cook remarks, "I could just as well have made it all of frosted cake . . . but 't wouldn't have been the right shade; the old house, as you observe, was never painted, and I concluded that plain gingerbread would represent it best" (123).

The artist/cook's economical art of representation participates in the scene's broader representation of economic principles. Her counterfoil is the poet Mary Anna who "harps too much" (124) when she delivers a "long faded garland of verses" at the reunion. "I'd laid half of that away for next time," Mrs. Todd says. Her acerbic appraisal of Mary Anna's effusions jibes with the artist/cook's plain-gingerbread stylistics: both advance a notion of artistic economy grounded in principles of economic probity. Laying half away for next time derives from the same sort of frugal housekeeping that presumably led to the house never being painted; it respects an economy of the necessary and sufficient; it grasps the deficiencies of Mary Anna's "painted" poetry as a corollary of poor household management. And it implicates still other social deficits. It leverages an assault on metropolitan cultures of excess—the "waste" of the human "inward force" in the "petty excitements of every day that belong to cities" (113), which the narrator witnesses in the propensity of some at the feast to "show off" (118).

Pastry, pie, and gingerbread texts—words good to eat, words that *are* goods—begin to formulate bioeconomic principles conducive to the functioning of a more perfect commonwealth. The artist/cook musters resources, invests labor, and produces nutritious goods for body (food), mind (language, precepts), and community (a feast and the shared ceremonies appropriate to it). She respects the Green Island logic of the "moderate sum," producing sufficient goods—the gingerbread house was "shared by a great part of the assembly" (123)—without waste or show. Laying away half for next time invokes theories about how societies accumulate capital to their advantage. Like digging potatoes on Green Island, pie-texts and gingerbread-essays construct narratives about how people distribute resources such that the "condition of mankind, or of any society of human beings . . . is made prosperous or the reverse."[3] The Bowden's kitchen commonwealth pays particular attention to the function of women's capital. The artist/cook produces a frugally decorated gingerbread house capable of feeding a community, and the gourmand/narrator in turn reinscribes it in a fictional order, a frugal realism, which implies new forms of literary and cultural capital women can now produce for the marketplaces of fiction. In comparison to Mary Anna's gush, plain-gingerbread stylistics promises a better-compensated future for women of letters.

To what sort of model commonwealth does Jewett's gingerbread re-creation of the Bowden house aspire? That peculiar trope of eating words offers one way to approach this question on the grounds of its seemingly utopian aspiration toward transcending the modality of the sign. The chapter's essays in cookery seem to want to collapse Claude Lévi-Strauss's distinction between the raw (the natural) and the cooked (the cultural). Once cooked and ingested in the form of pastry and gingerbread, signs such as "Bowden reunion" seem to circumvent the concept of *sign of* because the body interprets the signs as raw nutritious material. The material and aesthetic economies of a body (politic) nourished on edible texts could not run to excess since production and consumption, being sized to the stomach, would stand in an easily achieved equilibrium. Cultures of waste and Mary Anna's immoderate verse would be indicted equally. This argument overlaps Andrew Lawson's that the realist's fascination with material things is an attempt to "fix" something of immutable worth in a capitalist society given over to fluid values and precarious class formations.[4] Yet Jewett's essays in cookery lay claim to a much broader significance. Signs that become—that *are*—nutritious food point the way to a new sort of exchange-free utopian republic. Those who partake of the gingerbread house at the reunion know a healthy community physiologically, through the stomach, before the narrator ever articulates the meaning of the food in terms of sharing and pledges of loyalty. The body leads the way for the body politic. In line with Jean-Joseph Goux's argument that utopias attempt to dispel all that is a "parasite upon . . . healthy use-values,"[5] this confusion of "raw" and "cooked" comes about in part because the cooks offer their confections potlatch style; they are gifts to the reunion attendees. Being liberated from the marketplace is the reciprocal of being liberated from the domain of the sign. Pie-texts free both from their cultural function in market-based symbolic economies so that value-in-use becomes all.

What might grant legitimacy to this utopian freedom from the market is the fact of gendered asymmetries of power in the late nineteenth-century United States, which means that men and women are not equivalent under the regime of the general equivalent. An equivalent in a society controlled by and for men measures invidious differences. It does not translate one value into another so much as devalue women's productions. The quotidian work of the kitchen, which appears to have no cultural and little economic value to men, is a case in point. But speaking in pastry and gingerbread reveals that the long-suppressed imaginative work of the kitchen and the cook can be an effective way to establish truly general values. Offered gratis, pie and gingerbread texts demonstrate the extent to which they have been freed from the tyranny of money systems and the social power those systems underwrite. "Equivalents" now measure things equitably: pies are words and words are pastry, all pies go to feed all bodies, everyone takes a piece of gingerbread, and a "general sigh" (123) greets the consumption of the gingerbread house when it falls to ruin. Like the chowder feast on Green Island, the kitchen productions of the Bowden reunion have the capacity to level a potent critique of capitalist relations by satisfying everyone's simple wants—the wants of bodily appetite—without a market.

Nonetheless, the gingerbread house aligns with what looks to be the house of Bowden's broader duty to act as a general equivalent to a fractured United States, impartially translating its diverse value systems into one. The Bowden reunion reminds the narrator of soldiers' reunions during the "great national anniversaries which our country has lately kept" (125)—among them the thirtieth anniversary of the termination of the Civil War (in 1895) and the (relatively) unified nation it enacted.[6] Guided by Jewett's own democratically plain-gingerbread style realism, a new "Common Sense" for the fractious late nineteenth century, the scene gestures toward a utopian representation of the United States healed and redeemed after the ruin of the Civil War—a moment when "old feuds had been overlooked" (125). The Bowden chapters work hard to rescript the concept of family so that the "great" Bowden family is more of a great*er* national family where "you're goin' to meet everybody" (105) and everyone is symbolically equal. Given over to amity, unifying pledges, and a shared commitment to key texts, the feast invokes the Thanksgiving discourses leveraged so effectively by Stowe and Cooke. Jewett imagines a nourished body politic rooted in family but extending generously outward, offering an abundance of (free) food to the other(s) invited to the table. By helping the narrator "generously to the whole word *Bowden*" (123) at the feast, Mrs. Todd registers her friend's honorary membership in the clan; it helps her to feel "like an adopted Bowden" (116). As much to the point, the narrator adopts the Bowden family by ingesting *it*.

This relationship between nutritious food and words/precepts seems to fictionalize a national "common inheritance" (125) as that which is raw (as Lévi-Strauss puts it), universal, beyond interpretation or debate. But the relationship is a reciprocal one. Words good to eat effect a transformation of pies into discourse, which lays somewhat stronger claim than an actual apple pie to being shared with everybody. As noted in Stowe's *Oldtown* meditation on the lineage of American pies, *symbolic* pies speak to broader and more abstract relationships with others. The narrator recognizes this function of pie-speech when she remarks "you are safe to be understood if the spirit of your speech is the same for one neighbor as for the other" (123). Her barely registered shifting of the ground of shared precept-making from kinship to neighborliness is a crucial step. The concept of a pie-text suggests that neighbors not at the reunion's feast can participate by reading "The Bowden Reunion" and "The Feast's End." The reunifying practices modeled by the Bowden house are ultimately contractual—they aim at a civil society organized around shared precepts, thrusting its meanings into the mainstream of liberal political thought.

Even conceived of as a symbolic civil society, the notion of a Bowden (gingerbread) house capable of housing everybody seems to most scholars little more than a ruse. Philip Joseph points out that the narrator's cosmopolitan leanings are compromised by the fact that she only visits—*can* only visit—all-white communities.[7] From this perspective, the house functions as a model community—"model" here in the sense of something to be aspired to and emulated—but renders its vision of a social totality in terms of an extended and neighborly but, at heart, thoroughly white, and rural, family. A symbolic correlative for privileged assumptions about race, class, and metropolitan diversity held by the elite classes of the United States, Bowden generosity becomes a way to produce a folk or gemeinschaft capable of managing the struggles of the United States to enter modernity. The reunion's nascent critique of market capitalism looks more like a phantasmatic resolution to problems of immigration, urbanization, and all other socioeconomic inequalities in the United States. In that respect, the scene squares with Goux's conclusions about utopian republics, which is that writers trying to evade the imperatives of a general equivalent are forced to construct a totalitarian society. They expunge a principle of exchange by imagining a society that cannot be transformed and that cannot be exchanged for the real (in this case richly diverse) society from which it departs.

Many late nineteenth-century food discourses working to interpret and legislate momentous social issues lend support to this approach to Jewett's model feast. Anglo-Americans often expressed their opprobrium for what they saw as the perils of mass immigration in terms of peculiar-seeming food and eating habits, odd utensils, and outré traditions. Labor issues—poverty, strikes, socialism—could be addressed by a counterintuitive discourse of working-class indulgence, frequently linked to foreign ways. George Frederic Parsons weighs in on the Haymarket massacre by lamenting the fact that "we have agreed to open the door wide to all the world, and all the world has accepted our invitation."[8] "America for Americans" would have been a better policy, for, ignorant of "American" values of "thrift and temperance and reasonableness," immigrants spend "enormous sums" on alcohol.[9] "There may be no bread at home, but there is always beer and whiskey at the bar." And "the men who consider themselves the victims of circumstances or the 'thralls' of capital squander their earnings, spend their savings, in these dens."[10] The solution is "the man who has force to deny himself indulgences."[11] A surfeit of poor quality food accomplishes similar ends for Jonathan Baxter Harrison, who inveighs against the "poor cookery" that led mill operatives to "fry too much of their food." Many "do not know how to extract the nutritive elements from beef-bones by long boiling"; they could have "better food and more of it without additional expense" did they not "throw out to their dogs what would give them the basis for a valuable and delicious soup." For Harrison, these kitchen failures can be redeemed by a proper attention to kitchen economies. "Much good might be done," he argues, "by an arrangement for instructing these women and girls in economical methods of preparing wholesome and appetizing food. Perhaps the good women of the city who possess the advantages of wealth and culture can do something to aid their less fortunate sisters."[12]

For both Parsons and Harrison, the notion of a republic built on resisting luxury determines the difference between frugal Americans and the excessive appetites of foreigners and lower-class people. Taming the appetite for food and drink is one way to manage symbolically a body politic by means of superior middle-class know-how: a physiological knowledge of what makes for a healthy body in the case of Parsons, nutrition and cookery lessons by "good women of . . . wealth and culture" in the case of Harrison. Being economical with food encodes broad principles of what is thought to pertain to the national character and its political and cultural value systems. It is possible to read the gingerbread house scene as Jewett's cookery-culture lesson to the others invited or adopted into the Bowden house. If the Bowden door is open wide to all the world, then the secrets of the (white) rural cook passed on to the middle-class narrator may well stand as a pedagogy in how to become one of the pieces the cook assembles into the gingerbread house. At a minimum, that pedagogy would require an economical plain-gingerbread style matched to a frugal domestic economy (laying half away for next time), a plenitude of wholesome food as opposed to an excess of poor food, and largesse rather than large amounts spent on intemperance—all underpinned by a miniature history lesson that, in the spirit of Stowe's *Oldtown* discourse, touts the superiority of the all-American pie, baked on Anglo foundations.

This approach places a different construction on the literary capital that Jewett's trope of the pastry-text might be thought to claim. For Harrison and Parsons, pursuing the circulation of food in the body politic allows them to investigate the kitchen, the bar, the (empty) savings account, and fiery socioeconomic debates as manifestations of the same principle of excessive foreign appetite. American letters and public discourse are also implicated. The labor/capital debate will never be reasonable so long as "labor takes its arguments from the mouths of its worst enemies, and starves itself to feed fat a crowd of chattering demagogues."[13] Workingmen receive their socialist and populist "knowledge"—of demonetizing gold and silver, holding land in common—from newspapers that are no more than a "a kind of entertainment, a stimulus or opiate for the mind, and these people resort to it and feel a necessity for it in much the same way that others feel they must have whisky or opium."[14] A few years later, Charles Dudley Warner, Mark Twain's collaborator on *The Gilded Age* (1873), placed an elaborate capstone on this discourse. Though in the modern United States there is no longer any need to diet on "sodden pie," selecting appropriate "mental food for millions of people" is in serious jeopardy. Public discourse bears witness to an immense but superficial variety: it "creates dyspepsia when it is excessive, and when the literary viands are badly cooked and badly served the evil is increased. . . . The taste is lowered, and the appetite becomes diseased." People "fritter away their time upon a hash of literature"; concentrated reading has given way to "snatch[ing] a hasty meal at a lunch counter"; the "taste for a good book has not kept pace with the taste for a good dinner."[15] Warner's critique of the common school of letters casts it in terms of an emergent fast food nation defined by excess, disease, dyspepsia, sloppy cooking, and deteriorating taste(buds).

Looked at this way, Jewett's pastry-texts signify a sort of slow food Americanism. Cooked in (the last of the) brick ovens, eaten with care and in comity, these pies/letters link wholesome food to refined literary fare within a mazy discourse correlating poor food/taste/cooking and eating habits with various types of foreign appetites. Words good to eat circumvent the issue of taste, which might be thought increasingly problematic in a United States suddenly home to new cuisines and to more cosmopolitan palates. As Warner and Harrison make clear, poor taste is known viscerally by the dyspepsia and addiction it brings. Conversely, delicious pie/letters bring contentment before their precepts are brought to consciousness. Here, what looks to be Jewett's attempt to politicize the American pie allows her to invent a remarkable role for her artist/cook. Over against a foreign culture/fast-food nation, regionalism comes to embody a principle of homespun plain-gingerbread realism; and femina economica working from the kitchen becomes responsible for cooking and building a model "house" fit to house, feed, and nurture an extended body politic—head chef for a model polity constructed on traditional lines. This would also have Jewett putting the symbolic resources of the kitchen at the service of a white, rural body, seated together in joy and amity around a feast-table reminiscent of a long tradition of female regionalist Thanksgivings. In this sense femina economica might be said to come into her political state and accrue cultural capital at the very moment when the very meaning of an American pie is dramatically changing under the influx of new and diverse cuisines and cultures.

But interpretations positioning the gingerbread house as a general equivalent—whether understood as a counter to the invidious values of male-dominated US financial systems or as a domestic backstop to the house of Bowden's utopian republic—cannot account for the full range of rhetorical confections on display at the Bowden feast. Studying the economic implications of Jewett's kitchen is no simple exercise in slow-food Americanism. If the model gingerbread house in some sense implies a model commonwealth, it also opens an inquiry into the heuristic value of *models*. Analyses of Jewett (and female regionalism more broadly) overwhelmingly think of "model" in terms of a utopian construction: that which one wishes, or should wish, to emulate, in the sense that one can speak of a model citizen or community. Utopia seems a necessary corollary of counterworld thinking. It is implicit in the argument that Jewett's femina economica (the artist/cook) fashions a model kitchen commonwealth, a fantastic miniature United States, within which all are invited to a wholesome feast, while disregarding the actual material conditions of 1890s modernity. It is explicit in the moves some feminists have made to wall off female regionalist narrative from structures of male power. But we can also think of a model in terms of a heuristic device designed to elicit some underlying pattern that might otherwise be obscured by a too-rich multiplicity of features. Model-making can privilege the pattern it elicits as the deep structure of the system under scrutiny, or it can conceive of its function as a strategy designed to test out certain possibilities, in which case it can do little more than hazard a claim, or perhaps diverse claims, on truth. Model-building from this latter perspective is "adventure travel through concepts and ideas," as theoretical physicist Lisa Randall says of scientific inquiries, which are (so far) not susceptible to empirical testing.[16]

The example most pertinent to female regionalist writing in terms of its theoretical interest and its historical import is economic modeling. Political economic thought constantly turned to exemplary narratives enunciating what were considered to be the core principles of human development and sociality, such as the importance of capital accumulation to the progress of civilization and to the psychosocial life of the representative human, homo economicus. The value of those expository, narrative, and historical descriptions of economic knowledge began to come to an end by the end of the nineteenth century as neoclassical economists established their insights in market data susceptible to mathematical analysis. To them, stories about the stages of human civilization and fabulous islands, or arguments about whether market capitalism is worthwhile, did not meet the standards of scientific rigor achieved by models that could be empirically tested against actual data. This shift to abstract mathematical modeling proved to be foundational for the modern discipline of economics. Today this form of modeling is "what economics is all about."[17] To those critical of orthodox economics, such models possess serious drawbacks. They are "absurd fictions,"[18] turning out elegant solutions to useless models,[19] largely because they are "deterministic."[20] Solutions are a function of, and in accord with, the model that generated them. Such models run the risk of being wrong in the sense of being invalidated by data. But they cannot be invalidated by appeal to broader socioeconomic issues—whether, for example, it is worth addressing the issue that the model models in the first place. Mainstream economics ensures the narrow scope of its "parsimonious models" by building "ahistorical and acultural generalities" into the framework that generates them.[21] The infinitely desiring or wholly self-interested nature of human beings or the ineluctable value of market capitalism become core assumptions that are themselves not subject to scrutiny in the process of model-making.

The most substantive definitions of economics developing under the auspices of neoclassical thought in the late nineteenth century help to explain why cooking potlatch style and parsimonious household practices—marks of the artist/cook's aeconomia and of female regionalism more generally—seem so residual. Neoclassical economics reduces speculations about what constitutes the common good to the assumption that all individuals seek to maximize their utility and that the marketplace aggregates their numerous and diverse goods. Human desires and wants can be interpreted only through market processes and through the logic of self-interest. Speculations about what utility maximization might look like outside the marketplace are not rational, in part because they are not quantifiable and in part because no other mechanism for achieving the social good respects the equal right of all individuals to optimize their self-interested behavior. We might imagine a greater good from which all individuals would in fact benefit whether they know it or not, but it would not be one from which self-interested individuals could opt out: the greater good would have to trump any self-interested individual's conception of good.

Neoclassical definitions of the rational behavior of humans in the marketplace are especially hostile to the concept of parsimony, despite the fact that neoclassicism purports to respect the fact of scarce resources. In neoclassical economic theory, value is held to be a function of relative and comparative (dis)advantage only. The implication is that economic actors maximize their utility up to the very limit of their means and confront the fact of scarce resources not by ceasing their activities but by transferring their attention to other ranked preferences. Utility functions are plotted on a curve registering one's incrementally increasing unwillingness to pay more for more of the same commodity—its increasing disutility—given the presence of competing claims on one's attention and pocketbook. And those claims are omnipresent if humans are held to be creatures of infinite wants driven by self-interest and by an "obvious psychological law" such as "a greater gain is preferred to a smaller one."[22]

The logic of pricing one's wants and satisfactions by looking to the market insists on a merely abstract measure of utility. It cannot develop a theory of whether there should be limits to expenditure, or whether some forms of expenditure are more worthwhile than others, or whether it is a problem that different people have vastly unequal sums to expend. Only a transmarket theory of value—a definition of value outside the logic of price points in the market—could do so. The neoclassical theory of marginalism obviates any such possibility of developing a theory of absolute value. Pleasure (utility) or pain (disutility) cannot be measured as a whole quantity. "I never attempt to estimate the whole pleasure gained by purchasing a commodity," William Stanley Jevons announces, arguing that "the theory merely expresses that, when a man has purchased enough, he would derive equal pleasure from the possession of a small quantity more as he would from the money price of it."[23] What can be measured is the changing rate of (dis)satisfaction as other wants or needs come into view, and finally, a certain amount of money is switched to other uses. Reading human economic choices in terms of the market allows economists to understand loss in relative terms. To refrain from purchasing a small quantity more of a particular commodity could not be seen as an absolute loss since its absence exchanges for increased purchasing power and the pleasure of obtaining some other commodity.

By contrast, parsimony implies an absolute value. In the idiom of economics, it has a cardinal (whole) rather than ordinal (comparative) value. It comes into effect even if one supposes that there are no competing goods. On Green Island, the narrator's pleasure in her task never diminishes. She derives all of her satisfaction from digging just the right amount of potatoes (and no more). She experiences no other call on her time and pleasure. There is no last increment of disutility from the hard work of digging potatoes beyond which she might prefer to visit a store or to pay someone else to dig for her. Similarly, the value to the artist/cook of leaving the gingerbread house unadorned is not relational or fungible but absolute. Given that the house is unpainted, her aesthetic fulfils her purposes completely; no other aesthetic competes for her attention. Existing as an a priori good, not to achieve a comparative advantage, the concept of parsimony implies that though resources are indeed scarce, humans are not creatures of infinite wants, and moreover, they are capable of being parsimonious before the last degree of utility is reached. It would suggest, to rephrase Jevons, that humans might derive equal pleasure from some quantity less. If so, Jevons's axiom that humans prefer a greater gain to a smaller either seems false, or the function of a neoclassical dependence on a general equivalent whereby "quantities less" are exchangeable for the "money price"—the potential for purchasing more.

If utility for female regionalists can be described otherwise than in terms of the final degree—if parsimony must be distinguished from neoclassical concepts of scarcity—one key reason is that parsimony is underwritten by a principle of the common good. In *Country*, creating gingerbread houses and digging potatoes for free challenges the neoclassical principle of methodological individualism: the notion that all humans are self-interested and intent upon maximizing their utility in an environment where others, insatiably wanting, compete for the same scarce resources. Kitchen commonwealths have the capacity to interpret scarcity differently. The narrator's potato-digging necessarily observes the finite size of the potato patch and the future uses to which it must be put, but the principle of the moderate sum transforms the underlying economic mechanism from scarcity to sufficiency. What motivates the narrator to stop digging is not the fear of future scarcity but the knowledge that scarcity need never become an issue if she digs no more than a sufficient amount. The gingerbread house models a similar situation. Its parsimonious aesthetic of unadorned gingerbread reminds us of economic strategies that have worked well enough to sustain the human species from its forgotten childhood till now. Nonmarket economies are still up to the task of feeding a community—granted that the appetites of the feasters are not inspired by (metropolitan) cultures of excess and waste.

Economic modeling gingerbread style cannot be confined to the artist/cook's ethic of parsimony and potlatch. Other stakeholders—the narrator and the author (Jewett)—are implicated in the enterprise of modeling. The gingerbread artistry of the rural housewife constitutes the middle-class narrator's literary capital. The fiction includes what the artist/cook produces, but works to resituate—to recapitalize, really—its political economic meanings within a new discourse cognizant of the value of elaborate reading matter. The passage pursues a complicated rhetorical play with house, kitchen, models, and modelers. Chiasmic reversals, for example, are everywhere. Plain-style realism represents the gingerbread house's plain style. The Bowden house adopts the narrator; the narrator swallows *Bowden* whole. Houses contain kitchens, and kitchens contain ovens. But here an oven encloses the (miniature) Bowden house. The gingerbread house then serves to bring the house of Bowden together, only to be enclosed piecemeal by the Bowdens (in their stomachs). Modelers reprise this strategy. The cook turns out to be an artist and the narrator something of a gourmand. Moreover, the kitchen and its cook/artist model a sort of chiasmic history. "All such households from which this had descended" produce the Bowden house; the house in turn is said to reanimate the "tokens" it inherits from the past; and the gingerbread house incorporates both in miniature, even as, baked in "one of the last" brick ovens, it seems also to represent the apocalypse, the ruin, of the very history it recuperates. Left over is the undecipherable fragment from Mrs. Todd's meal, announcing a supplement—meaning(s) in excess of the facile assumption that *Bowden* is merely equivalent to Bowden.

Adding to the scene's accumulating conundrums, the gingerbread house's plain-gingerbread style demands to be rewritten as the fairy tale of Hansel and Gretel. This writing at the end of history—writing that is concurrent with the national anniversaries that have been lately kept—appears, perplexingly, to restore a child's story as a persuasive interpretive model. This particular fairy tale resists the logic of frugal economy that might have placed the food discourses of the Bowden reunion at the service of an Anglo-American-flavored nationalism. Ventriloquizing the gaudy house of fairy tale, the artist/cook's version is indeed frugally plain—but never quite rises to the level of critique. Admonishing readers about excess (candy), the tale also warns against the perilous lure of precisely what the artist/cook offers: free gingerbread. And it concludes with Hansel and Gretel returning home laden with the witch's riches. The scene cajoles us into reading one chiasmus—plain-style gingerbread/frugal realism—in terms of still another. The witch's rich gingerbread inverts the plain gingerbread of the artist/cook. Realism begins to look like fairy tale written backwards. There is, in short, no plain gingerbread reading of a gingerbread house that urges us to negotiate so many rhetorical positions. If anything, the house presides over its own rhetorical collapse as chiasmic reversals and unsettling paradoxes eat away at our certainty about what this model is supposed to model.

Political economic concepts are constantly implicated and elaborated in this gingerbread house discourse. The essay in cookery, for example, implies multiple, and not necessarily concordant, plots of polity. The making of the gingerbread house/text recapitulates common nineteenth-century conceptions about how societies evolve over time as, moving from raw materials to cooked food to language, it gestures with a sort of murky historicism toward an unfolding plot of social progress. An odd sense of historical positioning places this passage's culinary productions at the very dawn and at the very end of history. Cooked in an age of waste and excessive appetite, the gingerbread house urges us to look backward to a "far, forgotten childhood" when household management was thought to be characterized by subsistence. The child's story of Hansel and Gretel, its hungry children scavenging in the woods for any food they can find, seconds this interpretation. From that perspective, the essay in cookery seems to lay claim to a premodern economy pertinent to a rude state of society in which nothing is wasted and nothing accumulates, and which was thought to exist prior to a world of capital accumulation and market exchange. Yet realist verisimilitude—writing plain-gingerbread style—critiques, and supersedes, the passing mode of Mary Anna's verses. In this respect, plain-gingerbread realism seems to represent modernity itself, theorized in terms of a rupture with traditional lifestyles and cultural forms. One sign of that advance is the ability of women to parlay realism into capital: the cook's plain-gingerbread style inspires the narrator, and Jewett's account of it ushers *Country* into the marketplace.

Principles of capital accumulation supplement these nomadic plots of polity. The artist/cook's gingerbread gets eaten, but her fabrication becomes the capital from which the narrator and Jewett generate symbolic meaning and ultimately make it pay. The chapter adopts at least three conceptions of capital to underpin its account of writing styles: one where a good (the gingerbread house) is consumed immediately; one where a good is salted away to satisfy future consumption ("I'd laid half of that away for next time"); and one (Mary Anna's poetry; metropolitan showing-off) where a good is consumed to excess. That spectrum of possibilities aligns with discussions in classical theories of commonwealth about the fundamental role of capital accumulation in the dynamics of market economies and in the development of civilized societies. Laying half away for next time idiomatically rephrases Adam Smith's "general stock," which allows civilization to emerge by freeing humans from the "immediate consumption" characterizing a hand-to-mouth subsistence.[24] This model was itself being revised as late nineteenth-century writers promoted the necessity of excessive capital accumulation. Reprising Green Island's salute to moderation, the scene seems specifically to disavow this conception of capital—though, in another strange reversal, Mary Anna's poetry is thrust squarely into the past, where it functions as a sign of excess superseded by more economical modern forms.

A modeling of women's literary traditions proves to be an unexpected vector of this chapter's play with political economic principle. The efficiencies of pragmatic household economizing disclose the faults of Mary Anna's old-fashioned sentimental verse and the fading female poetic tradition it implies. Economies that fail to lay enough away for the future cannot survive for long. This was the principle that compelled the narrator to give up her enjoyable task in Mrs. Blackett's potato patch. The gingerbread house represents a more effective use of (cultural) capital: not because anything gets laid away—it is entirely consumed at the feast in fact—but because a woman's work in the kitchen and a woman's work in fiction capitalize each other under the sign of artist. The gingerbread is produced by the artist/cook, consumed by the narrator at the feast, reproduced as narrative by the narrator and Jewett, and consumed yet again in the marketplace for fiction. Material (gingerbread) becomes sign (*Bowden*) becomes marketed fiction in a series of incorporative gestures that grow the significance of the kitchen/fiction. Mary Anna's fading verse thereby attains a new status. Once assembled into the cook's, and the narrative's, symbolic reconstruction of the Bowden house, it can be thought of as the general stock that makes subsequent enterprises possible. Freeman's "An Autobiography," observed the same logic: it grew the capital of the original "The Revolt of 'Mother'" by repositioning it in a new market.

One implication of the gingerbread scene is that the sort of slow growth once pertinent to household economies has less and less contemporary value amid metropolitan cultures of excess and waste. Economizing itself may be a "last of," like the brick oven. What appears to be an urge to build a modern female literary tradition out of plain-gingerbread realism seems already out of step with the socioeconomic contexts of modernity. That style looks irretrievably past, even as it appears for the first time at the end of history (in the 1890s). Like "An Autobiography," Jewett's gingerbread discourse speaks of plain truths but enacts an unruly surplus of signification, contemplating new forms of cultural capital whose elaborate reading matter urges readers to adopt elaborate interpretive strategies. Those strategies privilege the cooked over the raw. If so, the passage's open-ended consideration of a model built, deconstructed, and remade as fable, metonym, sign of the Bowden house and the commonwealth it represents, would seem a much more persuasive way forward for female literary enterprises than the making of pie. It predicts the new forms of cultural capital soon to accrue to complex forms of writing under modernism. It would also suggest that Jewett, unlike her artist/cook counterpart, does assume the presence of competing aesthetic goods. For her, plain gingerbread realism has comparative or marginal value; it is not her last word in aesthetics. It partakes of a neoclassical economic logic.

Merely to say that the model gingerbread house models a commonwealth does scant justice to the complexity of gingerbread-style economics. Its miniature polity generates a discourse on an array of cultural practices and knowledge systems that weave into and around the economic: the interests of the body politic and of the common good; processes of historical change; various modes of capital accumulation and how to use them most efficiently. That discourse is, like the gingerbread house itself, pieced together out of heterogeneous materials and concepts. Incorporative and open-ended, it yokes its economical plain-style to an elaborate fabulism in order to produce a discourse on acts of modeling. The model compels attention most strikingly when, falling into ruin at the feast's end, it unmodels itself. Whatever meanings it has generated up to that point have to be reconciled with its curiously incomplete and indeterminate narrative architecture: pie-texts leave undecipherable fragments; a model falls apart; an essay fails to disclose its argument; precepts are never defined; pies lead to a practice of elaborate reading; and plain-gingerbread realism, as it keeps going back over its own ground in chiasmic reversals, wants to become as lavish and ornate as the gingerbread house of fairy tale. The elaborate reading matter on display at the Bowden feast urges us to elaborate—to develop, to think through, to enrich—the logic of model-making that underpins various discourses on economics. In the process it resists economic determinism—the notion that its conclusions are merely produced by its premises. And it resists the notion that the formal goal of the Bowden reunion is to produce a utopian republic, whether understood as a model female literary tradition, or US social relations as they are or could be.

To a mainstream economics grounding its scientific principles in mathematical formalism and market utilities, Jewett's hesitant and playful recuperation of the historicist and narrative underpinnings of political economic thought barely registers as economic knowledge of any kind. The complex and intriguing question is the extent to which literary and cultural studies of female regionalism participate in a neoclassical discursive regime when they overlook the diverse forms of kitchen economics. There would seem to be persuasive evidence to the contrary. Scholars responsible for the wealth of historically based studies of female regionalists exhibit no uncritical embrace of the ideologies of mainstream economics. It is nonetheless possible to uncover a compelling link between a late nineteenth-century paradigm shift in economics and the assumptions literary historians tend to make about what counts as economic knowledge. The very common counterworld hypotheses—the various ways scholars read female regionalism as a "counterworld to 1890s modernity"—provide an excellent example.[25] Scholars have contested the extent to which, and for what purpose, female regionalist writing constitutes a counterworld. What in contrast seems transparent and even irrefutable is the fact of modernity. A commonly accepted account of the late nineteenth century posits the shocking irruption of the new as the United States shifted from rural premodernity to a modern society marked by the ubiquity and transformative energies of markets. Socioeconomic turmoil and unsettling new market behaviors went hand in hand with the slow collapse of old authorities and certainties, with the emergence of diverse subjectivities and voices—and with a science dedicated to understanding economics in terms of markets, subjective experience, and relative utility.

Scholars seeking the most percipient responses to the economic transformations of the late nineteenth century have looked to works that acknowledge new material and psychic conditions consonant with the shock of modernity: Theodore Dreiser's *Sister Carrie* (1900), in which Carrie's fantasies of upwardly mobile consumerism offer a way "of imagining and managing the contradictions of a burgeoning consumer society;"[26] Frank Norris's *McTeague* (1899), with its representation of an "economics of desire" and its obsession with discourses about gold and money;[27] Henry James's *The Golden Bowl* (1904), its narrative epistemology "saturated with the imagery of the market";[28] and Edith Wharton's *The House of Mirth* (1905), whose characters, like Wharton herself, are both "consumer and commodity in the culture of commodity aesthetics."[29] All of these approaches emphasize a market-driven modernity characterized by fractured subjectivities and diverse and clashing cultural formations. From that perspective, a gingerbread house model of the old Bowden house registers as a quaint vestige of, or nostalgia for, premodern conditions: one (Anglo-American) nation, one (white) people, one (village) community, characterized by republicanism, nativism, slow-paced rural life, and rudimentary potlatch economies. This "regionalist body" is "fundamentally an obsolescent body."[30]

As this formulation implies, historical accounts emphasizing the transformative effects of market society can resemble what I call a plot of polity. This is not to say that they conform to nineteenth-century stadialist assumptions about civilization or that they accept that historical events are shaped by metahistorical principles. But they replicate two crucial aspects of stadialist practice. First, they appraise modernity from the standpoint of the end of history—that is to say, the late twentieth and early twenty-first century—so that accounts of the advent of modernity imply a still broader plot of postmodernity. Underpinning histories of the 1890s is an entire coordinating narrative that includes a grasp of what modernity led to: mercurial flows of capital and fluid movements of people around the globe under postcolonial conditions; the rapid shuffling of work forces; ever-increasing disruptions to established work patterns and lifestyles; mantras of creative destruction, rapid development, and substitutability; a consumerist milieu of surfaces, simula-cra, and schizophrenia; the breakup of stable categories of nationality, race, ethnicity, and gender. The fact that the 1890s partook of radical transfor-mations that are known to have intensified in subsequent decades—indeed they are held to define global conditions in the early twenty-first century—consolidates a sense that we have accurately described the most important socioeconomic features of modernity.

Second, the challenges (post)modernity posed and still pose to social and cultural forms governed by homogeneity means that premodern soci-ality is not held to be merely past but obsolescent. Since our most intellectu-ally agile interpreters of postmodernity have demonstrated the importance of challenging totalizing thinking as a matter of political and philosophical progress, the attitudes scholars adopt toward late capitalist and postcolonial conditions rarely include any desire to recuperate an outmoded allegiance to stable values and homogeneous forms. Historicist perspectives governed by the prefix post- (modern, colonial, capitalist, and so forth) exert a pressure on literary histories to account for late nineteenth-century writing in terms of its embrace of ever greater complexities, contested subjectivities and cul-tures, and eroding centers. The problem with taking parsimony and potlatch as serious economic solutions to complex late nineteenth-century socioeco-nomic dilemmas is not merely that they represent a simplistically retrograde answer to a bewildering situation in which one is both consumer and com-modity. They seem simplistic because we know them now to be solutions incapable of countenancing postness. To the extent that they were offered as authentic and stable solutions, they were out of step with the broader plot of postmodernity to which we are now privy.

A number of second-wave feminists who wrote the first hagiographic re-evaluations of female regionalists and then went on to rescind or compli-cate them offer evidence for the power of such historicist approaches. In New Essays on "The Country of the Pointed Firs," Sandra A. Zagarell acknowl-edges the accuracy of her earlier approach to Country while admitting its limits. Amid the turmoil of a modernizing United States, the book's radial, concentric structure looks less radical than repetitively static; its matrifocal world favors a sense of community built around narrow family ties.[31] Eliza-beth Ammons writes dismissively of her earlier fondness for the precapital-ist, prepatriarchal, matrifocal world of the Bowden reunion, where women seem to have real status and power. The reunion is in fact "about racial pu-rity and white cultural dominance," its design "protofascist."[32] Sarah Way Sherman emphasizes the fact that Jewett's "celebration of the preindustrial world, while powerful . . . evades the difficulty of applying its lessons to the task of healing a society structured through the inequalities of imperialism and industrial capitalism."[33] For Zagarell, Ammons, and Sherman—like Glazener—a new awareness of what counts as the material historical facts of the late nineteenth-century sets limits to Jewett's (and other regionalists') critique; the fantasy of a preindustrial world could never prove fully relevant to an industrializing one.[34]

That awareness also has the effect of aligning these scholars' careers with a plot of postmodernity. Their earlier, one-dimensional appraisals, their nostalgia for a cultural discourse ratifying unity, purity, and totality—albeit of and for women—have been revolutionized. They are now alive to complex alterations and competing paradigms, newly alert to imagining and managing contradiction. Unlike the regionalists they study, they are prepared to address the problem of our age. These scholars' mea culpas imply a standpoint situated far enough along the timeline of (post)modernity to be aware of their own protomodern yearnings. To recognize the fact of colonial exotica at the reunion means that Ammons must be looking backward from a postcolonial vantage; for her to write off the "female worlds of love and ritual" approach is to acknowledge the limits of "white feminist readings," among which, in a neat sleight of hand, she places her younger self.[35] Mapping her career onto the progress of feminist thought, Ammons brings an entire plot of (post)modernity into view: the category of white feminist shifts from what once seemed ontologically secure—something she was—to an unstable political category capable of affiliating with all manner of diverse beings. Perhaps Ammons's most subtle maneuver is the claim that the Bowden reunion is protofascist. That claim shapes two historical perspectives, only one of which is evident. It is not unimaginable that Jewett's (supposed) yearning for a racially pure community participates in the West's half-century-long plunge toward fascism. But the reunion could not be thought of as protofascist until a postfascist moment fully aware of the horrors of twentieth-century fascism has arrived. Ammons and her readers must be capable of looking back from a postmodern end of history to see how multiple plots of progress march in synchrony. Modernity leads to rupture (fascism, but also feminism), to a nostalgic infatuation with pure, stable categories (fascist and racist ideology, but also the naive celebration of woman power in Ammons's early career and in second-wave feminism); thence to the crucial postmodern moment when feminism effects what fascism cannot: a critique of totalitarian thinking, beginning with its own original yearning for stable categories and strict oppositions.

Though Ammons's approach is in many ways at odds with Fetterley and Pryse's *Writing out of Place*, the latter work also exemplifies what I call a plot of postmodernity: the inevitable advance from homogeneity into diversity and difference. Fetterley and Pryse call on the powerful forces of modernity—socioeconomic forces governed by male ideologies of nation, property, and capital—in order to produce the difference of female regionalism as a counterworld that resides somewhere outside economic relations of property and ownership. That difference celebrates all that is decentered, diverse, and queer in female regionalist writing against the aggressive attempts of male power to homogenize, totalize, discipline, and silence—to make obsolete—all that is Other. For them, female regionalists represent what we know now modernity was capable of becoming. Regionalists are precursors of postmodernity, able to represent difference and diversity without nostalgia or mourning. Part of the subtle cultural work Fetterley and Pryse perform is to thoroughly update second-wave feminists who used to read the oppositional strategies of female regionalism in terms of the premodern and preindustrial. This was in its time a radical and ambitious move, but one that that would hardly suffice for third-wave feminists cognizant of the historical evolution of woman into an extraordinarily diverse and problematic category—cognizant of how relatively stable (pre)modern categories can and must unravel into (post)modern diversity. In this, they share an interpretive orientation with new historicist thinking. Fetterley and Pryse historicize female regionalism by way of a trope of decenteredness, new historicists do so by way of a trope of contested centers—all respect the fact that the place of modernity can no longer be represented authentically by premodern formations. And from these diverse positions they emphasize the fact that kitchen economics is not congruent with economic knowledge.[36]

Exerting pressure on scholars to conceptualize the late nineteenth century in terms of a modernizing economy, a plot of postmodernity enacts a weak version of nineteenth-century stadialism. Concepts such as parsimony, potlatch, and the moderate sum are automatically consigned to a premodern stage, which led to the now familiar structures of global capitalism. My remarks about "Miss Beulah's Bonnet" in the introduction could be construed in this fashion. Miss Beulah makes perfectly rational economic decisions in her kitchen commonwealth, but Janey's admiration at the end of the story for the new hat ("Pitty, pitty bonnet!" [213]) coming "express" (213) from Chicago might be thought consonant with the socioeconomic changes structuring the real world of modernity. Because the "tasty" bonnet underscores a link between Miss Beulah's material economizing and her psychic repression, it appears to consign acts such as stewing up old hens and making do with one old bonnet to an unmourned economic oblivion. My analysis of Freeman's predilection in "An Autobiography" for fluid values liberated from cows and barns follows a similar pattern. And gingerbread-style economics seems to align itself with a neoclassical regime of markets and comparative values to the extent that Jewett's unruly rhetorical play—*her* elaborate reading matter—marks a difference from, and capitalizes upon, the artist/cook's faith in an imaginary body politic, homogeneous, easily sated, and plainly visible to the modeler's eye. Kitchens become heterotopias and relevant to the critical understanding, it seems, when introduced to market forces.

In this final section I set out to complicate that stadial model in two ways. First, accounts of aeconomia need not resolve in favor of readings where modern market forces irrupt into the once-homogeneous environs of the late nineteenth-century kitchen. The concept of heterotopia can instead be employed to reveal the principles of order underlying various constructions of "the economic." It need not adjudicate between them. Second, and as a contribution to that work of investigating our structuring assumptions, I seek to restore economic significance to what has always caused so much unease about the kitchen commonwealth: its counterworld or premodern aspects. Here, twenty-first century efforts to challenge the hegemony of neoclassical economics are of paramount importance. That goal overlaps the concerns of nineteenth-century political economy to the extent that it attempts to make the study of economics historically aware, ethically engaged, and open to raising philosophical questions about the rational framework within which the science of markets proceeds. A relatively small number of works have in fact taken on the specific task of returning mainstream economics to a "rich, diverse, multidimensional and pluralistic" conception of political economy.[37] But calls for a historically based and socially engaged alternative to neoclassical economic formalism have emerged more broadly from our contemporary landscape of ecological crisis. Writing from this end of history, a moment that may prove to be the end of history-writing as a scholarly activity—if not actual extinction—affords a new context for understanding the advent of modernity, the fictional forms appropriate to it, and the historical models we assume when we address them. The effects of this new context are especially acute when it comes to the aspects of a kitchen economic idiom that seems most out of step with the advent of modern market society: plain-gingerbread economies inscribed in principles of parsimony, sufficiency, and slow capital accumulation, all placed at the service of the common good.

The artist/cook's arguments about economic sustainability in a kitchen commonwealth dovetail neatly with twenty-first century analyses of the shortcomings of mainstream economic theory and practice in the face of impending ecological collapse. In a metaphor addressed to the carrying capacity of the earth, Herman E. Daly observes that however efficiently one distributes the cargo of a boat, too much cargo will still sink it.[38] The central fact of the "scale of human activity relative to the biosphere" is that it has "grown too large."[39] Throughput—the life of material resources from production to disposal—has become unsustainable because natural resources are being exploited at an alarming rate and because waste sinks are already overloaded. Climate change is one index of the inability of the biosphere to process increasing pollution; fears of a catastrophic collapse of the biosphere are growing. An August 2018 headline in the *Economist* announced: "The world is losing the war against climate change."

The threat of profound climate change "changes everything" when it comes to long-term human survival.[40] In large part that depends on dramatically transforming hegemonic socioeconomic structures and principles. There are numerous possibilities, most of which challenge in some way the logic of free-market capitalism. One is that human beings "have limited wants and needs."[41] Another promising avenue is localism. Focusing on the economy of specific regions offers one way to diminish external costs. Eating food locally produced, for example, reduces transport costs and pollution and fosters small markets. "In my backyard" thinking—taking control of the infrastructure and economies of one's locality—can help raise awareness of the actual costs and benefits of building a road or power plant. The new economic regionalism may help assuage some of the worst effects of global capitalism: the enormous expenditure of moving goods around the world and the sense that decisions of great import to a particular area are made anonymously elsewhere. Localism can also advance more extreme solutions to environmental crisis, such as small self-sufficient communities off-grid and off-market. In all cases, green economic solutions imply sometimes spiritual but certainly ethical aspirations about the directions economies should take. These, like an ethic of parsimony, must be logically prior to market pricing and methodological individualism. If, following the logic of laying half away for next time, we were to mandate a reduction in pollution by half in the next decade, such a procedure would circumvent any question of (market) cost as well as of cost-benefit analysis. There would be no trade-off between benefit and cost to analyze—no conceivable disutility compared to the good of saving global life. Green economics celebrates the "transcendence of moral values."[42]

Among the consequences of such a change is the fact that markets, if markets are to remain a necessary component of human economic life, "will have to learn to function without expansion."[43] Concepts linked to earlier manifestations of environmentalism such as sustainable growth and sustainable development would come under scrutiny, since both imply an enlargement of the economy as well as, probably, an unequal distribution of wealth. In our contemporary idiom, developers are those responsible for supplying new capital goods and infrastructure. The neoclassical assumption that healthy economies must grow to assuage infinite wants seems especially suspect. Green economists have increasingly argued in favor of sufficiency marked by a state of equilibrium between economic and ecological systems—a steady-state economy—maintained by the lowest possible rates of throughput.[44] For people and nations characterized by overconsumption, a steady-state economy implies degrowth and the end of progress.[45] Such measures are designed to downsize economies and throughput, and to bolster new forms of sociality and subjectivity no longer transfixed by (over)consumption. It may also involve a return to scarcity—a move to make the bottom line of economic planning reflect the fact that natural resources are not simply finite but actually diminishing.[46]

One important aspect of an ecologically minded economics is its critique of neoclassical theories of relative value. Market-based approaches—even in this moment of ecocrisis—still refuse to contemplate the possibility of absolute disutility. Economists (including many environmental economists) are drawn to the logic that in a free market disutility can be assumed to exchange for a potential market: pollution, for example, incentivizes new markets in green energy and carbon permits, as well as new technologies and industries; the depletion of one natural resource incentivizes the exploiting of another. Human ingenuity expressed in the shape of markets can be thought to cope with, say, the depletion of oil reserves or even the extinction of certain plant and animal species. Many green economists disagree. Taking measures merely to reduce pollution may do little more than extend the life of a fragile biosphere. The cumulative effects of even reduced calls on waste sinks might cause catastrophic change. Such an approach leaves intact the terrifying possibility of a black swan event—a once-in-a-thousand-years phenomenon. Ecosystems may not function on the principle of incremental change familiar to analysts of economic systems, leaving open the (wholly unpredictable) chance that the biosphere might suffer a nonlinear collapse—sudden, critical, and irrevocable.

Green economic thought comports with the artist/cook's kitchen economics and with many other moments of *Country*: Mrs. Todd's careful lading of the boat to keep it afloat; Mrs. Blackett's housekeeping; the narrator's digging potatoes. Each addresses ethical concerns and moors them to the balanced and efficient allocation of scarce resources. These are sufficient, and even plentiful, within the specified constraints of each scene: one basket of potatoes, but no more; one haddock, with which Mrs. Blackett will "make . . . do"; one boat, that carries all that is needed to Green Island; one wheelbarrow with enough room for a load of lobsters; and one gingerbread house that was enough to satisfy a great part of the assembly. Markets, to the extent that they intrude (such as Mrs. Todd's sale of William's lobsters), are small and local. And all characters operate with one eye on sustainability (leaving potatoes in the ground; laying half away for next time; conveying no more than a wheelbarrow-full of lobsters). This form of kitchen commonwealth is consistent with abstract classical economic principles. Participants at the Bowden feast consider their preferences (English pies or American pies? plain pies or adorned? realism or sentimental poetry?) and act rationally to ensure that there is enough for everyone. Such moments, however, typically resist the implication of comparative (dis)utility. Making a gingerbread house is not subject to a theory of marginal utility. Building it takes all of the artist/cook's time, energy, and artistic enterprise; there is no other once it is consumed. The gingerbread house is inconsistent with a neoclassical theory of markets insofar as it recognizes the possibility of an absolute good, an absolute loss, and a principle of consumption that conforms to those absolutes.

Green economics accords a new legitimacy to key principles of economics gingerbread style. It also compels us to rethink how we model the socioeconomic history of the late nineteenth century. This is not to deny the import of massive socioeconomic and psychological transformations produced by a corporatizing economy fomenting a newly potent ethos of consumerism—there would be no crisis without them—but rather to resituate them in a differently constructed historical narrative. The concept of 1890s modernity typically invokes a plot, or narrative arc, of postmodernity, leading from the explosive rise of corporate capitalism and consumerism to the historical moment that seems to seal the story—our moment of postcolonial global capitalism. The threat of incipient ecocatastrophe transforms that plot in two ways. First, it compels us to interpret our present moment in terms of forthcoming massive changes, which will consist of either embracing a new green ethic of sufficiency or facing the collapse or (at a minimum) serious disruption of global economic systems. This is not a conjecture about the future of the global economy but the logical outcome of staying the present course of ecological degradation. (Ecosystems do not necessarily obey any law of economic systems.) To the extent that we are scientifically sure that the consequences of (post)modernity will lead to its demise, descriptions of modernity need to extend their arc into the future. This approach creates an inverted stadial model. Instead of the certainties accruing to the backward glance of nineteenth-century stadialism, we look to the certainties of the proleptic glance, anticipating the new shape of history that ecocrisis will inevitably cause.

Second, revaluing concepts such as frugality, commonwealth, sufficiency, the region, and the local community as what we (that is, everyone and everything on this earth) require to survive has important ramifications for interpreting the productions of the *oikos* and the histories we tell to contextualize it. Taking the perspective of a long ecohistory stretching back from the twenty-first century to the late nineteenth, it is possible to argue that frugality, self-sufficiency, gift and barter economies, small local markets, and questions about the common good—the frequent signs of kitchen common-wealths—are not premodern so much as a marker of modernity that current concerns make visible and, with increasing urgency, force us to revalue. The late nineteenth century then appears not so much as a rupture with the past but as the first major step along a continuum that leads toward the possibility of catastrophic rupture *now*—toward an era when new procedures for mass production, distribution, and consumption began in earnest the process of overloading earth's ecosystems, supported by neoclassical economic ideologies that interpreted humans as creatures of insatiable wants, that rescripted parsimony and frugality as vestigial signs of a premodern world, and that dismissed compelling questions about the common good. In the light of our imperative need for parsimony now, it is 1890s modernity that turns out to be premodern, and the prophetess of what comes after our postmodern moment is no longer Sister Carrie but Jewett's artist/cook. Put another way, a gingerbread-house and Green-Island economics of sufficiency and the moderate sum are nearly, and necessarily, upon us, either in the form of rational decisions taken to bring human socioeconomic life into equilibrium with ecosystems, or in the form of massive structural changes wrought, willy-nilly, by catastrophic climate change.

From this point of view, Jewett's economic fabulism is not an alternative to the artist/cook's frugal aeconomia but a way of keeping alive a number of economic options within an open-ended discourse on model-making. In keeping those options alive, it directs attention toward the models that structure what counts as economic knowledge—and, just as importantly, models that have been discounted as issues of no consequence to mainstream economics—and makes them part of its discourse too. Economics gingerbread style incorporates the tendency of nineteenth-century political economic discourse to adopt diverse modes of expression: from cultural fable to economic law, from markets to marvelous islands. It finds itself aligned nowadays with the new privilege being accorded a political economy predisposed toward raising broad social and historical issues. The strange amalgam of fabulism and abstract economic principles on display in the gingerbread scene suggests that the model commonwealth thus adumbrated is not consistent with an aspirational or utopian representation of the United States. Rather, it leaves open the manner in which the Bowden reunion can be scaled up to a nation—whether the sequence of metonyms leading us from the gingerbread house to the Bowden house to the house of Bowden can proceed a step further to the house of the nation. And it leaves open the question of whether the model of a small-market community can be imagined even though the community it represents fictionally is staunchly white. At a moment when we dearly need better economic models, Jewett's discourse on the political economy of a gingerbread house is a place to start. The abstract economic principles considered there, and the way of thinking about them, afford us—meaning everyone and everything on this earth—a better chance of survival. This is what our historical moment in modernity requires.

NOTES

Introduction

1. Rose Terry Cooke, "Miss Beulah's Bonnet," in *How Celia Changed Her Mind and Selected Stories*, ed. Elizabeth Ammons (Rutgers, NJ: Rutgers University Press, 1986), 196. Subsequent references in this chapter are incorporated within the text.

2. Timothy Sweet, *American Georgics: Economy and Environment in Early American Literature* (Philadelphia: University of Pennsylvania Press, 2002), 122.

3. Eric J. Sundquist, ed, *American Realism: New Essays* (Baltimore: Johns Hopkins University Press, 1982), 19.

4. I take the term "incorporation" from Alan Trachtenberg, *The Incorporation of America: Culture and Society in the Gilded Age* (New York: Hill and Wang, 1982). Other influential histories pinning cultural change in the United States to the striking emergence of corporate capitalism and consumerism are Warren I. Susman, *Culture as History: The Transformation of American Society in the Twentieth Century* (1973; New York: Pantheon, 1984) and James Livingston, *Pragmatism and the Political Economy of Cultural Revolution, 1850–1940* (Chapel Hill: University of North Carolina Press, 1994). Steeples and Whitten provide a succinct account of late nineteenth-century transformations of the American economy in *Democracy in Desperation: The Depression of 1893* (Westport, CT: Greenwood, 1998), 14–23; also useful are Michael Zakim and Gary J. Kornblith, "Introduction: An American Revolutionary Tradition," in *Capitalism Takes Command: The Social Transformation of Nineteenth-Century America*, ed. Gary J. Kornblith and Michael Zakim (Chicago: University of Chicago Press, 2012), 1–2; and Martin J. Sklar, *The Corporate Reconstruction of American Capitalism, 1890–1916* (Cambridge, UK: University of Cambridge Press, 1988), 1–33.

5. Regenia Gagnier, *The Insatiability of Human Wants: Economics and Aesthetics in Market Society* (Chicago: University of Chicago Press, 2000), 1. Among important histories of the rise of consumerism are Richard Wightman Fox and T. J. Jackson Lears, eds., *The Culture of Consumption: Critical Essays in American History, 1880–1980* (New York: Pantheon, 1983); Daniel Horowitz, *The Morality of Spending: Attitudes toward the Consumer Society in America, 1875–1940* (Baltimore: Johns Hopkins University Press, 1985); Rachel Bowlby, *Just Looking: Consumer Culture in Dreiser, Gissing, and Zola* (New York: Methuen, 1985); and William Leach, *Land of Desire: Merchants, Power, and the Rise of a New American Culture* (New York: Pantheon, 1993). Walter

Benn Michaels connected late nineteenth-century debates about money to the logic of naturalism in *The Gold Standard and the Logic of Naturalism* (Berkeley: University of California Press, 1987).

6. Sundquist, *Realism*, 19.

7. I take the term "consuming desire" from Lawrence Birken, *Consuming Desire: Sexual Science and the Emergence of a Culture of Abundance, 1871–1914* (Cornell, NY: Cornell University Press, 1988). I have also found invaluable Gagnier, *The Insatiability of Human Wants*, and Jeffrey Sklansky, *The Soul's Economy: Market Society and Selfhood in American Thought,* 1820–1920 (Chapel Hill: University of North Carolina Press, 2002).

8. I take the term here from Nancy Bentley, *Frantic Panoramas: American Literature and Mass Culture 1870–1920* (Philadelphia: University of Pennsylvania Press, 2009).

9. I am thinking here specifically of the connection T. J. Jackson Lears makes between the rise of consumer capitalism and a "therapeutic ethos" in *No Place of Grace: Antimodernism and the Transformation of American Culture, 1880–1920* (Chicago: University of Chicago Press, 1994).

10. Rosalind H. Williams, *Dream Worlds: Mass Consumption in Late Nineteenth-Century France* (Berkeley: University of California Press, 1982), 67. For studies of new urban marketplaces, consumerist "dream worlds," and ad cultures, see Williams, *Dream Worlds*; Bowlby, *Just Looking*; Simon J. Bronner, *Consuming Visions: Accumulation and Display of Goods in America, 1880–1920* (New York: Norton, 1989); and Ellen Gruber Garvey, *The Adman in the Parlor: Magazines and the Gendering of Consumer Culture, 1880s to 1910s* (New York: Oxford University Press, 1996).

11. I refer here to Mary McAleer Balkun's argument in *The American Counterfeit: Authenticity and Identity in American Literature and Culture* (Tuscaloosa: University of Alabama Press, 2006).

12. I summarize Rita Felski's analysis of the complex forms of women's experience as they entered the new, burgeoning marketplaces of the late nineteenth century in *The Gender of Modernity* (Cambridge, MA: Harvard University Press, 1995).

13. Mark Seltzer, *Bodies and Machines* (New York: Routledge, 1991), 122.

14. Richard Brodhead, *Cultures of Letters: Scenes of Reading and Writing in Nineteenth-Century America* (Chicago: University of Chicago Press, 1993), 146.

15. June Howard, introduction to *New Essays on "The Country of the Pointed Firs,"* ed. June Howard (New York: Cambridge University Press, 1994), 11.

16. Susan V. Donaldson, *Competing Voices: The American Novel, 1865–1914* (New York: Twayne, 1998), 43.

17. Amy Kaplan, *The Social Construction of American Realism* (Chicago: University of Chicago Press, 1988), 21.

18. Howard, introduction, 4.

19. Herbert G. Gutman, *The Black Family in Slavery and Freedom, 1750–1925* (New York: Pantheon, 1976), 532.

20. Amy Kaplan, "Manifest Domesticity," *American Literature* 70, no. 3 (September 1998): 581, 582.

21. Ben Railton, *Contesting the Past, Reconstructing the Nation: American Literature and Culture in the Gilded Age, 1876–1893* (Tuscaloosa: University of Alabama Press, 2007), ix.

22. William Tabb, *Reconstructing Political Economy: The Great Divide in Economic Thought* (London: Routledge, 1999), 53.

23. John Stuart Mill, *Principles of Political Economy* (London: John W. Parker, 1848; reprint New York: Augustus M. Kelley, 1987), 176.

24. Mill, *Principles of Political Economy*, 13.

25. Murray Milgate and Shannon C. Stimson, for example, argue that later economists progressively narrowed the rich social implications of Adam Smith's work; see, for example, *After Adam Smith: A Century of Transformation in Politics and Political Economy* (Princeton, NJ: Princeton University Press, 2009), 5–6. For a similar argument, see Tabb, *Reconstructing Political Economy*, 39–51.

26. Tabb, *Reconstructing Political Economy*, 15.

27. Drucilla K. Barker and Edith Kuiper provide an excellent overview of these issues in their introduction to *Toward a Feminist Philosophy of Economics* (London: Routledge, 2003), 1–18.

28. Charlotte Perkins Gilman, *Women and Economics* (Boston: Small, Maynard, 1898; reprint Berkeley: University of California Press, 1998), 13, 118.

29. Claudia Tate, *Domestic Allegories of Political Desire: The Black Heroine's Text at the Turn of the Century* (New York: Oxford University Press, 1992), 142.

30. Ann Romines, *The Home Plot: Women, Writing, and Domestic Ritual* (Amherst: University of Massachusetts Press, 1992), 77.

31. Elizabeth Ammons, "Going in Circles: The Female Geography of Jewett's *The Country of the Pointed Firs*," *Studies in the Literary Imagination* 16, no. 2 (Fall 1983): 89.

32. Sarah Way Sherman, *Sarah Orne Jewett, an American Persephone* (Hanover, NH: University Press of New England, 1989), 195. My phrase "female world of love, ritual, and community" invokes Carroll Smith-Rosenberg's 1975 essay, "The Female World of Love and Ritual: Relations between Women in Nineteenth-Century America," *Signs* 1, no. 1 (Autumn 1975): 1–29. For other feminist-inspired perspectives privileging female regionalist "counterworlds," see Josephine Donovan, *New England Local Color Literature: A Women's Tradition* (New York: Frederick Ungar, 1983); Sandra A. Zagarell, "Narrative of Community: The Identification of a Genre," *Signs* 13, no. 3 (Spring 1988): 498–527; Elizabeth Ammons, *Conflicting Stories: American Women Writers at the Turn into the Twentieth Century* (New York: Oxford University Press, 1991); Helen Fiddyment Levy, *Fictions of the Home Place: Jewett, Cather, Glasgow, Porter, Welty, and Naylor* (Jackson: University Press of Mississippi, 1992); Margaret Roman, *Sarah Orne Jewett: Reconstructing Gender* (Tuscaloosa: University of Alabama Press, 1992); Romines, *The Home Plot* (1992); Laurie Shannon, "The Country of Our Friendship: Jewett's Intimist Art," *American Literature* 71, no. 2 (June 1999): 227–62; Laura Nicosia, "Jewett's *The Country of the Pointed Firs*," *Explicator* 62, no. 2 (2004): 89–91, https://doi.org/10.1080/00144940409597181.

33. Donovan, *New England*, 56.

34. Catriona Sandilands, "The Importance of Reading Queerly: Jewett's Deephaven as Feminist Ecology," *Interdisciplinary Studies in Literature and Environment* 11, no. 2 (Summer 2004): 69, 72, https://doi.org/10.1093/isle/11.2.57.

35. Judith Fetterley and Marjorie Pryse, *Writing out of Place: Regionalism, Women, and American Literary Culture* (Urbana: University of Illinois Press, 2003), 267. I follow Fetterley and Pryse in using the term "regionalists" rather than "realists" in order to draw attention to the specific domain of female regionalism.

36. Nancy Glazener, *Reading for Realism: The History of a U. S. Literary Institution, 1850–1910* (Durham, NC: Duke University Press, 1997), 223.

37. Andrew Lawson, *Downwardly Mobile: The Changing Fortunes of American Realism* (New York: Oxford University Press, 2012), 9.

38. Lawson, *Downwardly Mobile*, 7.

39. Glazener, *Reading for Realism*, 221. Like Glazener, Gillian Brown argues in *Domestic Individualism: Imagining Self in Nineteenth-Century America* (Berkeley: University of California Press, 1990) that domesticity was not antithetical to market society or to (white male) ideologies of possessive individualism.

40. Beth Sutton-Ramspeck, *Raising the Dust: The Literary Housekeeping of Mary Ward, Sarah Grand, and Charlotte Perkins Gilman* (Columbus: Ohio State University Press, 2004), 3–4.

41. Lora Romero, *Home Fronts: Domesticity and Its Critics in the Antebellum United States* (Durham, NC: Duke University Press, 1997), 65.

42. Gilman, *Women and Economics*, 30–31, 39.

43. Claudia C. Klaver, *A/Moral Economics: Classical Political Economy and Cultural Authority in Nineteenth-Century England* (Columbus: Ohio State University Press, 2003), xxiv.

44. Dimitris Milonakis and Ben Fine, *From Political Economy to Economics: Method, the Social and the Historical in the Evolution of Economic Theory* (London: Routledge, 2009), 2.

45. Tabb, *Reconstructing Political Economy*, 6.

46. Howard Horwitz, *By the Law of Nature: Form and Value in Nineteenth-Century America* (New York: Oxford University Press, 1991), 127.

47. For incisive critiques from a feminist perspective of the history and significance of homo economicus, see Julie A. Nelson's *Feminism, Objectivity, and Economics* (New York: Routledge, 1996) and Gillian J. Hewitson's *Feminist Economics: Interrogating the Masculinity of Rational Economic Man* (Cheltenham, UK: Edward Elgar, 1999).

48. Michael Kimmel and Amy Aronson, introduction to *Women and Economics* (Berkeley: University of California Press, 1998), vii.

49. Charlotte Perkins Gilman's *What Diantha Did* (1909), a novel about a young woman's (successful) struggle to enter the marketplace, in fact seems a natural and compelling sequel to the more covert female regionalist concern with political economy.

50. Laura Brown, *Fables of Modernity: Literature and Culture in the English Eighteenth Century* (Cornell, NY: Cornell University Press, 2001), 1–3, 114.

51. The phrase "supposing an island" is taken from John Locke's classic account of how humans enlarge their capital stock beyond the level of subsistence.

52. Catherine Gallagher, *The Body Economic: Life, Death, and Sensation in Political Economy and the Victorian Novel* (Princeton, NJ: Princeton University Press, 2006), 3.

53. Aristotle, *The Politics*, translated by Carnes Lord (Chicago: University of Chicago Press, 1984), 101.

54. Here and in subsequent chapters I refer to Julia Kristeva's work on abjection in *Powers of Horror: An Essay on Abjection*, trans. Leon S. Roudiez (New York: Columbia University Press, 1982). Abjection describes a process in which the symbolic expelling of impurities or improper bodies helps to secure hegemonic definitions of normalized identities.

55. Annabel Patterson, *Fables of Power: Aesopian Writing and Political History* (Durham, NC: Duke University Press, 1991).

56. Leo Bersani, *A Future for Astyanax: Character and Desire in Literature* (Boston: Little, Brown, 1976), 61.

57. Foucault, "Of Other Spaces," translated by Jay Miskowiec, http://foucault.info/doc/documents/heterotopia/foucault-heterotopia-en-html, n.p.

58. Keith Hetherington, *The Badlands of Modernity: Heterotopia and Social Ordering* (London: Routledge, 1997), viii.

59. Robert J. Topinka, "Foucault, Borges, Heterotopia: Producing Knowledge in Other Spaces," *Foucault Studies* 9 (September 2010): 56, 60–61.

60. Ben Fine and Dimitris Milonakis, *From Economics Imperialism to Freakonomics: The Shifting Boundaries between Economics and Other Social Sciences* (London: Routledge, 2009), 134.

61. Alfred Marshall, *Principles of Economics* (New York: Macmillan, 1891), 5.

62. William Stanley Jevons, *The Theory of Political Economy* (New York, Macmillan, 1871; reprint New York: Kelley and Millman, 1957), 21.

63. Milgate and Stimson, *After Adam Smith*, 5–6.

64. Milgate and Stimson, *After Adam Smith*, 6.

65. Quoted in Charles E. Staley, *A History of Economic Thought from Aristotle to Arrow* (Oxford, UK: Basil Blackwell, 1989), 133–34.

Chapter 1

1. Adam Smith, *The Wealth of Nations* (London: Strahan and Cadell, 1776; reprint, New York: Bantam, 2003), 22–24.

2. Smith, *Wealth*, 12, 25.

3. Smith, *Wealth*, 987.

4. Smith, *Wealth*, 988.

5. Smith, *Wealth*, 355–56.

6. Regenia Gagnier, *The Insatiability of Human Wants: Economics and Aesthetics in Market Society* (Chicago: University of Chicago Press, 2000), 73.

7. Lewis H. Morgan, *Ancient Society* (New York: Holt, 1877), 389, 390.

8. Henry Wood, *The Political Economy of Natural Law* (Boston: Lee and Shepard, 1894), 153. (Wood's italics.)

9. John Locke, "The Second Treatise of Government," in *The Selected Political Writings of John Locke* (New York: Norton, 2005), 32, 37.

10. I rely in this chapter on Ronald L. Meek's exemplary discussion of stages theory

in *Social Science and the Ignoble Savage* (New York: Cambridge University Press, 1976), 5–36.

11. See Cathy Boeckmann, *A Question of Character: Scientific Racism and the Genres of American Fiction, 1892–1912* (Tuscaloosa: University of Alabama Press, 2000) for an excellent discussion of pseudoscientific theories designed to buttress white supremacy in the late nineteenth century.

12. The reviewer was Florence Kelley; quoted in Amy Aronson and Michael Kimmel, introduction to *Women and Economics* (Berkeley: University of California Press, 1998), xxviii–ix.

13. The essay was first published in the *North American Review* (1889); it was better known as "The Gospel of Wealth" by the time it was reprinted in *The Gospel of Wealth and other Timely Essays* (1900). For an overview of the dissemination of "The Gospel of Wealth," see David Nasaw, introduction to *The "Gospel of Wealth" Essays and Other Writings* (New York: Penguin, 2006), viii–ix.

14. Andrew Carnegie, "Wealth," *North American Review* 148, no. 391 (June 1889): 653.

15. Carnegie, "Wealth," 661.

16. Andrew Carnegie, *The Gospel of Wealth and Other Timely Essays* (New York: Century, 1901), xxii; Carnegie, "Wealth," 655.

17. Carnegie, "Wealth," 657, 655.

18. William Graham Sumner, *What Social Classes Owe to Each Other* (New York: Harper, 1883; reprint New Haven, CT: Yale University Press, 1925), 59, 35, 38, 55.

19. Sumner, *What Social Classes Owe*, 38.

20. William Graham Sumner, "The Absurd Effort to Make the World Over," in *Essays of William Graham Sumner*, Vol 1, edited by Albert Galloway Keller and Maurice R. Davie (New Haven, CT: Yale University Press, 1934), 97.

21. I take the term from Regenia Gagnier, *The Insatiability of Human Wants*, her excellent account of a late nineteenth-century turn toward philosophies of infinitely desiring humans. See especially pp. 1–60.

22. Sumner, *What Social Classes Owe*, 77.

23. Quoted in George R. Geiger, *The Philosophy of Henry George* (New York: Macmillan, 1933), 8.

24. Henry George, *Progress and Poverty* (New York: Appleton, 1879; reprint London: Kegan Paul 1883), 212, 216, 217.

25. Jeffrey Sklansky, *The Soul's Economy: Market Society and Selfhood in American Thought, 1820–1920* (Chapel Hill: University of North Carolina Press, 2002), 122.

26. George, *Progress*, 77, 133, 126, 127.

27. Morgan, *Ancient Society*, 390.

28. Charlotte Perkins Gilman, *Women and Economics* (Boston: Small, Maynard, 1898; reprint Berkeley: University of California Press, 1998), 22, 60, 73, 8, 73, 9.

29. Morgan, *Ancient Society*, 390.

30. Gilman, *Women*, 74.

31. Gilman, *Women*, 8.

32. William Stanley Jevons, *The Theory of Political Economy* (New York: Macmillan,

1871; reprint New York: Kelley and Millman, 1957), xvi; Alfred Marshall, *Principles of Economics*, (New York: Macmillan, 1890), 4, 47, 6, 46 https://ia802605.us.archive.org/13/items/principlesecono00marsgoog/principlesecono00marsgoog.pdf. 6, 46.

33. Marshall, *Principles*, 44.

Chapter 2

1. Mary E. Wilkins Freeman, "Who's Who—and Why: Mary E. Wilkins Freeman, an Autobiography," *Saturday Evening Post*, (December 8, 1917): 75. I refer to this article as "An Autobiography." Subsequent references in this chapter are incorporated within the text.

2. Mary Wilkins Freeman, "The Revolt of 'Mother,'" in *A New England Nun and Other Stories*, edited by Sandra A. Zagarell (New York: Penguin, 2000), 75. Subsequent references in this chapter are incorporated within the text.

3. Francesco Lorrigio, "Regionalism and Theory," in *Regionalism Reconsidered: New Approaches to the Field*, edited by David Jordan (New York: Garland, 1994), 16.

4. Leah Blatt Glasser, *In A Closet Hidden: The Life and Work of Mary E. Wilkins Freeman* (Amherst: University of Massachusetts Press, 1996), xviii.

5. Elizabeth A. Meese, *Crossing the Double-Cross: The Practice of Feminist Criticism* (Chapel Hill: University of North Carolina Press, 1986), 22.

6. Thomas Maik, "Dissent and Affirmation: Conflicting Voices of Female Roles in Selected Stories by Mary Wilkins Freeman," *Colby Library Quarterly* 26, no. 1 (March 1990): 59, Proquest.

7. Michael Grimwood, "Architecture and Autobiography in 'The Revolt of "Mother,"'" *American Literary Realism* 40, no. 1 (Fall 2007): 73, https://doi.org/10.1353/alr.2008.0004. Martha J. Cutter also speaks of the way that some of Freeman's female characters have to achieve a "balance between the selflessness prescribed by the 19th-century Cult of True Womanhood and their need for autonomy." "Mary E. Wilkins Freeman's Two New England Nuns," *Colby Quarterly* 26, no. 4 (1990), 213–14. Josephine Donovan laments the fact that the "preindustrial values" of Freeman's "female-identified" world are "going down to defeat before the imperialism of masculine technology and patriarchal institutions." *New England Local Color Literature: A Women's Tradition* (New York: Frederick Ungar, 1983), 119. And Mary R. Reichhardt argues that "although many of Freeman's stories provide devastating critiques of sentimental ideology, others paradoxically uphold its tenets." *Mary Wilkins Freeman: A Study of the Short Fiction* (New York: Twayne, 1997), 12.

8. In a similar vein, Michael Grimwood reads Mother's move to the commercial realm of the barn as a metaphor for Mary Wilkins Freeman's engagement with the literary marketplace—"her commodification of a local culture for profitable distribution to a national market." "'The Revolt of "Mother"' and Consumer Culture," *American Literary Realism* 45, no. 3 (Spring 2013): 250, https://doi.org/10.5406/amerlitereal.45.3.0248.

9. The readership of the *Post* had burgeoned from 1 to 2 million between 1908 and 1913. For a history of the *Post*'s meteoric rise, see Jan Cohn, *Creating America: George Horace Lorimer and the Saturday Evening Post* (Pittsburgh: University of Pittsburgh

Press, 1989), 60–65. For an interesting account of how it manipulated the gender of its readership, see Helen Damon-Moore, *Magazines for the Millions: Gender and Commerce in the Ladies' Home Journal and the Saturday Evening Post, 1880–1910.* (Albany: State University of New York, 1994), 151–54.

10. Meese, *Crossing*, 34.

11. Virginia L. Blum, "Mary Wilkins Freeman and the Taste of Necessity," *American Literature* 65, no. 1 (March 1993): 72, https://doi.org/10.2307/2928080.

12. Lorne Fienberg, "Mary Wilkins Freeman's 'Soft Diurnal Commotion': Women's Work and Strategies of Containment," *New England Quarterly* 62, no. 4 (December 1989): 504, https://doi.org/10.2307/366394. Glasser, *In a Closet*, 26. Julia Bader argues that female regionalists "purposefully develop value systems in the domestic realm, where the desires and ambitions of women are allowed scope." "The Dissolving Vision: Realism in Jewett, Freeman, and Gilman," in *American Realism: New Essays*, ed. Eric J. Sundquist (Baltimore: Johns Hopkins University Press, 1982), 178. Martha J. Cutter contends that "The Selfishness of Amelia Lamkin" critiques patriarchal notions of womanhood—the domestic saint and the New Woman—but offers little sense of what might replace them. "Beyond Stereotypes: Freeman's Radical Critique of Nineteenth-Century Cults of Femininity," *Women's Studies* 21, no. 4 (1992): 383–95, https://doi.org/10.1080/00497878.1992.9978952. Monika M. Elbert, "The Displacement of Desire: Consumerism and Fetishism in Mary Wilkins Freeman's Fiction," *Legacy* 19, no. 2 (2002), 192, 197.

13. James Bucky Carter, "Princes, Beasts, or Royal Pains: Men and Masculinity in the Revisionist Fairy Tales of Mary E. Wilkins Freeman," in *Marvels and Tales: Journal of Fairy Tale Studies* 20, no. 1 (2006), 31.

14. To complete the Homeric associations, Charlotte is blind.

15. Carter, "Princes," 31.

16. Mary E. Wilkins Freeman, "A Mistaken Charity," in *A Humble Romance and Other Stories* (New York: Harper, 1887), 244. Subsequent references in this chapter are incorporated within the text.

17. Glasser, for example, speaks of their escape from the Home as the "heroism of their final act of self-determination." *In a Closet*, 209.

18. Agnes Repplier, "Esoteric Economy," *Atlantic Monthly* 62, no. 372 (October 1888): 533, Cornell University Library Making of America Collection.

19. "A Mistaken Charity" was first printed in *Harper's Bazar* in 1883 and then reprinted in *A Humble Romance and Other Stories* in 1887.

20. Henry Wood, *The Political Economy of Natural Law* (Boston: Lee and Shepard, 1894), 135.

21. Francis A. Walker, "What Shall We Tell the Working Classes?" *Scribner's Magazine* 2, no. 5 (November 1887): 622, Cornell University Library Making of America Collection.

22. "People of a New England Factory Village," *Atlantic Monthly* 46, no. 276 (October 1880): 460, Cornell University Library Making of America Collection.

23. "The City in Modern Life," *Atlantic Monthly* 75, no. 450 (April 1895): 555, Cornell University Library Making of America Collection.

24. Lucy Larcom. "Among Lowell Mill-Girls: A Reminiscence." *Atlantic Monthly* 48, no. 289 (November 1881): 596, Cornell University Library Making of America Collection.

25. Larcom, "Among Lowell Mill-Girls," 611.

26. Walker, "What Shall We Tell," 625.

27. Repplier, "Esoteric Economy," 533.

28. Larcom, "Among Lowell Mill-Girls," 596.

29. Eric Hobsbawm and Terence Ranger, eds, *The Invention of Tradition* (Cambridge, UK: Cambridge University Press, 1983), 1.

30. Nancy Glazener, *Reading for Realism: The History of a U. S. Literary Institution, 1850–1910* (Durham, NC: Duke University Press, 1997), 190.

31. Donna M. Campbell, *Resisting Regionalism: Gender and Naturalism in American Fiction, 1885–1915* (Athens: Ohio University Press, 1997), 109.

32. Richard Brodhead, *Cultures of Letters: Scenes of Reading and Writing in Nineteenth-Century America* (Chicago: University of Chicago Press, 1993), 18.

33. Fetterley and Pryse, *Writing out of Place*, 267.

34. For excellent introductions to the vexed question of how charity work in the nineteenth century formulated class identities for women, see Lori D. Ginzberg, *Women and the Work of Benevolence: Morality, Politics, and Class in the Nineteenth-Century United States* (New Haven, CT: Yale University Press, 1990), and Jill Bergman and Debra Bernardi, eds, *Our Sisters' Keepers: Nineteenth-Century Benevolence Literature by American Women* (Tuscaloosa: University of Alabama Press, 2005).

35. Lewis H. Morgan, *Ancient Society* (New York: H. Holt, 1877), 42, 26.

36. Glasser, *In a Closet*, 23.

37. Susan Allen Toth, "Defiant Light: A Positive View of Mary Wilkins Freeman," in *Critical Essays on Mary Wilkins Freeman*, edited by Shirley Marchalonis (Boston: G. K. Hall, 1991), 123.

38. Several scholars read Mother's territorial acquisition as an incursion into patriarchal language and discourse: Glasser argues that Mother foments a "revolutionary language" which creates a "new means for communicating differing gender values so that long overlooked feminine principles can begin to receive some recognition," *In a Closet*, 26, 27. Similarly, Joseph Church observes that Mother "must alter [Father's] position within the discursive formation." "Reconstructing Woman's Place in Freeman's 'The Revolt of "Mother,"'" *Colby Library Quarterly* 26, no. 3 (September 1990), 197. And Martha J. Cutter notes that Mother "revises, reassigns, the fundamental oppositions which structure her and Father's systems of signification" in an ambitious, if somewhat precarious, reconstruction of the entire Symbolic. "Frontiers of Language: Engendering Discourse in 'The Revolt of "Mother,"'" *American Literature* 63, no. 2 (June 1991), 288.

39. Grimwood, "Architecture," 67.

40. Elbert, "Displacement of Desire," 194.

41. There are many other more mundane likenesses. Sammy "showed a face like his father's" (65), for example, and both of their faces are compared to their horse's.

42. Brian White, "'In the Humble Fashion of a Scripture Woman': The Bible as

Besieging Tool in Freeman's "The Revolt of "Mother,""" *Christianity and Literature* 58, no. 1 (Autumn 2008): 83, https://doi.org/10.1177/014833310805800106.

43. Thomas Hobbes, *Leviathan* (Harmondsworth, UK: Penguin, 1985), 77; Locke, "Second Treatise," 18.

44. Hobbes, *Leviathan*, 193, 196.

45. Hobbes, *Leviathan*, 193.

46. Hobbes, *Leviathan*, 196, 189.

47. Hobbes, *Leviathan*, 190.

48. Robert Dimand and Chris Nyland observe that though Locke thought men enjoyed a "natural advantage when bargaining over the provisions of the marriage partnership as a consequence of the fact that women were physically the weaker sex," his work depicted "women as beings who were rational and who were entitled to the natural law rights that automatically accrued to all rational beings. This meant they had the right to freely possess their lives, liberty, goods and the products of their labour" and the "right to strive to find ways to overcome men's natural advantages." *The Status of Women in Classical Economic Thought* (Cheltenham, UK: Edward Elgar, 2003), 55, 58.

49. John Locke, "The Second Treatise of Government," in *The Selected Political Writings of John Locke*, edited by Paul E. Sigmund (New York: W. W. Norton, 2005), 32, 31.

50. Locke, "Second Treatise," 32.

51. Locke, "Second Treatise," 31.

52. Locke, "Second Treatise," 28.

53. Locke, "Second Treatise," 37, 15.

54. This quiet sense in the story that competing models of land usage are at stake is significant enough to have caught the attention of several scholars. Martha J. Cutter, in particular, notes that Father's desire for more barn-space and cattle seems "peculiarly overdetermined"; that being the case, the story poses his concern with "making more money for the sake of the money itself" against Mother's "actual and symbolic realm of the home," which values not capitalism but the "generation and regeneration of human life." "Frontiers of Language," 281.

55. Locke, "Second Treatise," 32.

56. Locke, "Second Treatise," 38.

57. Locke, "Second Treatise," 32.

58. Locke, "Second Treatise," 38.

59. Locke, "Second Treatise," 116.

60. Susan B. Anthony, Susan B., Matilda Joslyn Gage, and Elizabeth C. Stanton, *History of Woman Suffrage, 1848–1861*, Vol. 1 (Rochester, NY: Susan B. Anthony and Charles Mann Press, 1881), 15, 26, 32–33, 15.

61. Anthony et al., *History*, 13.

62. Anthony et al., *History*, 70.

63. Janice Daniel, "Redefining Place: *Femes Covert* in the Stories of Mary Wilkins Freeman," *Studies in Short Fiction* 33, no. 1 (Winter 1996): 74.

64. White, "In the Humble Fashion," 82, 89.

65. See Fetterley and Pryse, 169–213, for a detailed examination of the sketch form in regionalist fiction.

Chapter 3

1. Sarah Orne Jewett, *The Country of the Pointed Firs*, edited by Deborah Carlin (Peterborough, Ontario: Broadview Press, 2010), 103. All subsequent chapter references are incorporated within the text.

2. Judith Fetterley and Marjorie Pryse, *Writing out of Place: Regionalism, Women, and American Literary Culture* (Urbana: University of Illinois Press, 2003), 277.

3. Fetterley and Pryse, *Writing out of Place*, 38.

4. Catriona Sandilands, "The Importance of Reading Queerly: Jewett's *Deephaven* as Feminist Ecology," *Interdisciplinary Studies in Literature and Environment* 11, no. 2 (Summer 2004): 69, https://doi.org/10.1093/isle/11.2.57.

5. Sarah Orne Jewett, "The King of Folly Island," in *The King of Folly Island and Other People* (Boston: Houghton Mifflin, 1888), 12. Subsequent references in this chapter are incorporated within the text.

6. Sandilands, "Importance of Reading," 72.

7. E. H. Ropes, "Summering among the Thousand Isles," *Harper's New Monthly Magazine* 63, no. 376 (September 1881): 501, Cornell University Library Making of America Collection.

8. This assumption owes much to Richard Brodhead's reading of *The Country of the Pointed Firs* and female regionalism more broadly as part of a discourse on tourism and vacationing. See *Cultures of Letters: Scenes of Reading and Writing in Nineteenth-Century America* (Chicago: University of Chicago Press, 1993), 145–49.

9. For useful accounts of how female regionalists complicate the relationship between outsider-narrators and the regions they visit, see Sarah Way Sherman, *Sarah Orne Jewett, an American Persephone* (Hanover, NH: University Press of New England, 1989), 203–09; Philip Joseph, *American Literary Regionalism in a Global Age* (Baton Rouge: Louisiana State University Press, 2007), 23–33.

10. Robert S. Levine, *Dislocating Race and Nation: Episodes in Nineteenth-Century American Literary Nationalism* (Chapel Hill: University of North Carolina Press, 2008), 5–6, 179–236.

11. For a detailed account of the laborious, decade-long writing of *Pearl*, see E. Bruce Kirkham, "The Writing of Harriet Beecher Stowe's *The Pearl of Orr's Island*," *Colby Library Quarterly* 16, no. 3 (September 1980): 158–65, http://digitalcommons.colby.edu/cgi/viewcontent.cgi?article=2461&context=cq. For histories of US attempts to annex St. Domingo during the presidencies of Johnson and Grant, see G. Pope Atkins and Larman C. Wilson, *The Dominican Republic and the United States: From Imperialism to Transnationalism* (Athens: University of Georgia Press, 1998), 24–7; and William Javier Nelson, *Almost a Territory: America's Attempt to Annex the Dominican Republic* (Newark: University of Delaware Press, 1990), 54–94. The United States had already considered annexation in 1845 during President Polk's administration, and later (1854) President Pierce pursued the possibility of establishing a naval base there. See Atkins and Wilson, *Dominican Republic*, 16–18.

12. Edward Said, *Orientalism: Western Conceptions of the Orient* (New York: Pantheon, 1978; reprint New York: Penguin, 1991), 7.

13. George Black, *The Good Neighbor: How the United States Wrote the History of Central America and the Caribbean* (New York: Pantheon, 1988), xiii.

14. Helen S. Conant, "Life in Cuba," *Harper's New Monthly Magazine* 43, no. 255 (August 1871): 350, Cornell University Library Making of America Collection.

15. This topos was, as J. Michael Dash notes, part of a broader discourse placing the Caribbean "in a posture of sexual surrender, awaiting the valorizing presence of the white, male colonizer." *Haiti and the United States: National Stereotypes and the Literary Imagination*, 2nd ed (New York: St Martin's Press, 1997), 3.

16. Rousseau, Jean-Jacques. "The Second Discourse: Discourse on the Origin and Foundations of Inequality Among Mankind" (Amsterdam: Marc-Michel Rey, 1755; in *The Social Contract and The First and Second Discourses*, edited by Susan Dunn (New Haven, CT: Yale University Press, 2002), 117–18.

17. For useful accounts of the American roots of Locke's philosophy of natural law and property, see David Armitage, "John Locke: Theorist of Empire?" in *Empire and Modern Political Thought*, edited by Sankar Muthu (Cambridge, UK: Cambridge University Press, 2012), 84–111; and a number of fine essays by Barbara Arneil, including "The Wild Indian's Venison: Locke's Theory of Property and English Colonialism in America," *Political Studies* XLIV, no. 1 (March 1996): 60–74.

18. Peter Hulme, *Colonial Encounters: Europe and the Native Caribbean, 1492–1797* (New York: Methuen, 1986; reprint New York: Routledge, 1992), 222.

19. Chris Bongie, *Islands and Exiles: The Creole Identities of Post-Colonial Literature* (Stanford: Stanford University Press, 1998), 79.

20. Rebecca Weaver-Hightower, *Empire Islands: Castaways, Cannibals, and Fantasies of Conquest* (Minneapolis: University of Minnesota Press, 2007), 109.

21. Diane Loxley, *Problematic Shores: The Literature of Islands* (New York: St. Martin's Press, 1990), 3.

22. Crusoe's dog and two cats survive the shipwreck; King George is greeted by his dog and cat.

23. Harriet Beecher Stowe, *The Pearl of Orr's Island* (London: Sampson, Low, 1862; reprint New York: Houghton Mifflin, 2001), 251. Subsequent references in this chapter are incorporated within the text.

24. Gillian Brown, *Domestic Individualism. Imagining Self in Nineteenth-Century America* (Berkeley: University of California Press, 1990), 15–16.

25. The "real horror" about slavery for Stowe, Gillian Brown continues, is that "family life nurtured by women is not immune to the economic life outside it," *Domestic Individualism*, 16.

26. Reutter is thinking of moments when Moses is presented as a "black-eyed boy" (50), with his "great black eyes" (74) and "shining black curls" (75), and the "Spanish nature" (255) of his mother. Cheli Reutter, "Harriet Beecher Stowe's *Pear[l] of Orr's Island*: Novel of Passing and Cultural Gem," *CEA Critic: An Official Journal of the College English Association* 70, no 1 (Fall 2007): 48–65.

27. Dara E. Goldman, *Out of Bounds: Islands and the Demarcation of Identity in the Hispanic Caribbean* (Lewisburg, PA: Bucknell University Press, 2008), 10.

28. Ian Gregory Strachan, *Paradise and Plantation: Tourism and Culture in the Anglophone Caribbean* (Charlottesville: University of Virginia Press, 2002), 4, 79.

29. Samuel Hazard, *Santo Domingo: Past and Present, with a Glance at Hayti* (New York: Harper, 1873), 1, viii.

30. Hazard, *Santo Domingo*, viii, 1.

31. Hazard, *Santo Domingo*, 1.

32. Hazard, *Santo Domingo*, viii, 2.

33. Hazard, *Santo Domingo*, viii, 190, 194, 190.

34. Loxley, *Problematic Shores*, 102.

35. Hazard, *Santo Domingo*, 188.

36. Hazard, *Santo Domingo*, 213.

37. W. E. Sewell, "Cast-away in Jamaica," *Harper's New Monthly Magazine* 22, no. 128 (January 1861): 181, Cornell University Library Making of America Collection.

38. Lafcadio Hearn, *Two Years in the French West Indies* (New York: Harper, 1890; reprint New York: Harper, 1923), 85, 86.

39. Oran, "Tropical Journeyings en Route for California," *Harper's New Monthly Magazine* 16, no. 95 (April 1858): 579, Cornell University Library Making of America Collection.

40. Hazard, *Santo Domingo*, 188; An Artist, "Three Weeks in Cuba," *Harper's New Monthly Magazine* 6, no. 32 (January 1853): 165, Cornell University Library Making of America Collection; Oran, "Tropical Journeyings" (April 1858), 579.

41. Foster Crowell, "Training a Tropic Torrent. An Engineer's Glimpse of Hayti," *Scribner's Magazine* 10, no. 1 (July 1891): 115, Cornell University Library Making of America Collection.

42. Frank H. Taylor, "Street Scenes in Havana," *Harper's New Monthly Magazine* 58, no. 347 (April 1879): 684, Cornell University Library Making of America Collection 683, 684.

43. Sewell, "Cast-away," 176.

44. Howard Pyle, "Jamaica, New and Old," *Harper's New Monthly Magazine* 80, no. 477 (February 1890): 175, 385, Cornell University Library Making of America Collection.

45. Hazard, *Santo Domingo*, 182.

46. Lafcadio Hearn, "A Midsummer Trip to the West Indies," *Harper's New Monthly Magazine* 77, no. 458 (July 1888): 215, Cornell University Library Making of America Collection.

47. Sewell, "Cast-away," 176; Pyle, "Jamaica," 178.

48. Julia Ward Howe, *A Trip to Cuba* (Boston: Ticknor and Fields, 1860), 104, 105, 25. This is a compilation of earlier *Atlantic* articles.

49. Hearn, "A Midsummer Trip," 214.

50. Oran, "Tropical Journeyings en Route for California," *Harper's New Monthly Magazine* 16, no. 94 (March 1858): 470, Cornell University Library Making of America Collection.

51. Pyle, "Jamaica," 176.

52. Sewell, "Cast-away," 170, 176.

53. Sewell, "Cast-away," 170, 181, 176.

54. An Artist, "Three Weeks," 162.

55. Howe, *A Trip to Cuba*, 12.

56. John Weiss, "The Horrors of San Domingo," *Atlantic Monthly* 9, no. 56 (June 1862): 735, Cornell University Library Making of America Collection.

57. "The Fruits of Free Labor in the Smaller Islands of the British West Indies," *Atlantic Monthly* 9, no. 53 (March 1862): 273, Cornell University Library Making of America Collection.

58. Howe, *A Trip to Cuba*, 12.

59. An Artist, "Three Weeks," 165, 168, 169.

60. Helen S. Conant, "Life in Cuba," *Harper's New Monthly Magazine* 43, no. 255 (August 1871): 360, 365, Cornell University Library Making of America Collection.

61. Howe, *A Trip to Cuba*, 152.

62. T. Addison Richards, "The Valley of the Connecticut," *Harper's New Monthly Magazine* 13, no. 75 (August 1856): 291, Cornell University Library Making of America Collection.

63. N. H. Eggleston, "A New England Village," *Harper's New Monthly Magazine* 43, no. 258 (November 1871): 816, Cornell University Library Making of America Collection.

64. Helen S. Conant, "Rambles in the West Indies," *Harper's New Monthly Magazine* 43, no. 258 (November 1871): 846, Cornell University Library Making of America Collection.

65. "A Visit to Martha's Vineyard," *Atlantic Monthly* 4, no. 23 (September 1859): 281, Cornell University Library Making of America Collection.

66. D. H. Strother, "A Summer in New England," *Harper's New Monthly Magazine* 21, no. 124 (September 1860): 446, Cornell University Library Making of America Collection.

67. George William Curtis, "Newport—Historical and Social," *Harper's New Monthly Magazine* 9, no. 51 (August 1854): 296, Cornell University Library Making of America Collection.

68. Richards, "Valley of the Connecticut," 289.

69. Conant, "Life in Cuba," 350.

70. Monika Mueller, "New England Tempests? Harriet Beecher Stowe's *The Minister's Wooing* and *The Pearl of Orr's Island*," in *Beyond "Uncle Tom's Cabin": Essays on the Writing of Harriet Beecher Stowe*, edited by Sylvia Mayer and Monika Mueller (Madison, NJ: Fairleigh Dickinson University Press, 2011), 137.

71. Lisa Watt McFarlane, for example, speaks of Stowe's "utopian households that center around a kitchen" in *Pearl* and *Oldtown Folks*. "The New England Kitchen Goes Uptown: Domestic Displacements in Harriet Beecher Stowe's New York," *New England Quarterly* 64, no. 2 (June 1991): 273, https://doi.org/10.2307/366124. Monika Mueller argues that in her New England novels Stowe sets out to "invent a model society for the United States." "New England," 126. Dorothy Berkson concurs, noting that Stowe's reformist zeal finds expression in a "utopian vision of a reformed and regenerated society." "'So We All Became Mothers': Harriet Beecher Stowe, Charlotte Perkins Gilman, and the New World of Women's Culture," in *Feminism, Utopia, and Narrative*, edited by Libby Falk Jones and Sarah Webster Goodwin (Knoxville: University of Tennessee Press, 1990), 100.

72. The arranged marriage is, as Michael D. Pierson points out (16–17), a common trope in abolitionist literature of the era. "Antislavery Politics in Harriet Beecher

Stowe's *The Minister's Wooing* and *The Pearl of Orr's Island*," *American Nineteenth Century History* 3, no. 2 (2002): 16–17, https://doi.org/10.1080/713998990.

73. Pierson, "Antislavery Politics," 13.

74. Nina Bannett argues that readers have failed to appreciate the subversiveness of Stowe's "gynocentric plot" in which two women exchange one man. "Keepsakes, Promises, Exchange: Female Friendship in Harriet Beecher Stowe's *The Pearl of Orr's Island*," *New England Quarterly* 87, no. 3 (September 2014): 412–33.

75. Lora Romero, *Home Fronts: Domesticity and Its Critics in the Antebellum United States* (Durham, NC: Duke University Press, 1997), 65.

76. This is what Nancy Glazener means by a "stalled" regionalist response to the marketplace in *Reading for Realism*.

Chapter 4

1. Sarah Orne Jewett, *The Country of the Pointed Firs* (Boston; New York: Houghton, Mifflin, 1896; reprint Peterborough, Ontario: Broadview Press, 2010), 71. Subsequent references in this chapter are incorporated in the text.

2. A version of this chapter appeared as "The Kitchen Economics of Sarah Orne Jewett's *The Country of the Pointed Firs*" in *Legacy* 32, no. 1 (2015), 53–74.

3. Jean-Joseph Goux, *Symbolic Economies: After Marx and Freud*, trans. Jennifer Curtiss Gage (Cornell: Cornell University Press, 1990), 163, 164.

4. Helen Fiddyment Levy, *Fictions of the Home Place: Jewett, Cather, Glasgow, Porter, Welty, and Naylor* (Jackson: University Press of Mississippi, 1992), 54.

5. Judith Fetterley and Marjorie Pryse, *Writing out of Place: Regionalism, Women, and American Literary Culture* (Urbana: University of Illinois Press, 2003), 267.

6. Julia Bader, "The Dissolving Vision: Realism in Jewett, Freeman, and Gilman," in *American Realism: New Essays*, ed. Eric J. Sundquist (Baltimore: Johns Hopkins University Press, 1982), 182.

7. Josephine Donovan, *New England Local Color Literature: A Women's Tradition* (New York: Frederick Ungar, 1983), 56.

8. W. H. Harvey, *Coin's Financial School* (Chicago: Coin, 1894), 3.

9. Douglas Steeples and David O. Whitten, *Democracy In Desperation: The Depression of 1893* (Westport, CT: Greenwood, 1998), 1.

10. One of the very few essays to situate Jewett's work "not only in isolated, local communities but also in the broader spaces of transnational capitalism" is Hsuan L. Hsu's "Literature and Regional Production," *American Literary History* 17, no. 1 (Spring 2005): 37, https://doi.org/10.1093/alh/aji002.

11. James Livingston, *Pragmatism and the Political Economy of Cultural Revolution, 1850–1940* (Chapel Hill: University of North Carolina Press, 1994), 40.

12. More's *Utopia* was followed by Francis Bacon's *New Atlantis* (1624) and James Harrington's *Commonwealth of Oceana* (1656). Defoe's *Robinson Crusoe* belongs to this tradition, as does Karl Marx's meditation on *Crusoe* in *Capital* (1867).

13. Thomas More, *Utopia* (New York: Penguin 1965), 4, 66.

14. More, *Utopia*, 49–52.

15. More, *Utopia*, 59.

16. Adam Smith, *The Wealth of Nations* (London: Strahan and Cadell, 1776; reprint, New York: Bantam, 2003), 23.

17. Nancy Glazener, *Reading for Realism: The History of a U. S. Literary Institution, 1850–1910* (Durham, NC: Duke University Press, 1997), 221.

18. Joseph Rodes Buchanan, "Revolutionary Measures and Neglected Crimes. Part II," *The Arena* 4, no. 20 (July 1891): 200, https://ia601604.us.archive.org/12/items/ArenaMagazine-Volume04/9106-arena-volume04.pdf.

19. Harvey, *Coin's Financial*, 98–99.

20. Quoted in Walter Benn Michaels, *The Gold Standard and the Logic of Naturalism* (Berkeley: University of California Press, 1987), 146.

21. Gretchen Ritter, *Goldbugs and Greenbacks: The Antimonopoly Tradition and the Politics of Finance in America* (Cambridge, UK: Cambridge University Press, 1997), 172.

22. James A. Garfield, "The Currency Conflict," *Atlantic Monthly* 37, no. 220 (February 1876): 233, Cornell University Library Making of America Collection. Though W. H. Harvey saw silver as a way to liberate a money supply controlled by wealthy elites, he too undertakes a critique of excess in his assault on fiat money. He reads the "crime of 1873"—the demonetization of silver—in terms of the flood of fiat (or "credit") money he argues it brought in its wake. *Coin's Financial*, 19.

23. Gretchen Ritter notes that the money debate allowed Americans to tap into discourses on republicanism, labor, citizenship, monopoly capitalism, the financial system, and more. *Goldbugs*, 3–9. Michaels's chapter on Frank Norris's *McTeague* in *The Gold Standard and the Logic of Naturalism* aligns debates about the gold standard with the representational strategies of naturalism. *Gold Standard*, 137–80.

24. John Fiske, "The Paper Money Craze of 1786 and the Shays Rebellion," *Atlantic Monthly* 58, no. 347 (September 1886): 376, Cornell University Library Making of America Collection.

25. Jonathan Baxter Harrison, *Certain Dangerous Tendencies in American Life, and Other Papers* (Boston: Houghton, Osgood, 1880), 4, 27.

26. Harrison, *Certain Dangerous Tendencies*, 195, 156.

27. Harrison, *Certain Dangerous Tendencies*, 154.

28. Harrison, *Certain Dangerous Tendencies*, 175.

29. Harrison, *Certain Dangerous Tendencies*, 167, 185.

30. Harrison, *Certain Dangerous Tendencies*, 168.

31. Harrison, *Certain Dangerous Tendencies*, 30. Inventor and businessman Erastus B. Bigelow made much the same argument in an 1878 article in which he argued that credit and the associated inflation of the money supply was to blame for current economic problems: "Capital is the laborer's best friend; excessive credit his worst enemy." "The Relations of Labor and Capital," *Atlantic Monthly* 42, no. 252 (October 1878): 487, Cornell University Library Making of America Collection.

32. Harrison, *Certain Dangerous Tendencies*, 5, 6.

33. Relevant here is Irene van Staveren's provocative reading of Charlotte Perkins Gilman's *Herland* (1915). Van Staveren argues that the novel "shows how nonmarket production can be efficient" by observing important political economic principles concerning efficiency, specialization, economy of scale, externalities, and "intrinsic

motivation rather than the profit motive." "Feminist Fiction and Feminist Economics: Charlotte Perkins Gilman on Efficiency," in *Toward a Feminist Philosophy of Economics*, edited by Drucilla K. Barker and Edith Kuiper (New York: Routledge, 2003), 65. Though (I argue) Jewett never abandons the concept of markets on Green Island, van Staveren's argument dovetails neatly with my point that the narrator's potato digging abides by well-understood abstract laws of production and distribution.

34. Timothy Sweet, *American Georgics: Economy and Environment in Early American Literature* (Philadelphia: University of Pennsylvania Press, 2002), 122.

35. George, *Progress*, 212–17.

36. Though not primarily concerned with economic issues, Christine Wilson describes "how the ship functions as a site of (re)imagining the role of domesticity in women's lives" in Jewett's *Deephaven* (1877) by making domestic spaces fluid and transitional—by making them into "modified . . . heterotopias." "Delinquent Housekeeping: Transforming the Regulations of Keeping House," *Legacy* 25, no. 2 (2008), 299, 306.

Chapter 5

1. Rose Terry Cooke, "Miss Beulah's Bonnet," in *How Celia Changed Her Mind and Selected Stories*, edited by Elizabeth Ammons (Rutgers, NJ: Rutgers University Press, 1986), 210.

2. Rose Terry Cooke, "Mrs. Flint's Married Experience," in *Huckleberries: Gathered from New England Hills* (Boston: Houghton, Mifflin, 1892; reprint Charleston, SC: BiblioLife, n.d.), 106, 117. All subsequent references in this chapter are incorporated within the text.

3. Mary Wilkins Freeman, "A New England Nun," in *A New England Nun and Other Stories*, edited by Sandra A. Zagarell (New York: Penguin, 2000), 32, 23.

4. Mary Wilkins Freeman, "Louisa," in *A New England Nun and Other Stories*, edited by Sandra A. Zagarell (New York: Penguin, 2000), 62.

5. Rose Terry Cooke, "An Old-Fashioned Thanksgiving," in *Huckleberries: Gathered from New England Hills* (Boston: Houghton, Mifflin, 1892; reprint Charleston, SC: BiblioLife, n.d.), 125, 124. Subsequent references in this chapter are incorporated within the text.

6. Gallagher, *Body Economic*, 3, 46.

7. Thomas Malthus, "An Essay on the Principle of Population" (London: J. Johnson, 1798), 2, http://www.econlib.org/library/Malthus/malPop1.html).

8. Malthus, "An Essay," 2.

9. Gallagher, *Body Economic*, 36.

10. Jack Amariglio and David F. Ruccio, "From Unity to Dispersion: The Body in Modern Economic Discourse," in *Postmodernism, Economics and Knowledge*, edited by Stephen Cullenberg, et al. (New York: Routledge, 2001), 150.

11. Annabel Patterson, *Fables of Power: Aesopian Writing and Political History* (Durham, NC: Duke University Press, 1991), 43, 2, 4.

12. Sarah Orne Jewett, *The Country of the Pointed Firs* (Boston; New York: Houghton, Mifflin, 1896; reprint, Peterborough, Ontario: Broadview Press, 2010), 125.

13. Diana Karter Appelbaum, *Thanksgiving: An American Holiday, an American History* (New York: Facts on File, 1984), 129.

14. Not until 1941 was Thanksgiving proclaimed a national holiday to be celebrated on the fourth Thursday of November in perpetuity. See James W. Baker, *Thanksgiving: The Biography of an American Holiday* (Lebanon, NH: University Press of New England, 2009), 71.

15. Harriet Beecher Stowe, *Oldtown Folks* (Boston: Fields, Osgood, 1869; reprint New York: Houghton Mifflin, 1915), 396. Subsequent references in this chapter are incorporated in the text.

16. Claude Lévi-Strauss elaborates this distinction in *The Raw and the Cooked. Mythologiques*, Volume I. Trans. John and Doreen Weightman (Chicago: University of Chicago Press, 1983).

17. Rose Terry Cooke, "My Thanksgiving," *Harper's New Monthly Magazine* 26, no. 155 (April 1863): 636, Cornell University Library Making of America Collection. Subsequent references in this chapter are incorporated within the text.

18. Rose Terry Cooke, "How Celia Changed Her Mind," in *Huckleberries: Gathered from New England Hills* (Boston: Houghton Mifflin, 1892; reprint Charleston, SC: BiblioLife, n.d.), 315. Subsequent references in this chapter are incorporated within the text.

19. Rose Terry Cooke, "A Double Thanksgiving," in *Huckleberries: Gathered from New England Hills* (Boston: Houghton, Mifflin, 1892; reprint Charleston, SC: BiblioLife, n.d.), 257. Subsequent references in this chapter are incorporated within the text.

20. Rose Terry Cooke, "Home Again," in *Huckleberries: Gathered from New England Hills* (Boston: Houghton, Mifflin, 1892; reprint Charleston, SC: BiblioLife, n.d.), 269. Subsequent references in this chapter are incorporated within the text.

21. Carol Holly, "'You ain't no Christian, Not 'Cordin' to Gospel Truth': The Literary Theology of Rose Terry Cooke," *New England Quarterly* 83, no. 4 (December 2010): 676, https://doi.org/10.1162/TNEQ_a_00047.

22. Carol Holly, "The Cruelty of Husbands, the Complicity of Wives, and the Cooperation of Community in Rose Terry Cooke's 'Mrs. Flint's Married Experience,'" *American Literary Realism* 33, no. 1 (Fall 2000), 65. Eileen Razzari Elrod agrees that in her nonfiction work Cooke supported the "ideology of True Womanhood" and "vigorously opposed the women's movement, resisting any shift away from a thoroughly domestic notion of female identity." "Truth is Stranger than Non-Fiction: Gender, Religion, and Contradiction in Rose Terry Cooke," *Legacy* 13, no. 2 (1996), 113.

23. Sherry Lee Linkon, "Fiction as Political Discourse: Rose Terry Cooke's Antisuffrage Short Stories." in *American Women Short Story Writers: A Collection of Critical Essays*, edited by Julie Brown (New York: Garland, 1995), 22.

24. Holly, "Christian" 676.

25. Judith Fetterley and Marjorie Pryse, *Writing out of Place: Regionalism, Women, and American Literary Culture* (Urbana: University of Illinois Press, 2003), 162.

26. Fetterley and Pryse, *Writing*, 320.

Chapter 6

1. Alice Dunbar-Nelson. *The Goodness of St. Rocque and Other Stories. The Works of Alice Dunbar-Nelson.* New York: Dodd, Mead, 1896; reprint Schomburg Library of

Nineteenth-Century Black Women Writers, vol. 1, edited by Gloria T. Hull (Oxford: Oxford University Press, 1988), 223. Subsequent references in this chapter are incorporated within the text.

2. Kristina Brooks, "Alice Dunbar-Nelson's Local Colors of Ethnicity, Class, and Place," *MELUS* 23, no. 2 (Summer 1998): 122, https://doi.org/10.2307/468009.

3. Pamela Glenn Menke, "Behind the 'White Veil': Alice Dunbar-Nelson, Creole Color, and *The Goodness of St. Rocque*," *Songs of the Reconstructing South: Building Literary Louisiana, 1865–1945*, edited by Lisa Abney and Suzanne Disheroon-Green (Westport, CT: Greenwood, 2002), 80.

4. Violet Harrington Bryan, *The Myth of New Orleans in Literature: Dialogues of Race and Gender* (Knoxville: University of Tennessee Press, 1993), 126.

5. This is in fact the gist of my argument in "'You . . . Could Never Be Mistaken': Reading Alice Dunbar-Nelson's Rhetorical Diversions in *The Goodness of St. Rocque and Other Stories*," *Studies in American Fiction* 36, no. 1 (Spring 2008), 77–94.

6. For excellent accounts of New Orleans waterfront troubles in the 1890s, see Daniel Rosenberg, *New Orleans Dockworkers: Race, Labor, and Unionism 1892–1923* (Albany: State University of New York Press, 1988); and Eric Arnesen, *Waterfront Workers of New Orleans* (New York: Oxford University Press, 1991). Robert H. Zieger describes this history more briefly but in the broader context of US race/labor relations in *For Jobs and Freedom: Race and Labor in America Since 1865* (Lexington: University Press of Kentucky, 2007), 36–42.

7. Arnesen recounts that there were two ships from Stoddart and Co, plus four English ships, in October 1894; and the ships of the Harrison, the Ross, Howe and Merrow, and the Elder-Demster Lines in March 1895. *Waterfront*, 128, 140.

8. Rosenberg, *New Orleans*, 33.

9. Rich Cohen, *The Fish That Ate the Whale: The Life and Times of American's Banana King* (New York: Farrar, Straus and Giroux, 2012), 19.

10. Lafcadio Hearn, "Dead Sea Fruit," in *The New Orleans of Lafcadio Hearn: Illustrated Sketches from the Daily City Item*, edited by Delia LaBarre (Baton Rouge: Louisiana State University Press), 81–82.

11. John Quincy Adam, Letter to Hugh Nelson, April 28, 1823, US Congress, House of Representatives, 32nd Cong., 1st sess, House Document No. 121, Ser. 648, 7.

12. By the 1890s, 90 percent of Cuba's exports went to the United States. Louis Pérez Jr., *Cuba: Between Reform and Revolution*, 3rd ed (New York: Oxford University Press, 2005), 149.

13. In 1881 Southern Pacific acquired the Texas and New Orleans railroad, which included the Morgan Line's Louisiana and Texas railroad.

14. For excellent histories of US attempts to dominate the Caribbean trade, see Alison Acker, *Honduras: The Making of a Banana Republic* (Boston: South End Press, 1988); Peter Chapman, *Bananas: How the United Fruit Company Shaped the World* (Edinburgh: Canongate, 2007); and Rich Cohen, *The Fish That Ate the Whale* (2012).

15. Chapman, *Bananas*, 49.

16. Oran, "Tropical Journeyings en Route for California," *Harper's New Monthly Magazine* 16, no. 95 (April 1858): 579, Cornell University Library Making of America Collection.

17. Oran, "Tropical Journeyings," 579.

18. W. E. Sewell, "Cast-away in Jamaica," *Harper's New Monthly Magazine* 22, no. 128 (January 1861): 176, Cornell University Library Making of America Collection.

19. Helen S. Conant, "Life in Cuba," *Harper's New Monthly Magazine* 43, no. 255 (August 1871): 364, Cornell University Library Making of America Collection.

20. Frank H. Taylor, "Street Scenes in Havana," *Harper's New Monthly Magazine* 58, no. 347 (April 1879): 684, Cornell University Library Making of America Collection.

21. Lafcadio Hearn, "A Midsummer Trip to the West Indies," *Harper's New Monthly Magazine* 77, no. 458 (August 1888): 327, Cornell University Library Making of America Collection.

22. Sewell, "Cast-away," 176.

23. Conant, "Life in Cuba," 356.

24. Lafcadio Hearn, *Two Years in the French West Indies* (New York: Harper, 1923), 40, 92, 37.

25. Howard Pyle, "Jamaica, New and Old," *Harper's New Monthly Magazine* 80, no. 477 (February 1890): 175, Cornell University Library Making of America Collection.

26. Howard Pyle, "Jamaica, New and Old," *Harper's New Monthly Magazine* 80, no. 476 (January 1890): 178, 176, Cornell University Library Making of America Collection.

27. Conant, "Life in Cuba," 356.

28. G. O. Seilhamer, "Negro Life in Jamaica," *Harper's New Monthly Magazine* 44, no. 262 (March 1872): 555, Cornell University Library Making of America Collection.

29. Pyle, "Jamaica," January 1890, 175.

30. S. B. Hynes, "The Danish West Indies," *Harper's New Monthly Magazine* 44, no. 260 (January 1872): 200, Cornell University Library Making of America Collection.

31. Samuel Hazard, *Santo Domingo: Past and Present, with a Glance at Hayti* (New York: Harper, 1873), 222.

32. Pyle, "Jamaica," January 1890, 172, 175.

33. Lafcadio Hearn, "A Midsummer Trip to the West Indies," *Harper's New Monthly Magazine* 77, no. 458 (July 1888): 215, Cornell University Library Making of America Collection.

34. Pyle, "Jamaica," January 1890, 172.

Chapter 7

1. Quoted in Gwen L. Nagel, introduction to *Critical Essays on Sarah Orne Jewett* (Boston: G. K. Hall, 1984), 2.

2. Sarah Orne Jewett, *The Country of the Pointed Firs* (Boston; New York: Houghton, Mifflin, 1896; reprint, Peterborough, Ontario: Broadview Press, 2010), 123. Subsequent references in this chapter are incorporated within the text.

3. John Stuart Mill, *Principles of Political Economy* (London: John W. Parker, 1848; reprint New York: Augustus M. Kelley, 1987), 13.

4. Andrew Lawson elaborates this argument in *Downwardly Mobile*.

5. Goux, *Symbolic Economies*, 164.

6. The narrator is also probably thinking of the four-hundredth anniversary of

Columbus's voyage, as celebrated, for example, by the Chicago World's Fair [the Columbian Exposition] in 1893.

7. Philip Joseph, *American Literary Regionalism in a Global Age* (Baton Rouge: Louisiana State University Press, 2007), 26–9.

8. George Frederic Parsons, "The Labor Question," *Atlantic Monthly* 58, no. 345 (July 1886): 98, Cornell University Library Making of America Collection.

9. Parsons, "Labor Question," 108, 107, 106.

10. Parsons, "Labor Question," 106.

11. Parsons, "Labor Question," 106.

12. Jonathan Baxter Harrison, *Certain Dangerous Tendencies in American Life, and Other Papers* (Boston: Houghton, Osgood, 1880), 691, 692, 693.

13. Parson, "Labor Question," 107.

14. Harrison, *Certain Dangerous Tendencies*, 693.

15. Charles Dudley Warner, "The Novel and the Common School," *Atlantic Monthly* 65, no. 392 (June 1890): 721, 723, 724, Cornell University Library Making of America Collection.

16. Lisa Randall, *Warped Passages: Unraveling the Mysteries of the Universe's Hidden Dimensions* (New York: Harper Perennial, 2006), 8. Randall's scientific theories concern the possible existence of multiple, hidden dimensions.

17. Arjo Klamer, *Speaking of Economics: How to Get in the Conversation* (New York: Routledge, 2007), 7.

18. Tony Lawson, *Reorienting Economics* (New York: Routledge, 2003), 18.

19. See Tony Lawson, *Economics and Reality*, 6–8.

20. William Tabb, *Reconstructing Political Economy: The Great Divide in Economic Thought* (New York: Routledge, 1999), 14.

21. Tabb, *Reconstructing*, 7; Geoffrey M. Hodgson, *How Economics Forgot History: The Problem of Historical Specificity in Social Science* (New York: Routledge, 2001), 6.

22. William Stanley Jevons, *The Theory of Political Economy* (New York: Macmillan, 1871; reprint New York: Kelley and Millman, 1957), 16.

23. Jevons, *The Theory*, 13.

24. Adam Smith, *The Wealth of Nations* (London: Strahan and Cadell, 1776; reprint, New York: Bantam, 2003), 355.

25. Richard Brodhead, *Cultures of Letters: Scenes of Reading and Writing in Nineteenth-Century America* (Chicago: University of Chicago Press, 1993), 146.

26. Amy Kaplan, *The Social Construction of American Realism* (Chicago: University of Chicago Press, 1988), 143.

27. William E. Cain, "Presence and Power in *McTeague*," in *American Realism: New Essays*, ed. Eric Sundquist (Baltimore: Johns Hopkins University Press, 1982), 211; see Walter Benn Michaels, *The Gold Standard and the Logic of Naturalism* (Berkeley: University of California Press, 1987), 139–80. The bulk of Michaels's book—four chapters—concern works by Dreiser and Norris.

28. Jean-Christophe Agnew, "The Consuming Vision of Henry James," in *The Culture of Consumption: Critical Essays in American History, 1880–1980*, edited by Richard Wightman Fox and T. J. Jackson Lears (New York: Pantheon, 1983), 94.

29. Jennifer Shepherd, "Fashioning an Aesthetics of Consumption in *The House of Mirth*," in *Memorial Boxes and Guarded Interiors: Edith Wharton and Material Culture*, edited by Gary Totten (Tuscaloosa: University of Alabama Press, 2014), 137. *Sister Carrie* is also James Livingston's first and most compelling example of the newly commodified subjectivity shaped by consumer capitalism. See *Pragmatism and the Political Economy of Cultural Revolution, 1850–1940* (Chapel Hill: University of North Carolina Press, 1994), 137–57.

30. D. K. Meisenheimer, "Regionalist Bodies/Embodied Regions: Sarah Orne Jewett and Zitkala-Sa," in *Breaking Boundaries: New Perspectives on Women's Regional Writing*, edited by Sherrie A. Inness, and Diana Royer (Iowa City: University of Iowa Press, 1997), 114.

31. See Sandra A. Zagarell, "*Country*'s Portrayal of Community and the Exclusion of Difference," in *New Essays on "The Country of the Pointed Firs"* (New York: Cambridge University Press, 1994), 39–60.

32. Elizabeth Ammons, "Material Culture, Empire, and Jewett's *Country of the Pointed Firs*," in *New Essays on "The Country of the Pointed Firs"* (New York: Cambridge University Press, 1994), 96.

33. Sarah Way Sherman, "Party out of Bounds: Gender and Class in Jewett's 'The Best China Saucer,'" in *Jewett and her Contemporaries: Reshaping the Canon*, edited by Karen L. Kilcup and Thomas S. Edwards (Gainesville: University of Florida, 1999), 244–45.

34. Sherman's recent work extends her critique. Though Alcott and Wharton may be concerned about the "seductions of the marketplace," they "still find readers in the twenty-first century because they speak so powerfully to the struggle to define identity and moral values in American consumer culture." *Sacramental Shopping: Louisa May Alcott, Edith Wharton, and the Spirit of Modern Consumerism* (Durham, NC: University of New Hampshire Press, 2013), 12. Monika M. Elbert makes explicit the notion that Freeman will have to be imagined as a naturalist if her "connection to larger cultural, economic concerns" is to be recognized. "The Displacement of Desire: Consumerism and Fetishism in Mary Wilkins Freeman's Fiction," *Legacy* 19, no. 2 (2002): 212.

35. Ammons, "Material Culture," 93, 98.

36. Stephanie Foote offers a version of this "postmodernizing" argument: Regional writing is a "form *about* the representation of difference," and it sets out to "transform rather than to passively resist the meaning of the social and economic developments of late-nineteenth-century urban life." *Regional Fictions: Culture and Identity in Nineteenth-Century American Literature* (Madison: University of Wisconsin Press, 2001), 4, 3.

37. Dimitris Milonakis and Ben Fine, *From Political Economy to Economics: Method, the Social and the Historical in the Evolution of Economic Theory* (London: Routledge, 2009), 9. William Tabb's *Reconstructing Political Economy* (1999), Geoffrey M. Hodgson's *How Economics Forgot History* (2001), and a handful of works by Ben Fine and Dimitris Milonakis are among those studies urging a return to political economy. Feminist economists also insist on the importance of the "community economy." J. K. Gibson-Graham, *The End of Capitalism (As We Knew It): A Feminist Critique of*

Political Economy (Cambridge, MA: Blackwell, 1996; reprint Minneapolis: University of Minnesota Press, 2006), xiv. The titles of some important contributions to feminist economics demonstrate a similar orientation: April Laskey Aerni and KimMarie McGoldrick (eds.), *Valuing us All: Feminist Pedagogy and Economics* (1999); Drucilla K. Barker and Susan F. Feiner, *Liberating Economics: Feminist Perspectives on Families, Work, and Globalization* (2004); Julie A. Nelson, *Economics for Humans* (2006).

38. Cited in Frank Fischer and Maarten A. Hajer, eds., *Living with Nature: Environmental Politics as Cultural Discourse* (New York: Oxford University Press, 1999), 40.

39. John B. Cobb and Herman E. Daly, *For the Common Good: Redirecting the Economy Toward Community, The Environment, and a Sustainable Future* (Boston: Beacon Press, 1989), 2.

40. See Naomi Klein, *This Changes Everything: Capitalism vs. the Climate* (New York: Simon and Schuster, 2014).

41. Wolfgang Hoeschele, *The Economics of Abundance: A Political Economy of Freedom, Equity, and Sustainability* (Farnham, UK: Gower, 2010), 1. Hoeschele goes on to argue that "capitalist institutions seek to continuously generate new forms of scarcity by creating ever new needs. . . . An economics that supports these institutions is not the science of the efficient allocation of scarce resources; it is instead the science of the profitable allocation of scarcity. Scarcity, then, is a means toward the end of profit maximization." *Economics of Abundance*, 1–2.

42. Quoted in Molly Scott Cato, *Green Economics: An Introduction to Theory, Policy and Practice* (Sterling, VA: Earthscan, 2009), 24.

43. Alan Gilpin, *Environmental Economics: A Critical Overview* (New York: John Wiley, 2000), 93.

44. I take the phrase "steady-state economy" from Herman E, Daly, ed., *Toward a Steady-State Economy* (San Francisco: W. H. Freeman, 1973).

45. I take the phrase "the end of progress" from Graeme P. Maxton, *The End of Progress: How Modern Economics Has Failed Us* (New York: John Wiley, 2011).

46. I take the phrase "return to scarcity" from H. C. Coombs, *The Return of Scarcity: Strategies for an Economic Future* (Cambridge, UK: Cambridge University Press, 1990).

WORKS CITED

Acker, Alison. *Honduras: The Making of a Banana Republic*. Boston: South End Press, 1988.

Adams, John Quincy. Letter to Hugh Nelson, April 28, 1823, US Congress, House of Representatives, 32nd Cong., 1st sess, House Document No. 121, Ser. 648: 7. https://babel.hathitrust.org/cgi/pt?id=loc.ark:/13960/t9j39k809;view=1up;seq=8

Aerni, April Laskey, and KimMarie McGoldrick, eds. *Valuing Us All: Feminist Pedagogy and Economics*. Ann Arbor: University of Michigan Press, 1999.

Agnew, Jean-Christophe. "The Consuming Vision of Henry James." In *The Culture of Consumption: Critical Essays in American History, 1880–1980*, edited by Richard Wightman Fox and T. J. Jackson Lears, 65–100. New York: Pantheon, 1983.

Amariglio, Jack, and David F. Ruccio. "From Unity to Dispersion: The Body in Modern Economic Discourse." In *Postmodernism, Economics and Knowledge*, edited by Jack Amariglio, Stephen Cullenberg, and David F. Ruccio, 143–65. New York: Routledge, 2001.

Ammons, Elizabeth. *Conflicting Stories: American Women Writers at the Turn into the Twentieth Century*. New York: Oxford University Press, 1991.

———. "Going in Circles: The Female Geography of Jewett's *The Country of the Pointed Firs*." *Studies in the Literary Imagination* 16, no. 2 (Fall 1983): 83–92.

———. "Material Culture, Empire, and Jewett's *Country of the Pointed Firs*." In *New Essays on "The Country of the Pointed Firs,"* edited by June Howard, 81–99. New York: Cambridge University Press, 1994.

An Artist. "Three Weeks in Cuba." *Harper's New Monthly Magazine* 6, no. 32 (January 1853): 161–75. Cornell University Library Making of America Collection.

Anthony, Susan B., Matilda Joslyn Gage, and Elizabeth C. Stanton. *History of Woman Suffrage, 1848–1861*. Vol 1. Rochester, NY: Susan B. Anthony and Charles Mann Press, 1881. https://books.google.com/books?id=wYgEAAAAYAAJ&pg=PA25&source=gbs_toc_r&cad=3#v=onepage&q&f=false.

Appelbaum, Diana Karter. *Thanksgiving: An American Holiday, an American History*. New York: Facts on File, 1984.

Aristotle. *The Politics*. Translated and introduced by Carnes Lord. Chicago: University of Chicago Press, 1984.

Armitage, David. "John Locke: Theorist of Empire?" In *Empire and Modern Political*

Thought, edited by Sankar Muthu, 84–111. Cambridge, UK: Cambridge University Press, 2012.

Arneil, Barbara. "The Wild Indian's Venison: Locke's Theory of Property and English Colonialism in America." *Political Studies* 44, no. 1 (March 1996): 60–74.

Arnesen, Eric. *Waterfront Workers of New Orleans*. New York: Oxford University Press, 1991.

Aronson, Amy, and Michael Kimmel. Introduction to *Women and Economics*. Berkeley: University of California Press, 1998.

Atkins, G. Pope, and Larman C. Wilson. *The Dominican Republic and the United States: From Imperialism to Transnationalism*. Athens: University of Georgia Press, 1998.

Bader, Julia. "The Dissolving Vision: Realism in Jewett, Freeman, and Gilman." In *American Realism: New Essays*, edited by Eric J. Sundquist, 176–98. Baltimore: Johns Hopkins University Press, 1982.

Baker, James W. *Thanksgiving: The Biography of an American Holiday*. Lebanon, NH: University Press of New England, 2009.

Balkun, Mary McAleer. *The American Counterfeit: Authenticity and Identity in American Literature and Culture*. Tuscaloosa: University of Alabama Press, 2006.

Bannett, Nina. "Keepsakes, Promises, Exchange: Female Friendship in Harriet Beecher Stowe's *The Pearl of Orr's Island*." *New England Quarterly* 87, no. 3 (September 2014): 412–33.

Barker, Drucilla K., and Susan F. Feiner. *Liberating Economics: Feminist Perspectives on Families, Work, and Globalization*. Ann Arbor: University of Michigan Press, 2004.

Barker, Drucilla K., and Edith Kuiper, eds. *Toward a Feminist Philosophy of Economics*. New York: Routledge, 2003.

Bentley, Nancy. *Frantic Panoramas: American Literature and Mass Culture 1870–1920*. Philadelphia: University of Pennsylvania Press, 2009.

Bergman, Jill, and Debra Bernardi, eds. *Our Sisters' Keepers: Nineteenth-Century Benevolence Literature by American Women*. Tuscaloosa: University of Alabama Press, 2005.

Berkson, Dorothy. "'So We All Became Mothers': Harriet Beecher Stowe, Charlotte Perkins Gilman, and the New World of Women's Culture." In *Feminism, Utopia, and Narrative*, edited by Libby Falk Jones and Sarah Webster Goodwin, 100–115. Knoxville: University of Tennessee Press, 1990.

Bersani, Leo. *A Future for Astyanax: Character and Desire in Literature*. Boston: Little, Brown, 1976.

Bigelow, Erastus B. "The Relations of Labor and Capital." *Atlantic Monthly* 42, no. 252 (October 1878): 475–87. Cornell University Library Making of America Collection.

Birken, Lawrence. *Consuming Desire: Sexual Science and the Emergence of a Culture of Abundance, 1871–1914*. Ithaca, NY: Cornell University Press, 1988.

Black, George. *The Good Neighbor: How the United States Wrote the History of Central America and the Caribbean*. New York: Pantheon, 1988.

Blaug, Mark. *The Methodology of Economics; or How Economists Explain*. Cambridge, UK: Cambridge University Press, 1980.

Blum, Virginia L. "Mary Wilkins Freeman and the Taste of Necessity." *American Literature* 65, no. 1 (March 1993): 69–94. https://doi.org/10.2307/2928080.

Boeckmann Cathy. *A Question of Character: Scientific Racism and the Genres of American Fiction, 1892–1912*. Tuscaloosa: University of Alabama Press, 2000.

Bongie, Chris. *Islands and Exiles: The Creole Identities of Post-Colonial Literature*. Stanford, CA: Stanford University Press, 1998.

Bowlby, Rachel. *Just Looking: Consumer Culture in Dreiser, Gissing, and Zola*. New York: Methuen, 1985.

Brodhead, Richard. *Cultures of Letters: Scenes of Reading and Writing in Nineteenth-Century America*. Chicago: University of Chicago Press, 1993.

Bronner, Simon. *Consuming Visions: Accumulation and Display of Goods in America, 1880–1920*. New York: Norton, 1989.

Brooks, Kristina. "Alice Dunbar-Nelson's Local Colors of Ethnicity, Class, and Place." *MELUS* 23, no. 2 (Summer 1998): 3–26. https://doi.org/10.2307/468009.

Brown, Gillian. *Domestic Individualism. Imagining Self in Nineteenth-Century America*. Berkeley: University of California Press, 1990.

Brown, Laura. *Fables of Modernity: Literature and Culture in the English Eighteenth Century*. Ithaca, NY: Cornell University Press, 2001.

Bryan, Violet Harrington. *The Myth of New Orleans in Literature: Dialogues of Race and Gender*. Knoxville: University of Tennessee Press, 1993.

Buchanan, Joseph Rodes. "Revolutionary Measures and Neglected Crimes. Part II." *The Arena* 4, no. 20 (July 1891): 192–208. https://ia601604.us.archive.org/12/items/ArenaMagazine-Volume04/9106-arena- volume04.pdf.

Cain, William E. "Presence and Power in *McTeague*." In *American Realism: New Essays*, edited by Eric Sundquist, 199–214. Baltimore: Johns Hopkins University Press, 1982.

Campbell, Donna M. *Resisting Regionalism: Gender and Naturalism in American Fiction, 1885–1915*. Athens: Ohio University Press, 1997.

Carnegie, Andrew. *The Gospel of Wealth and Other Timely Essays*. New York: Century Co., 1901.

———. "Wealth." *North American Review* 148, no. 391 (June 1889): 653–65. Cornell University Library Making of America Collection. https://babel.hathitrust.org/cgi/pt?id=uc1.c105438535;view=1up;seq=24

Carter, James Bucky. "Princes, Beasts, or Royal Pains: Men and Masculinity in the Revisionist Fairy Tales of Mary E. Wilkins Freeman." *Marvels and Tales: Journal of Fairy Tale Studies* 20, no. 1 (2006): 30–46.

Cato, Molly Scott. *Green Economics: An Introduction to Theory, Policy, and Practice*. Sterling, VA: Earthscan, 2009.

Chapman, Peter. *Bananas: How the United Fruit Company Shaped the World*. Edinburgh: Canongate, 2007.

Church, Joseph. "Reconstructing Woman's Place in Freeman's 'The Revolt of "Mother,"'" *Colby Library Quarterly* 26, no. 3 (September 1990): 195–200.

"The City in Modern Life." *Atlantic Monthly* 75, no. 450 (April 1895): 552–56. Cornell University Library Making of America Collection.

Cobb, John B, and Herman E. Daly. *For the Common Good: Redirecting the Economy Toward Community, The Environment, and a Sustainable Future*. Boston: Beacon Press, 1989.

Cohen, Rich. *The Fish That Ate the Whale: The Life and Times of American's Banana King*. New York: Farrar, Straus and Giroux, 2012.

Cohn, Jan. *Creating America: George Horace Lorimer and the Saturday Evening Post*. Pittsburgh: University of Pittsburgh Press, 1989.

Conant, Helen S. "Life in Cuba." *Harper's New Monthly Magazine* 43, no. 255 (August 1871): 350–65. Cornell University Library Making of America Collection.

———. "Rambles in the West Indies." *Harper's New Monthly Magazine* 43, no. 258 (November 1871): 837–55. Cornell University Library Making of America Collection.

Cooke, Rose Terry. "A Double Thanksgiving." In *Huckleberries: Gathered from New England Hills*, 227–58. Boston: Houghton, Mifflin, 1892. Reprint Charleston, SC: BiblioLife, n.d.

———. "Home Again." In *Huckleberries: Gathered from New England Hills*, 259–83. Boston: Houghton, Mifflin, 1892. Reprint Charleston, SC: BiblioLife, n.d.

———. "How Celia Changed Her Mind." In *Huckleberries: Gathered from New England Hills*, 284–315. Boston: Houghton, Mifflin, 1892. Reprint Charleston, SC: BiblioLife, n.d.

———. "Miss Beulah's Bonnet." In *How Celia Changed Her Mind and Selected Stories*, edited and introduced by Elizabeth Ammons, 196–213. Rutgers, NJ: Rutgers University Press, 1986.

———. "My Thanksgiving." *Harper's New Monthly Magazine* 26, no. 155 (April 1863): 636–45. Cornell University Library Making of America Collection.

———. "An Old-Fashioned Thanksgiving." In *Huckleberries: Gathered from New England Hills*, 122–51. Boston: Houghton, Mifflin, 1892. Reprint Charleston, SC: BiblioLife, n.d.

Coombs, H. C. *The Return of Scarcity: Strategies for an Economic Future*. Cambridge, UK: Cambridge University Press, 1990.

Crowell, Foster. "Training a Tropic Torrent. An Engineer's Glimpse of Hayti." *Scribner's Magazine* 10, no. 1 (July 1891): 111–16. Cornell University Library Making of America Collection.

Curtis, George William. "Newport—Historical and Social." *Harper's New Monthly Magazine* 9, no. 51 (August 1854): 289–317. Cornell University Library Making of America Collection.

Cutter, Martha J. "Beyond Stereotypes: Freeman's Radical Critique of Nineteenth-Century Cults of Femininity." *Women's Studies* 21, no. 4 (1992): 383–95. https://doi.org/10.1080/00497878.1992.9978952.

———."Frontiers of Language: Engendering Discourse in 'The Revolt of "Mother,"'" *American Literature* 63, no. 2 (June 1991): 279–91.

———. "Mary E. Wilkins Freeman's Two New England Nuns." *Colby Quarterly* 26, no. 4 (1990): 213–25.

Daly, Herman E, ed. *Toward a Steady-State Economy*. San Francisco: W. H. Freeman, 1973.

Damon-Moore, Helen. *Magazines for the Millions: Gender and Commerce in the Ladies' Home Journal and the Saturday Evening Post, 1880–1910*. Albany: State University of New York, 1994.

Daniel, Janice. "Redefining Place: *Femes Covert* in the Stories of Mary Wilkins Freeman." *Studies in Short Fiction* 33, no. 1 (Winter 1996): 69–76.

Dash, J. Michael. *Haiti and the United States: National Stereotypes and the Literary Imagination*. 2nd ed. New York: St Martin's Press, 1997.

Dimand, Robert, and Chris Nyland, eds. *The Status of Women in Classical Economic Thought*. Cheltenham, UK: Edward Elgar, 2003.

Donaldson, Susan V. *Competing Voices: The American Novel, 1865–1914*. New York: Twayne, 1998.

Donovan, Josephine. *New England Local Color Literature: A Women's Tradition*. New York: Frederick Ungar, 1983.

Dunbar-Nelson, Alice. *The Goodness of St. Rocque and Other Stories: The Works of Alice Dunbar-Nelson*. New York: Dodd, Mead, 1896. Reprint Schomburg Library of Nineteenth-Century Black Women Writers, Vol. 1, edited by Gloria T. Hull. Oxford: Oxford University Press, 1988.

———. "People of Color in Louisiana," Part I. *The Journal of Negro History* 1, no. 4 (October 1916): 361–76. http://www.jstor.org/stable/3035611.

Eggleston, N. H. "A New England Village." *Harper's New Monthly Magazine* 43, no. 258 (November 1871): 815–29. Cornell University Library Making of America Collection.

Elbert, Monika M. "The Displacement of Desire: Consumerism and Fetishism in Mary Wilkins Freeman's Fiction." *Legacy* 19, no. 2 (2002): 192–215.

Elrod, Eileen Razzari. "Truth is Stranger than Non-Fiction: Gender, Religion, and Contradiction in Rose Terry Cooke." *Legacy* 13, no. 2 (1996): 113–29.

Felski, Rita. *The Gender of Modernity*. Cambridge, MA: Harvard University Press, 1995.

Fetterley, Judith, and Marjorie Pryse. *Writing out of Place: Regionalism, Women, and American Literary Culture*. Urbana: University of Illinois Press, 2003.

Fienberg, Lorne. "Mary Wilkins Freeman's 'Soft Diurnal Commotion': Women's Work and Strategies of Containment." *New England Quarterly* 62, no. 4 (December 1989): 483–504. https://doi.org/10.2307/366394

Fine, Ben. *Social Capital versus Social Theory: Political Economy and Social Science at the Turn of the Millennium*. New York: Routledge, 2001.

Fine, Ben, and Dimitris Milonakis. *From Economics Imperialism to Freakonomics: The Shifting Boundaries between Economics and Other Social Sciences*. New York: Routledge, 2009.

Fischer, Frank, and Maarten A. Hajer, eds. *Living with Nature: Environmental Politics as Cultural Discourse*. New York: Oxford University Press, 1999.

Fiske, John. "The Paper Money Craze of 1786 and the Shays Rebellion." *Atlantic Monthly* 58, no. 347 (September 1886): 376–85. Cornell University Library Making of America Collection.

Foote, Stephanie. *Regional Fictions: Culture and Identity in Nineteenth-Century American Literature*. Madison: University of Wisconsin Press, 2001.

Foucault, Michel. "Of Other Spaces." Translated by Jay Miskowiec. http://foucault.info/doc/documents/heterotopia/foucault-heterotopia-en-html, n.p. Accessed July 15, 2015.

Fox, Richard Wightman, and T. J. Jackson Lears, eds. *The Culture of Consumption: Critical Essays in American History, 1880–1980*. New York: Pantheon, 1983.

Freeman, Mary E. Wilkins. "An Autobiography," "Who's Who—and Why." *Saturday Evening Post* 8 (December 1917): 25, 75.

———. "Louisa." 1890. In *A New England Nun and Other Stories*, edited by Sandra A. Zagarell. New York: Penguin, 2000.

———. "A Mistaken Charity." In *A Humble Romance and Other Stories*. New York: Harper, 1887.

———. "A New England Nun." In *A New England Nun and Other Stories*, edited by Sandra A. Zagarell, New York: Penguin, 2000.

———. "The Revolt of 'Mother.'" In *A New England Nun and Other Stories*, edited by Sandra A. Zagarell. New York: Penguin, 2000.

"The Fruits of Free Labor in the Smaller Islands of the British West Indies." *Atlantic Monthly* 9, no. 53 (March 1862): 273–82. Cornell University Library Making of America Collection.

Gagnier, Regenia. *The Insatiability of Human Wants: Economics and Aesthetics in Market Society*. Chicago: University of Chicago Press, 2000.

Gallagher, Catherine. *The Body Economic: Life, Death, and Sensation in Political Economy and the Victorian Novel*. Princeton, NJ: Princeton University Press, 2006.

Gardiner, Robin. *The History of the White Star Line*. Hersham, UK: Ian Allan, 2001.

Garfield, James A. "The Currency Conflict." *Atlantic Monthly* 37, no. 220 (February 1876): 219–36. Cornell University Library Making of America Collection.

Garvey, Ellen Gruber. *The Adman in the Parlor: Magazines and the Gendering of Consumer Culture, 1880s to 1910s*. New York: Oxford University Press, 1996.

Geiger, George R. *The Philosophy of Henry George*. New York: Macmillan, 1933.

George, Henry. *Progress and Poverty*. New York: Appleton, 1879. Reprint London: Kegan Paul, 1883.

Gibson-Graham, J. K. *The End of Capitalism (As We Knew It): A Feminist Critique of Political Economy*. Cambridge, MA: Blackwell, 1996. Reprint Minneapolis: University of Minnesota Press, 2006.

Gilman, Charlotte Perkins. *Women and Economics*. Boston: Small, Maynard, 1898. Reprint Berkeley: University of California Press, 1998.

Gilpin, Alan. *Environmental Economics: A Critical Overview*. New York: John Wiley, 2000.

Ginzberg, Lori D. *Women and the Work of Benevolence: Morality, Politics, and Class in the Nineteenth-Century United States*. New Haven, CT: Yale University Press, 1990.

Glasser, Leah Blatt. *In a Closet Hidden: The Life and Work of Mary E. Wilkins Freeman*. Amherst: University of Massachusetts Press, 1996.

Glazener, Nancy. *Reading for Realism: The History of a U. S. Literary Institution, 1850–1910*. Durham, NC: Duke University Press, 1997.

Goldman, Dara E. *Out of Bounds: Islands and the Demarcation of Identity in the Hispanic Caribbean*. Lewisburg, PA: Bucknell University Press, 2008.

Goux, Jean-Joseph. *Symbolic Economies: After Marx and Freud*. Translated by Jennifer Curtiss Gage. Ithaca, NY: Cornell University Press, 1990.

Grimwood, Michael. "Architecture and Autobiography in 'The Revolt of "Mother."'" *American Literary Realism* 40, no. 1 (Fall 2007): 66–82. https://doi.org/10.1353 /alr.2008.0004

———. "'The Revolt of "Mother"' and Consumer Culture." *American Literary Realism* 45, no. 3 (Spring 2013): 248–67. https://doi.org/10.5406/amerlitereal.45.3.0248.

Gutman, Herbert G. *The Black Family in Slavery and Freedom, 1750–1925.* New York: Pantheon, 1976.

Harrison, Jonathan Baxter. *Certain Dangerous Tendencies in American Life, and Other Papers.* Boston: Houghton, Osgood, 1880.

Harvey, W. H. *Coin's Financial School.* Chicago: Coin, 1894.

Hazard, Samuel. *Santo Domingo: Past and Present, with a Glance at Hayti.* New York: Harper, 1873.

Hearn, Lafcadio. "Dead Sea Fruit." In *The New Orleans of Lafcadio Hearn: Illustrated Sketches from the Daily City Item*, edited and introduced by Delia LaBarre, 81–82. Baton Rouge: Louisiana State University Press, 2007.

———. "A Midsummer Trip to the West Indies." *Harper's New Monthly Magazine* 77, no. 458 (July 1888): 209–26. Cornell University Library Making of America Collection.

———. "A Midsummer Trip to the West Indies." *Harper's New Monthly Magazine* 77, no. 459 (August 1888): 327–45. Cornell University Library Making of America Collection.

———. *Two Years in the French West Indies.* New York: Harper, 1890. Reprint New York: Harper, 1923.

Hetherington, Kevin. *The Badlands of Modernity: Heterotopia and Social Ordering.* New York: Routledge, 1997.

Hewitson, Gillian J. *Feminist Economics: Interrogating the Masculinity of Rational Economic Man.* Cheltenham, UK: Edward Elgar, 1999.

Hobbes, Thomas. *Leviathan.* London: Andrew Crooke, 1651. Reprint Harmondsworth, UK: Penguin, 1985.

Hobsbawm, Eric, and Terence Ranger, eds. *The Invention of Tradition.* Cambridge, UK: Cambridge University Press, 1983.

Hodgson, Geoffrey M. *How Economics Forgot History: The Problem of Historical Specificity in Social Science.* New York: Routledge, 2001.

Hoeschele, Wolfgang. *The Economics of Abundance: A Political Economy of Freedom, Equity, and Sustainability.* Farnham, UK: Gower, 2010.

Holly, Carol. "The Cruelty of Husbands, the Complicity of Wives, and the Cooperation of Community in Rose Terry Cooke's 'Mrs. Flint's Married Experience.'" *American Literary Realism* 33, no. 1 (Fall 2000): 65–80.

———. "'You ain't no Christian, Not 'Cordin' to Gospel Truth': The Literary Theology of Rose Terry Cooke." *New England Quarterly* 83, no. 4 (December 2010): 674–704. https://doi.org/10.1162/TNEQ_a_00047

Horowitz, Daniel. *The Morality of Spending: Attitudes toward the Consumer Society in America, 1875–1940.* Baltimore: Johns Hopkins University Press, 1985.

Horwitz, Howard. *By the Law of Nature: Form and Value in Nineteenth-Century America.* New York: Oxford University Press, 1991.

Howard, June. Introduction to *New Essays on "The Country of the Pointed Firs,"* edited by June Howard, 1–37. New York: Cambridge University Press, 1994.

Howe, Julia Ward. *A Trip to Cuba.* Boston: Ticknor and Fields, 1860.

Hsu, Hsuan L. "Literature and Regional Production." *American Literary History* 17, no. 1 (Spring 2005): 36–69. https://doi.org/10.1093/alh/aji002.

Hulme, Peter. *Colonial Encounters: Europe and the Native Caribbean, 1492–1797.* New York: Methuen, 1986. Reprint New York: Routledge, 1992.

Hynes, S. B. "The Danish West Indies." *Harper's New Monthly Magazine* 44, no. 260 (January 1872): 196–203. Cornell University Library Making of America Collection.

Jackson Lears, T. J. *No Place of Grace: Antimodernism and the Transformation of American Culture, 1880–1920.* Chicago: University of Chicago Press, 1994.

Jevons, William Stanley. *The Theory of Political Economy.* New York: Macmillan, 1871. Reprint New York: Kelley and Millman, 1957.

Jewett, Sarah Orne. *The Country of the Pointed Firs.* Boston: Houghton, Mifflin, 1896. Reprint, edited by Deborah Carlin, Peterborough, Ontario: Broadview, 2010.

———. "The King of Folly Island." In *The King of Folly Island and Other People,* 1–49. Boston: Houghton Mifflin, 1888.

Johanningsmeier, Charles. "Sarah Orne Jewett and Mary E. Wilkins (Freeman): Two Shrewd Businesswomen in Search of New Markets." *New England Quarterly* 70, no. 1 (March 1997): 57–82. https://doi.org/10.2307/366527.

Joseph, Philip. *American Literary Regionalism in a Global Age.* Baton Rouge: Louisiana State University Press, 2007.

Kaplan, Amy. "Manifest Domesticity." *American Literature* 70, no. 3 (September 1998): 581–606.

———. *The Social Construction of American Realism.* Chicago: University of Chicago Press, 1988.

Kelley, Mary. *Private Woman, Public Stage: Literary Domesticity in Nineteenth-Century America.* New York: Oxford University Press, 1984.

Kirkham, E. Bruce. "The Writing of Harriet Beecher Stowe's *The Pearl of Orr's Island.*" *Colby Library Quarterly* 16, no. 3 (September 1980): 158–65. Proquest.

Klamer, Arjo. *Speaking of Economics: How to Get in the Conversation.* New York: Routledge, 2007.

Klaver, Claudia C. *A/Moral Economics: Classical Political Economy and Cultural Authority in Nineteenth-Century England.* Columbus: Ohio State University Press, 2003.

Klein, Naomi. *This Changes Everything: Capitalism vs. the Climate.* New York: Simon and Schuster, 2014.

Kornblith, Gary J. and Michael Zakim. "Introduction: An American Revolutionary Tradition." In *Capitalism Takes Command: The Social Transformation of Nineteenth-Century America,* edited by Gary J. Kornblith and Michael Zakim, 1–12. Chicago: University of Chicago Press, 2012.

Larcom, Lucy. "Among Lowell Mill-Girls: A Reminiscence." *Atlantic Monthly* 48, no. 289 (November 1881): 593–612. Cornell University Library Making of America Collection.

Lawson, Andrew. *Downwardly Mobile: The Changing Fortunes of American Realism.* New York: Oxford University Press, 2012.

Lawson, Tony. *Economics and Reality.* New York: Routledge, 1997.

———. *Reorienting Economics.* New York: Routledge, 2003.

Leach, William. *Land of Desire: Merchants, Power, and the Rise of a New American Culture.* New York: Pantheon, 1993.

Levine, Robert S. *Dislocating Race and Nation: Episodes in Nineteenth-Century American Literary Nationalism.* Chapel Hill: University of North Carolina Press, 2008.

Lévi-Strauss, Claude. *The Raw and the Cooked. Mythologiques*, Volume I. Trans. John and Doreen Weightman. Chicago: University of Chicago Press, 1983.

Levy, Helen Fiddyment. *Fictions of the Home Place: Jewett, Cather, Glasgow, Porter, Welty, and Naylor.* Jackson: University Press of Mississippi, 1992.

Linkon, Sherry Lee. "Fiction as Political Discourse: Rose Terry Cooke's Antisuffrage Short Stories." In *American Women Short Story Writers: A Collection of Critical Essays*, edited by Julie Brown, 17–31. New York: Garland, 1995.

Littenberg, Marcia B. "From Transcendentalism to Ecofeminism: Celia Thaxter and Sarah Orne Jewett's Island Views Revisited." In *Jewett and Her Contemporaries: Reshaping the Canon*, edited by Karen L. Kilcup and Thomas S. Edwards, 137–52. Gainesville: University Press of Florida, 1999.

Livingston, James. *Pragmatism and the Political Economy of Cultural Revolution, 1850-1940.* Chapel Hill: University of North Carolina Press, 1994.

Locke, John. "The Second Treatise of Government." In *The Selected Political Writings of John Locke*, edited by Paul E. Sigmund, 17–125. New York: Norton, 2005.

Lorrigio, Francesco. "Regionalism and Theory." In *Regionalism Reconsidered: New Approaches to the Field*, edited by David Jordan, 3–27. New York: Garland, 1994.

Loxley, Diana. *Problematic Shores: The Literature of Islands.* New York: Palgrave Macmillan, 1990.

MacFarlane, Lisa Watt. "The New England Kitchen Goes Uptown: Domestic Displacements in Harriet Beecher Stowe's New York." *New England Quarterly* 64, no. 2 (June 1991): 272–91. https://doi.org/10.2307/366124.

Maik, Thomas. "Dissent and Affirmation: Conflicting Voices of Female Roles in Selected Stories by Mary Wilkins Freeman." *Colby Library Quarterly* 26, no. 1 (March 1990): 59–68. Proquest.

Malthus, Thomas. "An Essay on the Principle of Population." London: J. Johnson, 1798. http://www.econlib.org/library/Malthus/malPop1.html. Accessed October 10, 2012.

Marin, Louis. *Utopics: The Semiological Play of Textual Spaces.* Translated by Robert Vollrath. Atlantic Highlands, NJ: Humanities Press, 1990.

Marshall, Alfred. *Principles of Economics.* NewYork: Macmillan, 1890. https://ia802605.us.archive.org/13/items/principlesecon000marsgoog/principlesecon000marsgoog.pdf

Maxton, Graeme P. *The End of Progress: How Modern Economics Has Failed Us.* New York: John Wiley, 2011.

Meek, Ronald L. *Social Science and the Ignoble Savage.* Cambridge, UK: Cambridge University Press, 1976.

Meese, Elizabeth A. *Crossing the Double-Cross: The Practice of Feminist Criticism.* Chapel Hill: University of North Carolina Press, 1986.

Meisenheimer, D. K., Jr. "Regionalist Bodies/Embodied Regions: Sarah Orne Jewett and Zitkala-Sa." In *Breaking Boundaries: New Perspectives on Women's Regional Writing,* edited by Sherrie A. Inness and Diana Royer, 109–23. Iowa City: University of Iowa Press, 1997.

Menke, Pamela Glenn. "Behind the 'White Veil': Alice Dunbar-Nelson, Creole Color, and *The Goodness of St. Rocque.*" In *Songs of the Reconstructing South: Building Literary Louisiana, 1865–1945,* edited by Lisa Abney and Suzanne Disheroon-Green, 77–88. Westport, CT: Greenwood, 2002.

Michaels, Walter Benn. *The Gold Standard and the Logic of Naturalism.* Berkeley: University of California Press, 1987.

Milgate, Murray, and Shannon C. Stimson. *After Adam Smith: A Century of Transformation in Politics and Political Economy.* Princeton, NJ: Princeton University Press, 2009.

Mill, John Stuart. *Principles of Political Economy.* London: John W. Parker, 1848. Reprint New York: Augustus M. Kelley, 1987.

Milonakis, Dimitris, and Ben Fine. *From Political Economy to Economics: Method, the Social and the Historical in the Evolution of Economic Theory.* London: Routledge, 2009.

More, Thomas. *Utopia.* London, 1516. Reprint. Translated by Paul Turner. New York: Penguin 1965.

Morgan, Lewis H. *Ancient Society.* New York: H. Holt, 1877. https://archive.org /details/ancientsociety035004mbp

Mueller, Monika. "New England Tempests? Harriet Beecher Stowe's *The Minister's Wooing* and *The Pearl of Orr's Island.*" In *Beyond "Uncle Tom's Cabin": Essays on the Writing of Harriet Beecher Stowe,* edited by Sylvia Mayer and Monika Mueller, 125–44. Madison, NJ: Fairleigh Dickinson University Press, 2011.

Nagel, Gwen L. Introduction to *Critical Essays on Sarah Orne Jewett.* Boston: G. K. Hall, 1984, 1–23.

Nasaw, David. Introduction to *The 'Gospel of Wealth' Essays and Other Writings,* edited by David Nasaw, vii–xiii. New York: Penguin, 2006.

Nelson, Julie A. *Economics for Humans.* Chicago: University of Chicago Press, 2006.

———. *Feminism, Objectivity, and Economics.* New York: Routledge, 1996.

Nelson, William Javier. *Almost a Territory: America's Attempt to Annex the Dominican Republic.* Newark: University of Delaware Press, 1990.

Nicosia, Laura. "Jewett's *The Country of the Pointed Firs.*" *Explicator* 62, no. 2 (2004): 89–91. https://doi.org/10.1080/00144940409597181.

Oran. "Tropical Journeyings en Route for California." *Harper's New Monthly Magazine* 16, no. 94 (March 1858): 457–71. Cornell University Library Making of America Collection.

———. "Tropical Journeyings en Route for California." *Harper's New Monthly Magazine* 16, no. 95 (April 1858): 577–93. Cornell University Library Making of America Collection.

Parsons, George Frederic. "The Labor Question." *Atlantic Monthly* 58, no. 345 (July 1886): 97–113. Cornell University Library Making of America Collection.

Patterson, Annabel. *Fables of Power: Aesopian Writing and Political History.* Durham, NC: Duke University Press, 1991.

"People of a New England Factory Village." *Atlantic Monthly* 46, no. 276 (October 1880): 460–64. Cornell University Library Making of America Collection.

Pérez, Louis, Jr. *Cuba: Between Reform and Revolution.* 3rd ed. New York: Oxford University Press, 2005.

Pierson, Michael D. "Antislavery Politics in Harriet Beecher Stowe's *The Minister's Wooing* and *The Pearl of Orr's Island.*" *American Nineteenth Century History* 3, no. 2 (2002): 1–24. https://doi.org/10.1080/713998990.

Pyle, Howard. "Jamaica, New and Old." *Harper's New Monthly Magazine* 80, no. 476 (January 1890): 169–86. Cornell University Library Making of America Collection.

———. "Jamaica, New and Old." *Harper's New Monthly Magazine* 80, no. 477 (February 1890): 378–96. Cornell University Library Making of America Collection.

Railton, Ben. *Contesting the Past, Reconstructing the Nation: American Literature and Culture in the Gilded Age, 1876–1893.* Tuscaloosa: University of Alabama Press, 2007.

Randall, Lisa. *Warped Passages: Unraveling the Mysteries of the Universe's Hidden Dimensions.* New York: Harper Perennial, 2006.

Reichardt, Mary R. *Mary Wilkins Freeman: A Study of the Short Fiction.* New York: Twayne, 1997.

Repplier, Agnes. "Esoteric Economy." *Atlantic Monthly* 62, no. 372 (October 1888): 529–36. Cornell University Library Making of America Collection.

Reutter, Cheli. "Harriet Beecher Stowe's *Pear[l] of Orr's Island*: Novel of Passing and Cultural Gem." *CEA Critic: An Official Journal of the College English Association* 70, no. 1 (Fall 2007): 48–65.

Richards, T. Addison. "The Valley of the Connecticut." *Harper's New Monthly Magazine* 13, no. 75 (August 1856): 289–302. Cornell University Library Making of America Collection.

Ritter, Gretchen. *Goldbugs and Greenbacks: The Antimonopoly Tradition and the Politics of Finance in America.* Cambridge, UK: Cambridge University Press, 1997.

Roman, Margaret. *Sarah Orne Jewett: Reconstructing Gender.* Tuscaloosa: University of Alabama Press, 1992.

Romero, Lora. *Home Fronts: Domesticity and Its Critics in the Antebellum United States.* Durham, NC: Duke University Press, 1997.

Romines, Ann. *The Home Plot: Women, Writing and Domestic Ritual.* Amherst: University of Massachusetts Press, 1992.

Ropes, E. H. "Summering among the Thousand Isles." *Harper's New Monthly Magazine* 63, no. 376 (September 1881): 501–18. Cornell University Library Making of America Collection.

Rosenberg, Daniel. *New Orleans Dockworkers: Race, Labor, and Unionism 1892–1923.* Albany: State University of New York Press, 1988.

Rousseau, Jean-Jacques. "The Second Discourse: Discourse on the Origin and

Foundations of Inequality among Mankind." Amsterdam: Marc-Michel Rey, 1755. In *The Social Contract and the First and Second Discourses*, edited and translated by Susan Dunn, 87–148. New Haven, CT: Yale University Press, 2002.

Said, Edward. *Orientalism: Western Conceptions of the Orient*. New York: Pantheon, 1978. Reprint New York: Penguin, 1991.

Sandilands, Catriona. "The Importance of Reading Queerly: Jewett's Deephaven as Feminist Ecology." *Interdisciplinary Studies in Literature and Environment* 11, no. 2 (Summer 2004): 57–77. https://doi.org/10.1093/isle/11.2.57.

Seilhamer, G. O. "Negro Life in Jamaica." *Harper's New Monthly Magazine* 44, no. 262 (March 1872): 553–61. Cornell University Library Making of America Collection.

Seltzer, Mark. *Bodies and Machines*. New York: Routledge, 1991.

Sewell, W. E. "Cast-away in Jamaica." *Harper's New Monthly Magazine* 22, no. 128 (January 1861): 166–81. Cornell University Library Making of America Collection.

Shannon, Laurie. "'The Country of Our Friendship': Jewett's Intimist Art." *American Literature* 71, no. 2 (June 1999): 227–62.

Shepherd, Jennifer. "Fashioning an Aesthetics of Consumption in *The House of Mirth*." In *Memorial Boxes and Guarded Interiors: Edith Wharton and Material Culture*, edited by Gary Totten, 135–58. Tuscaloosa: University of Alabama Press, 2014.

Sherman, Sarah Way. "Party Out of Bounds: Gender and Class in Jewett's 'The Best China Saucer." In *Jewett and Her Contemporaries: Reshaping the Canon*, edited by Karen L. Kilcup and Thomas S. Edwards, 223–48. Gainesville: University Press of Florida, 1999.

———. *Sacramental Shopping: Louisa May Alcott, Edith Wharton, and the Spirit of Modern Consumerism*. Durham, NH: University of New Hampshire Press, 2013. Proquest Ebrary.

———. *Sarah Orne Jewett, an American Persephone*. Hanover, NH: University Press of New England, 1989.

Sklansky, Jeffrey. *The Soul's Economy: Market Society and Selfhood in American Thought, 1820–1920*. Chapel Hill: University of North Carolina Press, 2002.

Sklar, Martin J. *The Corporate Reconstruction of American Capitalism, 1890–1916*. Cambridge, UK: University of Cambridge Press, 1988.

Smith, Adam. *The Wealth of Nations*. London: W. Strahan and T. Cadell, 1776. Reprint, edited by Edwin Cannan, New York: Bantam, 2003.

Smith-Rosenberg, Carroll. "The Female World of Love and Ritual: Relations between Women in Nineteenth-Century America." *Signs* 1, no. 1 (Autumn 1975): 1–29.

Staley, Charles E. *A History of Economic Thought from Aristotle to Arrow*. Oxford, UK: Basil Blackwell, 1989.

Staveren, Irene Van. "Feminist Fiction and Feminist Economics: Charlotte Perkins Gilman on Efficiency." In *Toward a Feminist Philosophy of Economics*, edited by Drucilla K. Barker and Edith Kuiper, 56–70. London: Routledge, 2003.

Steeples, Douglas, and David O. Whitten. *Democracy in Desperation: The Depression of 1893*. Westport CT: Greenwood, 1998.

Stowe, Harriet Beecher. *The Pearl of Orr's Island*. London: Sampson, Low, 1862. Reprint New York: Houghton Mifflin, 2001.

————. *Oldtown Folks*. Boston: Fields, Osgood, 1869. Reprint New York: Houghton Mifflin, 1915.

Strachan, Ian Gregory. *Paradise and Plantation: Tourism and Culture in the Anglophone Caribbean*. Charlottesville: University of Virginia Press, 2002.

Strother, D. H. "A Summer in New England." *Harper's New Monthly Magazine* 21, no. 124 (September 1860): 442–61. Cornell University Library Making of America Collection.

Strychacz, Thomas. "You . . . Could Never Be Mistaken": Reading Alice Dunbar-Nelson's Rhetorical Diversions in *The Goodness of St. Rocque and Other Stories*." *Studies in American Fiction* 36, no. 1 (Spring 2008): 77–94.

Sumner, William Graham. "The Absurd Effort to Make the World Over." In *Essays of William Graham Sumner*, edited by Albert Galloway Keller and Maurice R. Davie, 1:91–106. New Haven, CT: Yale University Press, 1934.

————. *What Social Classes Owe to Each Other*. New York: Harper, 1883. Reprint New Haven, CT: Yale University Press, 1925.

Sundquist, Eric J. ed. *American Realism: New Essays*. Baltimore: Johns Hopkins University Press, 1982.

Susman, Warren I. *Culture as History: The Transformation of American Society in the Twentieth Century*. New York: Pantheon, 1984.

Sutton-Ramspeck, Beth. *Raising the Dust: The Literary Housekeeping of Mary Ward, Sarah Grand, and Charlotte Perkins Gilman*. Columbus: Ohio State University Press, 2004.

Sweet, Timothy. *American Georgics: Economy and Environment in Early American Literature*. Philadelphia: University of Pennsylvania Press, 2002.

Tabb, William. *Reconstructing Political Economy: The Great Divide in Economic Thought*. New York: Routledge, 1999.

Tate, Claudia. *Domestic Allegories of Political Desire: The Black Heroine's Text at the Turn of the Century*. New York: Oxford University Press, 1992.

Taylor, Frank H. "Street Scenes in Havana." *Harper's New Monthly Magazine* 58, no. 347 (April 1879): 682–86. Cornell University Library Making of America Collection.

Topinka, Robert J. "Foucault, Borges, Heterotopia: Producing Knowledge in Other Spaces." *Foucault Studies* 9 (September 2010): 54–70.

Toth, Susan Allen. "Defiant Light: A Positive View of Mary Wilkins Freeman." In *Critical Essays on Mary Wilkins Freeman*, edited by Shirley Marchalonis, 123–31. Boston: Hall, 1991.

Trachtenberg, Alan. *The Incorporation of America: Culture and Society in the Gilded Age*. New York: Hill and Wang, 1982.

Tylor, Edward Burnett. *Researches in the Early History of Mankind and the Development of Civilization*. London: John Murray, 1865.

"A Visit to Martha's Vineyard." *Atlantic Monthly* 4, no. 23 (September 1859): 281–94. Cornell University Library Making of America Collection.

Walker, Francis A. "What Shall We Tell the Working Classes?" *Scribner's Magazine* 2, no. 5 (November 1887): 619–27. Cornell University Library Making of America Collection.

Warner, Charles Dudley. "The Novel and the Common School." *Atlantic Monthly* 65, no. 392 (June 1890): 721–31. Cornell University Library Making of America Collection.

Weaver-Hightower, Rebecca. *Empire Islands: Castaways, Cannibals, and Fantasies of Conquest*. Minneapolis: University of Minnesota Press, 2007.

Weiss, John. "The Horrors of San Domingo." *Atlantic Monthly* 9, no. 56 (June 1862): 732–54. Cornell University Library Making of America Collection.

———. "The Horrors of San Domingo." *Atlantic Monthly* 11, no. 65 (March 1863): 289–306. Cornell University Library Making of America Collection.

———. "The Horrors of San Domingo." *Atlantic Monthly* 11, no. 68 (June 1863): 768–85. Cornell University Library Making of America Collection.

White, Brian. "'In the Humble Fashion of a Scripture Woman': The Bible as Besieging Tool in Freeman's 'The Revolt of "Mother."'" *Christianity and Literature* 58, no. 1 (Autumn 2008): 81–92. https://doi.org/10.1177/014833310805800106.

Williams, Rosalind H. *Dream Worlds: Mass Consumption in Late Nineteenth-Century France*. Berkeley: University of California Press, 1982.

Wilson, Christine. "Delinquent Housekeeping: Transforming the Regulations of Keeping House." *Legacy* 25, no. 2 (2008): 299–310.

Wood, Ann Douglas. "The Literature of Impoverishment: The Women Local Colorists in America 1865–1914." *Women's Studies* 1, no. 1 (1972): 3–46.

Wood, Henry. *The Political Economy of Natural Law*. Boston: Lee and Shepard, 1894.

Woodmansee, Martha, and Mark Osteen, eds. *The New Economic Criticism: Studies at the Intersection of Literature and Economics*. New York: Routledge, 1999.

Zagarell, Sandra A. "*Country*'s Portrayal of Community and the Exclusion of Difference." In *New Essays on "The Country of the Pointed Firs,"* edited by June Howard, 39–60. New York: Cambridge University Press, 1994.

———. "Narrative of Community: The Identification of a Genre." *Signs* 13, no. 3 (Spring 1988): 498–527.

Zieger, Robert H. *For Jobs and Freedom: Race and Labor in America since 1865*. Lexington: University Press of Kentucky, 2007.

INDEX

195n46; and urbanism, 93, 105, 152; and women, 174n12

Caribbean islands: and economic disorder, 68, 69, 72, 75–77, 79–81, 83–84, 88–90, 139–44; and excess, 79–80; feminization of, 65, 69, 77, 89, 90, 140, 184n15; and filibusters, 138; and fruit discourses, 13–14, 139–44; and New England, 12, 67, 69, 71–72, 79–81, 84–90; and piracy, 76, 83; and "ripe fruit" theory, 66, 138, 139; and travelogues, 13, 65, 66, 68, 73, 139, 144; and slavery, 66, 72, 78; and US fruit trade, 13–14, 131, 137–39, 191n14; US political and economic interest in, 13–14, 65–69, 131, 138–39, 144, 146, 191n12. *See also* fruit sublime, concept of

Caribbeanism, 12, 13–14, 66, 68, 73–84, 88–90, 139–44.

Carnegie, Andrew, 10, 23, 24–26, 29–30, 36; and philanthropy, 24; and the Sioux, 24–25, 48; "Wealth," 10, 23, 24–26, 36

Carter, James Bucky, 37

Century, 10

charity, 11, 45–46, 181n34; and market relations, 45–46; and middle-class values, 46; and stadialism, 47; and women, 46

Child, Lydia Maria, 82

colonization of North America, 24–25, 61, 63

Columbus, Christopher, 74, 192–93n6

common good. *See* commonwealth

commonwealth, 5, 13, 17, 18, 63, 71, 94–96, 99, 101, 116, 117, 149

Conant, Helen S., 79, 140

Cooke, Rose Terry, 1, 6, 13, 19, 107–11, 117–29, 151; and Christianity, 122, 123, 124; and the Civil War, 117–21; and consumerism, 1, 9, 166; "A Double Thanksgiving," 110, 121, 125; "Home Again," 110, 121–24, 129; "How Celia Changed her Mind,"

13, 110, 121, 124–29; *Huckleberries: Gathered from New England Hills*, 13, 110, 121, 122, 128, 129; "Miss Beulah's Bonnet," 1–6, 9, 14, 16, 20, 107, 166; "My Thanksgiving," 110, 117–21, 125; "Mrs. Flint's Married Experience," 107; "An Old-Fashioned Thanksgiving," 107–8, 110, 111, 121, 126; and queerness, 128; and True Womanhood, 190n22

Crane, Stephen, 18

Crowell, Foster, 76

cultural fable, concept of, 10–11, 13, 20, 22, 30

Daily City Item, 137

Daly, Herman E., 167, 195n44

Defoe, Daniel: *Robinson Crusoe*, 12, 68, 69, 74, 83, 94, 184n22, 187n12

Dewey, John, 27

division of labor, 11, 20–21, 22, 27, 28, 104; efficiencies of, 20–21, 27, 104–5

domesticity: and class, 3, 8, 43, 44, 49; and female subjectivity, 6, 49, 50; and heterotopia, 39, 44, 48–50, 51, 52, 62–63, 70, 89–90, 102, 110, 115, 126; and public voice, 33; and relationship to marketplace, 7, 8, 9, 33–34, 70, 97, 123, 126, 165, 179n8, 187n76, 176n39; as resistance to capitalism, 7–8, 44, 180n12; as resistance to patriarchy, 7; and women's cultures, 7–8, 43, 87–88, 125–26. *See also* kitchen economics

Donovan, Josephine, 92, 175n32, 179n7

Douglass, Frederick, 73

Dreiser, Theodore, 18, 163, 193n27; *Sister Carrie*, 163, 171, 194n29

Dunbar-Nelson, Alice, 2, 13, 19, 66, 110, 130–47; and Christian imagery, 132; and Creole identity, 132–33, 144; and modernity, 130–31, 147; "Mr. Baptiste," 2, 13–14, 66, 130–37, 144–47; "Titee," 130; *Violets and Other Tales*, 130

ecohistory, 18, 148

economic behavior, 4, 5, 16; and competition, 5

economic fabling, 12, 14, 15, 16, 22, 27, 38, 110, 111, 131, 148, 149–50, 159–60, 162

economic modeling, 16, 18, 148, 155–62, 170

Economist, 168

Eggleston, N. H., 79

Elbert, Monika M., 36–37, 50, 51, 194n34

female regionalism, 176n35, 180n12; and class privilege, 3, 99–100, 152, 155; as counterworld to modernity, 3, 7–8, 9, 18, 19, 92, 97, 131, 155, 161, 162–63, 167, 175n32; as critique of male capitalism, 7–8, 9, 44, 63, 64, 65, 92, 93, 94, 106; and fabulism, 12, 14, 20; and queerness, 128, 166; as site of economic analysis, 4, 8–9, 12, 17; and nostalgia, 3, 12, 103; and role of readers, 65, 132–34; as tourist fiction, 65–66, 183nn8–9

femina economica, 6, 8–9, 16, 49, 70, 87–90, 94, 102–4, 106, 108, 110, 155

Fetterley, Judith, and Marjorie Pryse, *Writing out of Place*, 7, 44, 63, 64, 127, 165–66, 176n35, 182n65

Fienberg, Lorne, 36

Fiske, John, 100–101

Foucault, Michel, 15

Freeman, Mary Wilkins, 2, 11, 15, 19, 31, 32–63; "An Autobiography," 31, 32–37, 50, 57, 58, 161, 166; and Christianity, 62; "A Church Mouse," 32; and consumerism, 34, 36, 50, 194n34; and critique of capitalism, 37, 40, 44, 48; and fabling, 32, 33–34, 37–39, 48–49, 54, 61–62, 180n14; and feminist scholarship, 32–33, 36–37, 179n7; and literary markets, 33–36, 179n8; "Louisa," 107; "A Mistaken Charity," 2, 11, 15, 33, 37–49, 105, 180n19; "A New

England Nun," 32, 107; "The Revolt of 'Mother,'" 11, 15, 32–37, 49–63, 161, 180n17, 181n38, 181n41, 182n54; "A Village Singer," 32

Friedan, Betty: *The Feminine Mystique*, 7

fruit sublime, concept of, 13, 131, 139, 140, 143, 147

Gagnier, Regenia, 21, 178n21

Gallagher, Catherine, 13, 108, 109

Garfield, James, 99

general equivalent, 22, 141, 143

George, Henry, *Progress and Poverty*, 10, 23, 27–28, 29, 104, 105

Gilman, Charlotte Perkins, 7, 9, 10, 23, 28–29, 48; *Herland*, 188n33; *What Diantha Did*, 176n49; *Women and Economics*, 10, 23, 28, 48

gingerbread house: as economic model, 15, 16, 149–55, 158–62; and women's literary traditions, 149, 150, 158, 159, 160–62

Glazener, Nancy, 8, 9, 97, 165, 176n39, 187n76

Goux, Jean-Joseph, and utopian republic, concept of, 91–92, 103, 150–51, 152

Grant, Ulysses S., 73, 183n11

green economics, 18, 167–72; and "the end of progress," 195n45; and environmental collapse, 167–70; and localism, 168; and morality, 168; and scarcity, 195n46; and steady-state economy, 195n44; and sustainability, 167–71

Green Island, 11, 12, 13, 64, 91–106, 149, 150, 151, 157, 160, 169, 171, 189n33; as challenge to economic theory, 92, 94, 97, 102, 106; and symbolic relationship to Maine, 93, 103, 105–6

Hale, Sarah Josepha, 111–12

Hansel and Gretel, 1, 14, 38, 39, 40, 45, 48, 149, 159, 160

Harper's, 10, 33, 139, 142

political liberalism, 11, 21–22, 37, 44, 51–60; and emergence of civil society, 11, 22, 52–55, 104–6; and exchange relations, 51, 53, 55, 56, 104–6; and islands, 67; and markets, 51; and possessive individualism, 45, 51, 55, 60, 69; and property rights, 51, 53–54, 62, 104, 106; and scarcity, 58; and women, 56–61, 62, 182n48. *See also* Hobbes, Thomas; Locke, John

Polk, James K., 183n11

populism, 97–98, 100

postmodernity: economic conditions of, 163–64; narratives of, 163–66, 194n36

premodernism, 17, 18, 141, 163, 164, 166, 167

property rights, 21–22, 29, 62, 104; critique of, 65

Pyle, Howard, 76, 77, 140, 141

Randall, Lisa, 155, 193n16

rational economic agent, 4, 5–6, 9, 11, 28, 34, 49, 102; and self-interest, 5, 20, 22, 156–57

realism, literary, 2, 149, 159, 161, 162; critique of, 14

Reconstruction, 61, 73, 74, 110, 112, 116, 135, 136

republicanism, 2, 8, 11, 38–39, 41, 42, 43, 49, 60, 86, 97, 163, 188n23; and Jeffersonianism, 39, 40, 42, 44, 49, 103; nostalgia for, 40–42, 97, 103, 163

resource distribution, 5, 6

Ricardo, David, 4–5, 6, 26, 27, 29

robinsonade, 68, 69, 91. *See also* Defoe, Daniel: *Robinson Crusoe*

Romero, Lora, 8, 88

Rousseau, Jean-Jacques, 4, 67

Sandilands, Catriona, 7

Saturday Evening Post, 32, 33, 34, 36, 37, 50, 51, 57, 179n9

Scribner's, 10

Seilhamer, G. O., 140–41

Seneca Falls Convention, 57, 59, 60; and Declaration of Sentiments, 57, 59, 60

Sewell, W. E., 75, 76, 77, 140

Sherman, Sarah Way, 164–65, 183n9, 194n34

Smith, Adam, 4, 5, 11, 20-21, 25, 27, 96, 102, 104, 141, 143, 160, 175n25

southern Redeemers, 135

stadialism, 11–12, 14, 18, 20–31, 39, 47–49, 87, 105–6, 143, 166–67, 170, 177n10; challenges to, 20, 23, 25, 29, 49, 58–59; and emergence of civilization, 11, 20, 21, 22, 23, 24, 28, 71, 143; and imperialism, 22, 23; as metanarrative, 20, 30, 31; principles of, 11, 21, 29, 47–49; and privileged observer, 24, 25, 68–69, 143, 163, 165, 166; and race, 22; and women, 21, 28–29. *See also* plot of polity, concept of

stages theory. *See* stadialism

Stanton, Elizabeth Cady, Susan. B Anthony, and Matilda Joselyn Gage: and *History of Woman Suffrage*, 51, 57, 59, 61

state of nature, 22, 24, 26, 53–55, 58, 68, 75, 105

Steeples, Douglass, and David O. Whitten: *Democracy in Desperation: The Depression of 1893*, 93, 173n4

Stowe, Harriet Beecher, 12, 13, 14, 19, 64, 69–73, 80–90, 107, 109, 110, 111–17, 118, 127, 129, 131, 148, 151, 152, 154; and Christianity, 115–16; and gynocentric plot, 187n74; and marriage, 72, 81–82, 186n72; *The Minister's Wooing*, 83; *Oldtown Folks*, 111, 148; and opposition to market capitalism, 70, 184n25; *The Pearl of Orr's Island*, 12, 64, 65, 66, 69–73, 80–90, 131, 183n11, 184n26; and race, 80–84, 116; and slavery, 72–73, 80–83, 84, 113, 116, 184n25; and Thanksgiving, 111–17; *Uncle Tom's Cabin*, 82; and utopia, 81, 84, 89, 186n71